ALL IN

BECOMING

WORLD

CHAMPION

LAURA MASSARO

First edition June 2021

Written with Rod Gilmour.
Edited by Eleanor Preston.

Book design by Richard Salisbury

Photo credits: SquashSite - Steve Cubbins
PSA (Professional Squash Association) Nathan Clarke
TAGD Photography - Trevor Davies

ISBN 978-1-8383516-0-1 (paperback)
ISBN 978-1-8383516-1-8 (ebook)
978-1-8383516-3-2 (hardback)

Published by Marylebone Publishing

www.marylebonepublishing.com

MARYLEBONE
PUBLISHING

ACKNOWLEDGMENTS

Writing and editing this book has been much harder but also a lot more fun than I ever expected.

To start, thank you to Danny Massaro, my husband. You have sacrificed so much for me to achieve my dreams. You said the difficult things – the things I didn't always want to hear but needed to hear to progress. Thank you for putting up with my strops, stubbornness and single-mindedness along the way. You are special in your positivity and outlook and I am lucky to have learned some of that from you. Thank you and I love you!

To my parents, John and Jill, and my brother, Christopher, I simply would not be the person I am without the support, dedication and love over many years. Thank you for supporting me in so much more than just squash. My roots are deep because of the person you helped me become.

To my coach David Pearson 'DP', without your support, kindness and skill I would not be where I am. I put my 'big titles' down to you and the subtleties you could see, your 'squash eye' is second to none. You were soft when I needed it and hard when I really needed it. You supported not only me but provided Danny support too. Together you both kept my feet on the ground. Always with a smile and a twinkle in your eye, a funny story or a deliberately mis-pronounced name, you always put things wonderfully into perspective. Thank you.

Mark Campbell, I am beyond grateful for your time, effort and wealth of knowledge. You went above and beyond the task of training me to become a better athlete. Your understanding of squash and its unique requirements were like no trainer I have ever worked with. Your confidence and steadiness in every situation were calming. You coached me, the person who I am, brilliantly. Thank you.

I also want to thank *'the witch'*, Caroline Glain, my fasciotherapist. I could never get across in the book how many times you saved the match, literally! You're a witch in the nicest possible way. I will never understand how you work your magic but I am grateful for all the rescues you provided. I thank you not only for the 16 years of treatment but for helping me get through those years more injury free than most athletes could hope for.

I also want to thank physiotherapists Jade Leeder, Vicky O'Donnell, Ian Horsley and Rachel Carter. You each brought a sense of reassurance and high expertise to my treatments. Jade and Vicky, you both travelled with me around the world and not only helped get me recovered, rested and repaired but you listened to my endless and repeating worries. I think you genuinely stopped me and, in turn, Danny from going nuts.

And to Sylvan Richardson. Your understanding of the human body is superbly special. I count myself lucky to have had your specialist skills to count on over the all those years.

To Lawrence and Gail Jones, thank you for your support. Out of nowhere, you guys stepped up, not only sponsoring but supporting me in many more ways. Lawrence, you went above and beyond, never asking for anything in return. From that random meeting I have met a unique friend. I am so grateful for you opening up my mind to a different way of thinking and forcing me to step out of my 'thinking comfort zone'.

Everyone talks about my strength of mind. They have for many years but because of you Peter McNab, you took my personality and made the strong parts of it a strength and helped me figure out my weaknesses. You helped me grow and understand myself more than anyone. You worked with and grew the parts of me that later became the 'ice queen'.

To all my friends. Your loving support has been more than one can expect. Thanks for accepting those missed occasions, birthdays and even weddings! I hope I can pay it back to you in retirement.

I thank everyone who I couldn't mention in the book and who has helped me on my journey. At the start everyone at Clayton Green, Alan Robinson, Bob Wigmore, Mike Farrington, Steve and Ian Johnson, and all the women who did my homework in return for me playing ladies' league! Later, Annette Pilling, Nigel Willis, Matt Cooke, Nick Taylor and John Kiely.

Towards the end, Andy Whipp, Mick Todd, Chris Gelder, Phil Whitlock, Lee Beachill, Jeff Shurr and Nick Matthew. I learnt valuable lessons from each of you – things I will take forward all my life.

My unbelievable sponsors: HEAD who now continue to support me post career. Christine, Stuart and Chris Haworth and everyone at CSH. James Greenwell and everyone at Proto-col, Simon McCabe, Andy Wyn-Jones, Richard Bury, Ian and Mel White, Andy Hosgood and Richard Ingle.

To all at England Squash for all the support since I was 15 years old. To David Campion who was in my corner for countless 'big matches' in the heat of the battle, I always knew I could count on you.

To Faye Andrews and Eleanor Preston, two amazing and strong friends from the Emilia Group, who guided and supported me professionally and personally. Faye, you fought for what I deserved and taught me my own worth as a woman in professional sport. Thank you for creating opportunities for me and always being on the end of the phone when I needed help or support. Eleanor, thank you for the huge effort and time you put into this book. You encouraged me and drew out my deepest thoughts in making this book sound like me. I am forever grateful of your time, guidance and edit after edit after edit.

To Rod Gilmour for working so closely with me to produce this book. Thanks for listening to me talk and talk. Thank you for all that you do in trying to get squash and us as athletes out to a wider audience.

Lastly, to Alice Gibson and everyone at the Marylebone Publishing in making the book come together. It was an idea and a dream, and you helped it become a reality. To have it finished, feels like a huge accomplishment. Thanks for the hours and hours reading and re-reading it for me. I am beyond proud, thank you.

Not forgetting you the reader, the sports fan or the squash supporter. Thank you for trusting me with your valuable time in picking up this book. I hope I have shed some light on the life of a professional female squash player. If you've supported me over the years, thank you!

FOREWORD BY TRACEY NEVILLE MBE

I first met Laura when I was still playing netball and we were among the first athletes who began training at the English Institute of Sport in Manchester. I was rehabbing from a serious knee injury, which meant a lot of time in the gym. The only athlete who was in that gym more than me was Laura.

When it comes to training, there are two types of athletes; those who think 'nobody is looking at me or monitoring me so I'll just do what I have to do' and those athletes, like Laura, who always seem to be in the gym, always doing that little bit extra and staying that little bit longer.

That's what champions do. All the incredible things that she achieved in her career – being world champion, becoming World No.1, winning Commonwealth Games medals – were built on her drive and her work ethic.

Laura also seemed to have a strong desire to prove people wrong. When I first knew her, she was what I would call an 'underdog athlete', not the No.1 in the country, not the one that everyone was focussed on or who the coaches were investing much time in. Sport is hierarchical. Netball was the same and I saw it with cycling too when we trained at the National Velodrome in Manchester. It takes drive to overcome that and move yourself up that hierarchy. Even then, I could see that drive in Laura.

In those days she wasn't yet the No.1 in England. She changed that by learning, listening and persisting. She knew that if she kept driving, her time would come and she had the resilience and the willingness to keep putting herself on the line, time after time. A lot of athletes wouldn't do that. They won't keep trying; they will give up. It's one of the reasons why we have such a big drop-out rate in sport among female athletes in particular.

There are so many challenges for female athletes to overcome, especially in an individual sport like squash, which, like netball, has its roots in an amateur culture. When you are starting out, you are always conscious that a lot of people are investing a lot of time in you for free, often the people closest to you, like your family. As you get better, you have to make a massive commitment to your career because there isn't a lot of money in the sport, and you are asked when you will be able to make a living from it. Then you have to worry about losing your funding if you don't get the results, which can be a massive pressure.

I was lucky in that I came through a team sport. I can only imagine how much tougher that is in an individual sport where when you play at the very highest level, you might have a team supporting you but you are the boss and, however much they are there to help, everything ultimately comes down to you. In a team sport like netball, when things go wrong the coach gets blamed but in an individual sport, it's the athlete who loses the match.

Another challenge is that, in my view, female athletes often have a more pronounced fear of failure than men do. I think it's because we feel that we're judged by society more than men are; told that we have to look a certain way and if we don't then we've failed, if we don't buy certain products, we've failed. Both my brothers were professional footballers at the highest level and I don't think I recall that fear of failure being a factor for them.

Even when she had become the best in England, which is no mean feat, Laura then had to fight her way to get out of the shadow of a huge international star in Nicol David. She did that by never giving up and always trying to find different ways of getting better. You are never the finished article as a professional athlete. You're always trying to find that extra one per cent and then when you do find it, you realise that other people have also got one per cent better and you have to start again.

It takes a huge character to keep doing that. That's exactly what Laura is, a huge character. There is a steeliness and a sassiness about her, which, as a fellow Northern lass, I recognise!

Most important of all, Laura should be a role model for young female athletes everywhere because hers is a story of resilience and of always striving to be better.

And what an inspiring story it is.

PROLOGUE

'Click' marks the sound of the glass back door opening. I know this isn't squash etiquette but I'm already on my way to remonstrate with the central referee. The adrenaline is pumping, my heart is racing and it feels like I'm yelling as I momentarily take in the thousand or so spectators looking on in the bright sun.

'I actually have my thumb up her nose,' I tell the ref.

The 'her' in question is Nicol David, the world's best player and unbroken, undisputed No.1 for years and often my nemesis in big matches. Christ, this is a crucial time. It's the 2013 British Open final, the pinnacle of my sport. 'The decision is … Yes, let,' the ref replies. My heart is racing. 'Review!' I say immediately, before the ref has barely finished speaking. I'm 11-10, game ball up, in the crucial third. I know it's a huge moment and I know I have Nicol rattled. She so rarely sprays the ball down the middle of the court, never mind at game ball down off a return of serve. Coming out of court and yelling at the referee isn't my style either. Maybe I'm a bit rattled myself.

Spectators like player-referee interaction. I get it; it's compelling and entertaining to see those discussions (or arguments) in the heat of the moment. But watching the match back a few weeks later I am mortified at the 'thumb up her nose' comment. Where did that come from?

In squash, you are awarded a stroke if the ref decides that you would have won the rally if your opponent had not impeded you. It happens all the time in our supposedly non-contact sport. The 'nose' comment was my way of saying that Nicol had put her body in the way to stop me being able to hit a shot. I might have found a nicer way of putting it but the video ref agreed with me; I didn't have room for a swing. As one of the TV commentators put it: 'Wow, Massaro would have taken her head off if she'd hit that!'

Suddenly I'm sitting in my chair, one game away from winning the Open, a tournament known as the 'Wimbledon of squash'. I reach for my gel pack. Taking a load of sugar on seems like a good idea to me. I take a big gulp and Danny, my husband and coach, comes over to talk to me. He sounds pretty calm in his advice but he's absolutely adamant that I take fluid on quickly.

Why is he trying to make me drink my energy drink, I think.

'I'm okay,' I say.

'Take it,' he replies forcefully.

I trust in him knowing what I need almost more than I do myself. He talks tactics, how I need to stay up the court and be positive. He mentions a couple of technical things that have worked for me all week. 'Stay tall and use the shoulder,' he shouts as I stride away from him. Danny loves a yell of something technical. He senses that in that moment I need a simple, clear instruction to focus my mind. Maybe making me take on fluid was his way of focussing on the details and not what was at stake.

I make a dream start to the fourth game. I can't believe how relaxed I am. I'm playing possibly the greatest female squash player of all time, the living legend who seemingly no one can beat, but I'm on home turf and at that moment I have belief coursing through me. The crowd are sitting outside in seats behind the Hull FC goal, as if watching Hull City put in crosses or defending at the far post. Instead there are two women smashing a tiny rubber ball against a glass wall in a court positioned at one end of the pitch. Squash has been played in some mad places before, and this is one of them.

A few days earlier, the spectators had blankets and the players wore jackets in between games in some of the coldest playing conditions we had ever experienced. Now, the fans are wearing sunglasses and, as the game goes on, they shout more forcibly between points. They are the twelfth man here and I'm glad to have them on my side.

I get a lead, stay calm and tell myself the score is different to what it is. Anything to trick my mind out of relaxing, thinking I've already won. I know from bitter experience that complacency when you're winning is often a route to painful defeat later. At 9-6, I'm two points away from the title. Nicol is ready to serve, I give myself a good talking to and turn to see her start her mechanical service motion. As the ball comes off the front wall and goes up I'm thinking, 'That's going out, that's going OUT!' I can't believe my luck. A smile starts to emerge and the voice in my head goes: 'Don't smile, what are you doing that for? Nothing's happened yet.'

This is Nicol David I'm playing. This is the player who has been World No.1 for nearly seven years in a row. I've been in this position before against her and she's beaten me many times, but this time I'm not going quietly. Nicol's excellence has forced me to look at myself and my game since the first moment I stood across from her on a squash court but every bead of sweat, every sacrifice and every teardrop has led me to this moment. This is mine.

CONTENTS

1.   FROM PONTINS TO PENANG

2.   INVISIBLE PECKING ORDER

3.   FEAR OF LOSING

4.   THE PSYCHOLOGIST

5.   CHASING NICOL

6.   A HULL OF A VICTORY

7.   LIFE ON THE ROAD

8.   BECOMING WORLD CHAMPION

9.   THE MANAGEMENT TEAM

10.   AT THE HEART OF CHANGE

11.   'THAT'S IT, I'M DONE'

12.   THE BIG SHAKE-UP

13.   THE FITNESS TRAINER

14.   SCALING NEW HEIGHTS

15.   THE THERAPISTS

16.   'YOU DO REALISE, IF YOU WIN YOU'RE NO.1?'

17.   THE HUSBAND

18.   HUNTER BECOMES HUNTED

19.   CHICAGO COMEBACK

20.   THE COACH

21.   STEPPING OFF THE ROLLERCOASTER

22.   I FOUND MY INNER WARRIOR

      EPILOGUE

      MY NOTEBOOK

1. FROM PONTINS TO PENANG

I was born Laura-Jane Lengthorn in November 1983. As Laura Lengthorn, I was told that I had no hope of making it as a top professional yet I ended my playing career in 2019, playing under my married name of Laura Massaro, as a world champion and World No.1.

I can tell you honestly that I was never the most talented or gifted player but I had an intensively competitive nature that drove me to become a perfectionist and left me obsessed with improving, and even more driven to win. Every time I was dealt a loss, whether I was in the under-11s or ranked No.1 in the world, I set about rectifying it. My career saw me battle against many difficult opponents, not least the world's best ever female squash player in Nicol David, but the biggest fight was always going on inside me. It meant overcoming a deep well of self-doubt, nerves and anxiety and finding a way to be the best I could be in spite of the voices inside asking myself if I was really good enough.

My motto in life is, 'You get out of life what you put in'. For a long time I thought that meant working as hard as I could physically but I realised that putting in the effort as a professional athlete was so much more than just the physical sweat I left on the court or in the gym. It was about putting the work in mentally as well, making sure that you could win those inner battles when you needed to.

That motto was really our family's philosophy. I always wanted to do things 'right' and there's no denying that this is down to my dad, John. Dad was never one for taking the easy path in life. He decided to join the Army in a bid to gain some discipline into his life and be able to provide for his family. He had spells in Germany and Northern Ireland, where he was a sniper with the Royal Green Jackets in the early Seventies. He later saved up to buy himself out of the Army but his playing squash while he served paved my entry into the game.

Dad is one of the most competitive people I know and it is safe to say I get my spirit and work ethic from him. While he may have been tough on me, especially as a young player, I value what he taught me and I am absolutely sure it helped me become successful. Dad is a success story in my eyes. He grew up in Deptford, a tough part of London in the 50s, and his early childhood was brutal at times. He always wanted life to be different for my brother and I. It's not something he's talked about over the years but I know that he had a rough upbringing and he was raised without much money. He wanted to give his kids the best life possible and he worked very hard to make that happen for us. When I was growing up, he and my mum were a team, they gave us everything they could.

My mum, Jill, was born in Yorkshire, which I think is partly why I've always felt so connected to the north of England, even though I was actually born in a seaside town in Norfolk.

My parents met at a Pontins holiday camp in Lowestoft, on England's east coast, when they were both working there. Mum worked in the cafe and Dad worked his way up the Pontins ranks from bartender to bar manager before finally getting a promotion to area manager. We stayed there until I was six before moving to Prestatyn in North Wales where we lived on a Pontins campus for two years, in a bungalow by the entrance gates.

It wasn't a bad place to be a little kid at all. I learnt to swim in the pool when the camp was closed – I think Dad swapped a bottle of whisky in return for my lessons. I remember riding my bike on the carpeted floor in the big ballroom and Dad taking me to feed the ducks in the camp pond on a Sunday. Captain Croc, the famous Pontins mascot, even came to visit me and my friends for birthday parties. Eventually, though, Dad got another promotion to manage all of Pontins' bars nationwide and that meant a move further north. It's where I stayed and it's why I now speak with the lilt of a proud Lancastrian.

We moved into a four-bedroom newbuild on an estate in Chorley, about 10 miles south of Preston, in January 1990, when I was seven years old. It was freezing cold and the move was hard on us all as Mum got pneumonia and spent a spell in hospital while the rest of the family tried to get unpacked and settled. Even though Mum is a Yorkshire lass she quite clearly didn't handle being back in the cold weather!

My brother Christopher and I always felt well supported and we never needed anything in life but our lives were very structured and we were certainly never indulged. Instead we had to earn everything that we wanted and we weren't allowed chocolate apart from on Saturdays. We didn't ever bother asking. To earn extra pocket money I had to clean the car or pick up the extra clumps of grass at the back of the mower, following Dad as he went up and down the lawn. The military-style house we settled into felt like a showroom; bedrooms super tidy. We were taught to appreciate what we had.

Dad was spending a lot of time away from home for work, so that he could make sure we have everything we needed. He sacrificed a huge amount for us as a family and I appreciate that even more now that I am old enough to realise it. The Army made him into a tough, disciplined and no-nonsense character. There was always some fun and the rewards came, but only after the hard work and chores were completed. I didn't want to create arguments, so I strived to do things in the right way and do my bit to keep the home environment happy.

If Dad had something to say, he said it and I learned to take his honesty on board even when it stung. It taught me an important lesson that stayed with me for the next two decades – that criticism can make you better. Either it shows you where you are going wrong or you can use your indignation and determination to shut people up as a motivator. As my career developed, if someone said I wasn't good enough, I listened – however much it hurt or made me angry – because it's what I had throughout my whole childhood from my dad. I knew he cared and I know that's what counted the most. If I hadn't been to the gym enough, I hadn't practised enough, I hadn't done my homework or my room wasn't tidy enough, my dad told me straight.

It was Dad who helped me get my first paid job when I was around aged 14, boxing up eggs on a chicken farm. It was a 7am start, which meant an early start on a Saturday morning. Both parents instilled great discipline in us with money – it had to be earned and it was down to us to fund the treats and extras we needed. I would stand collecting eggs off a conveyor belt boxing them up in trays of 30. The farm smelled of sulphur, as well as the strong smell of chickens and everything that goes with that. Occasionally we would go in the chicken hut to see where the chickens lay their eggs. There were hundreds of chickens in a single massive chicken house but the birds all seemed happy enough, clucking and chirping away. I can still remember the noise of that hut, not to mention the smell. I would get £12 to work until noon and I was always careful with it.

My brother took on the job after me and he was very free and generous with his money. He's always been more relaxed and less of a worrier than me. It took me ages to save and build up the courage to spend my money from the chicken farm before I eventually bought a new pair of Nike Air trainers, splashing out £120 – a fortune to me back then. I think my mum still uses them to do the gardening.

There is a picture of me on holiday in Lanzarote on a squash court at about two years old, running around with a ball on court. We were there for four weeks and my dad's love of squash meant we spent a lot of time there on the court. I caught chickenpox on the way home from that holiday and cried on the plane all the way back. That might have put me off squash for life, fortunately it didn't. What followed were countless hours at my local squash club, shadowing my dad when he played and hitting ball after ball myself.

There were plenty of squash courts in the 80s and 90s with three-bar heaters in the gallery, tired flooring and cold walls. It sounds harsh but Clayton Green Leisure Centre was a bit of the same; soulless, the court roof miles high and the walls quite dark. It didn't matter to me in the least. It might as well have been the Royal Albert Hall as far as I was concerned. All I needed was a ball and a wall.

The local club was quiet most days before players emerged to play when the bar opened at around 7pm. I remember the old vending machines and making £1 last an hour waiting to go on court, while Christopher ended a lesson or Dad played. I would get a can of Tango and my goal would be to make the precious liquid last as long as possible because we weren't normally allowed fizzy drinks at all. I would pull the ring of the can down ever so slightly, just a few millimetres, so that only a few drops would come out at a time. It had to last for the whole 45 minutes that my brother was going to be on court. Self-discipline wasn't just reserved for the squash court.

When I went on court on my own to hit against the wall, it just felt natural. Dad had encouraged me to play because the first time we stepped on court he said I had volleyed the ball, which he thought showed natural hand-eye coordination. I loved the fact I could close the door and that the empty feeling was so intimate; cosy but comforting at the same time. This may sound weird but it reminded me of pubs I used to go to with Dad on his business travels. It was my happy place.

While trying to improve my squash, I was also trying to balance life at my high school. I was a model student looking back; I did everything right and I never once got a detention – mainly because Dad would have hit the roof. However, to be honest, despite all that I don't have the best memories from my school days. The school itself was a bit rough around the edges and I wasn't the most popular either. It was hard trying to balance everything with school and squash. Balancing friendships was sometimes a step too far. I was away almost every weekend going to sports competitions, which meant that I was always up and on the road on Friday night or early Saturday morning, and exhausted by the time I got back to school on Monday. The teachers who liked me, or liked squash, didn't give me a hard time but there's no denying that it was tough.

I can understand why so many kids drop out of sport or, vice versa, focus on sport so much that they end up leaving school with no qualifications. It takes a lot of dedication and discipline at a time when your body is changing a lot (this is especially hard for teenage girls in my view) and your friends are all starting to go out more, to find themselves and get boyfriends or girlfriends. It's never easy as a sportsperson to balance training and competition with the rest of your life, especially as you get better and you have to go further away from home. Throw school, exams, being a teenager and, in my case, a job at a chicken farm into that mix and it means only the most driven – or the best supported – stay on the road to becoming professional athletes.

I got a lot of attention at school when the local press picked up on my squash through my junior days. For all that I found that time difficult, I was lucky because my school embraced what I was doing. I was one of the best all-round athletes and played netball, hockey and athletics. I played everything and the school was positive towards my sport.

I got a sports scholarship to Preston College to do my A-levels. They tried to sign me up for the hockey team but I was told it was quite dangerous, which put me off because squash was my priority. Then I chipped a bone in my left hand playing netball. That was it for me and team sports. To be honest, I prefer to be out there alone, to be in control of my own performance. It used to annoy me that I could play a really good netball game or hockey match and still lose. And I really did not like losing.

The day I started at Preston College, I met the tutor who was running the scholarship programme. It turned out he was also a squash player. He had recently started playing again, so we arranged to play. It meant that I could get some training in against a decent level of opponent and he could get some matches. He was called Danny Massaro.

The main thing I remember about that time is that Danny was really unreliable. We kept arranging matches on the two new courts at Preston College and then he didn't turn up, which really wound me up (he's more reliable these days I'm pleased to say!). There were no thoughts in either of our heads about anything except playing squash and having a laugh. He was nine years older than me and a tutor at college, and even though I was 18 and he never actually taught me, because of our situation it just wasn't on the radar.

Yet something was obviously happening, unbeknownst to both of us. We began to spend more time together away from college (where Danny was much more reliable), playing at the David Lloyd Club in Chorley. Slowly, slowly, and probably without even realising it, the feelings that we had for each began to creep up on us. I remember one night getting a phone call around 2am. Danny had got home from a night out. He was a little drunk but I remember being pleased he had rung and that we were chatting, regardless of the time. I was whispering on my Nokia phone with my parents across the hall. Without really discussing it, I think we both knew from then that you don't ring someone at 2am unless you're really wanting to talk to them. Even then it took a long, long time for either of us to say out loud that we wanted to be more than just training partners, let alone act on those feelings. Talk about a slow burner.

When I look back further, to my childhood, it was basically a mix of school and squash with tournaments at the weekend. I played my first British Closed Championships at under-12 level in Welwyn Garden City and lost in the last eight to a player from Guernsey. As I had won the county championships, I went over to Yorkshire to play their top girls.

Awaiting us was a rich pool of squash players and new challenges. It was always a mindset my dad used to tell me: First win the regionals, especially by beating the Yorkshire girls, and then compete down south. I did just that in 1997 when I was seeded second at the Under-14 British Closed against Alison Waters. It was my first big win against Alison during what would turn out to be a long British rivalry against her lasting up until my retirement.

It didn't always go right and however good you are in a sport like squash you will usually lose more than you win. It doesn't get any easier. I remember one such loss at a junior tournament like it was yesterday. Leanne Gilmartin on a back court with the small crowd watching from high above on the balcony. She was older, stronger and better than me and she was thrashing me. I was getting angry and more than that, frustrated. After losing one of the games I walked to the door quickly and dropped my racket. I reached for the door and flung it open so hard it nearly whacked me on the bum as I walked out the door.

Dad came over. He wasn't happy. 'Go back on that court, stand your racket up and apologise to Leanne.'

'What for?'

'You never drop your racket on the floor. Go and pick it up.'

I protested but he was adamant.

'Go and pick your racket up; apologise to Leanne. You nearly hit her with the door when it flung back in her face. Go and do it or you are not playing the rest of this match.'

I was mortified, of course. I hadn't realised. Still, I was seething about losing and I didn't want to do what he said. 'Go,' he said. I got up, walked on the court, stood my racket up and walked to Leanne. Probably a bit sheepishly, I said, 'Sorry about the door.' Dad was fine after that. He gave me a couple of technical tips and I went back on.

This stuck with me the rest of my career. From that moment I never dropped my racket, much less threw it. In fact, I rarely lost my temper full stop. Maybe it's because I knew that Dad wouldn't approve.

I had also started to play in the Lancashire women's leagues and this was undoubtedly one of my favourite times as a junior. Away from the cut and thrust of junior tournaments, these midweek nights were such a relaxing environment to play in. I was with older, wiser women – away from all the shenanigans and pressurised parenting politics of the junior game. There were plenty of laughs and a huge amount of love and care from these brilliant women. They were my first female sporting role models.

I was usually picked up by one of the other players so I could go on my own. I was really well looked after and I learnt so much playing women who didn't want to lose to a junior.

Those league nights were the making of me. It was the one time of the week where squash was genuinely fun. I was also learning a lot about taking more responsibility for myself. Before I could drive, at least Dad had the brilliant insight of making me write down the directions in my notebook on the way to regional matches so that I had them all to hand and couldn't get lost. When I passed my test a year later, I was on my own and Dad never came to another squash match; he rarely came to another match until later in my career. At 17 and a half, he pretty much sat me down and said, 'Over to you now.' At the time, I didn't really notice it but looking back I think there was real wisdom in him letting me go on my own. I wonder now if it was hard for him – I know so many other parents of talented young athletes struggle with letting go when the time comes – or whether it was a relief to be free of the endless hours on the motorway taking me to tournaments. He'd given up an enormous amount to support my dream of playing squash. The older I get, the more I understand the impact of the sacrifices both my parents made and the more I feel profoundly grateful to them.

People talk a lot about the expectation put on young sportspeople. Some of that came from my parents – of course it did – but it was kind of everywhere around me at that time. People in Lancashire are plain-spoken so there wasn't a lot of sugar-coating or massaging my ego from neighbours, friends and relatives. 'What happened there? Why didn't you win that one, then?' All of that stuff intensifies when you become successful and even when I was at the height of my career I'd still have to go home and answer to straight-talking Lancastrians, most of whom didn't know very much about squash other than that I played it and was meant to be quite good at it. I remember when I got to No.2 in the world and the first thing someone asked me was, 'Well, when are you going to get to No.1 then?'

Back then, I would overhear conversations people had with my dad about me. 'Well, she would be an alright player if she wasn't so tubby or was a bit faster wouldn't she?' These comments rubbed me up the wrong way but I tried to do something about it over the years. I wanted to be able to prove him and them wrong and say: 'Remember once when 'so and so' said I couldn't move? Well, I showed them!'

I also had to deal with weeks like the British Junior Open held a couple of hours away in Sheffield. It was the unofficial World Championship for juniors and every year, just after Christmas and New Year, kids from all over the world turned up to battle it out. The pressure I felt was enormous. I would be panicking that I was another year older and I still hadn't won an age group title at the most prestigious junior event in squash.

Looking back, the pressure I put on myself as a junior seems utterly ridiculous – some of which also came from family, school, coaches and squash-playing friends. It made it feel like every competition, every match, was all or nothing. The expectation of being No.1 in my country was something I loved and hated at the same time. I was still just a young teenager and I really wish I could have been told to just enjoy it and relax.

Generally, though, it was a dad-and-daughter team off to conquer the junior squash world. We would stop off on the way to squash events so Dad could have work meetings and check up on the pubs he ran for the company he had started working for.

I would sleep and chill in the car or occasionally go into the pub with him in the middle of the day. Sitting in a corner with a magazine, that nostalgic smell of stale beer and the feeling of the sticky floor underfoot is still there in my nostrils to this day. As meetings overran, there would often be a time when Dad would announce: 'You better get warmed up, we might be pushing it for your match.' I would then throw a leg out on the dashboard and stretch my hamstring. It seemed completely normal to me at the time. Who needs to warm up as a junior? I never would have believed that a decade later my warm-ups would sometimes be longer than my matches.

We would spend hours in the car together. Talking, laughing and joking. Dad painfully wanted to listen to BBC Radio 5 Live for hours on end and on the drive to events he would see how far we could keep the signal. At one point, on arrival in Germany for the Junior Open, the signal was hanging on by a thread because this was before the advent of digital radio. The sound of crackly voices and bursts of whistling radio interference still take me back there even now.

There are so many little things I remember about those endless hours together, with me and Dad and the motorway or hanging around at tournaments. As much as there were difficult times, we were also a team and we definitely had fun along the way. In the late 90s one of the petrol companies had a campaign where you could collect scratch cards to win chocolate bars when you stopped at a garage. I'm not going to go into details in case anyone from the garage chain or the chocolate manufacturer is reading this, but let's just say we found a loophole in the system and ended up with countless chocolate bars in the cupboard and more scratch cards than we knew what to do with. We collected so many that we even won a family trip to watch ITV's *Gladiators* being filmed.

The thing with Dad was, he just hated failure. When he was hard on me, it was really only ever about my squash. I always felt loved and supported by him and Mum and I'm sure my brother did too. Mum is the least competitive person you'll ever meet so they made a great team during those years. Mum was and still is so caring and loving to me and my brother. I like to think that I got the best parts of both of my parents – my mum's softer side and my dad's drive and discipline, as well as his sense of humour. I also feel genuinely lucky to have a little brother, especially one that I could pick on a little bit until he got big enough to fight back, upon which I decided I was much too old to bother with fighting him anymore. Christopher was brilliant to have around. He was cheeky and mischievous but cute growing up. He had a kind of calm confidence which was the exact opposite to me. He cared so much less what people thought of him and he was always much more popular than I was because he didn't ever seem to feel awkward in social situations like I did. As adults, we're not just siblings but really close friends.

My awkwardness and shyness wasn't helped by the cliquey and sometimes bitchy atmosphere around the junior tournaments in those days. Some of it was because Dad and I didn't really mix with other players and their families because he was trying to hold down a full-time job at the same time as supporting me. That meant he would often have to drop me off at a tournament while he went for work meetings at the pubs nearby that he was responsible for as an area manager. He only told me recently that this was because we didn't have a lot of money; he needed to be able to combine the squash trips with work to claim back the mileage and the hotel to be able to afford to take me. As a kid you are oblivious to what your parents are doing to make it all work.

Maybe other families on the junior circuit didn't have those worries. They certainly didn't seem to. I remember one occasion where I was waiting to play a third/fourth place play-off after losing in the semi-finals at a tournament in Sussex. It was Sunday afternoon, we had a five-hour drive back to Lancashire ahead of us and Dad would have to be up early and on the road again for work the next morning. He went to the parents of my opponent and explained this, asking if we could play the match a bit earlier so we could leave. They gave him a flat 'no', saying that she was much too tired to play another match so soon and that we would just have to sit around for a few more hours. Dad trudged back to tell me, only to later spot the whole family – including the girl who was much too tired to play – messing about energetically in the club pool.

That trip was particularly memorable too because Dad and I had a bet going. He was super competitive – which is where I get it from – and he loved to play squash, so, as I was improving, he bet me that I wouldn't beat him before I turned 14. Not long before my 14th birthday I got my first win, even copying the backhand flick drop that he always beat opponents with. I was especially proud of that! The bet was £50 and I was absolutely over the moon. Dad challenged me again 'double or quits'. We played again – I won! It was brilliant. Dad being Dad, he wouldn't let it go and he kept challenging me again. I kept winning. It was up to about £500 by the time we were travelling back from Germany and he turned to me and said: 'You know the bet? With the cost of this trip, do you think we could call it quits?' I was high from the event I'd just played, not to mention the brand new portable ghetto blaster sitting on my lap which had been second prize. Of course we could call it quits.

The problems came when the inevitable happened and I had an off-day on court. Generally, if I played badly and won it didn't matter to Dad but it still did to me and he didn't seem to understand that. If I lost and played someone older or better, that seemed acceptable. If I lost and it was to someone ranked lower or because I played poorly, this was when the trouble started. It fed a desperation in me on court and more nerves and more desperation followed. It was as if I was already looking ahead to the sick feeling in my stomach and the disappointment – mine and Dad's – that would be there if I lost. When you feel like that it becomes a self-fulfilling prophecy. I was panicking on the inside during matches, which stopped me from playing well, which just made me panic more and play worse. It's a very hard cycle to break, especially when you're just starting out.

On this particular January day in 2000, the Sheffield air was crisp and cold. Inside Abbeydale Squash Club, the air was heavy and steamy. For as long as I can remember I had been coming to Sheffield to play the British Junior Open, held two days into the New Year.

We headed off in the car, carefully crossing over the county border in the frosty weather, usually with the New Year sporting fixtures on the radio. Depending on match times we would travel back and forth until the latter stages of the event and this year was no different. I made it through the rounds relatively easily and found myself, as second seed, in the semi-finals against Swiss No.1 Manuela Zehnder.

We stayed at a local hotel and, as we did at most events, Dad and I were sharing a room. He was snoring and there I was lying wide awake, worrying about the next day's big match. I rooted around in my bag for my portable CD player in the hope it would get me to relax. I took some deep breaths to the same rhythm as my snoring father next to me. I didn't help.

The next morning, we dragged ourselves down to breakfast. It was a familiar pre-match routine. I felt like someone was whisking eggs in my stomach and I struggled to eat anything at all. I managed a small bowl of cereal as a full English breakfast was placed in front of me – Dad's idea, 'No point in wasting it if we have paid for it.'

I hardly ate anything.

I warmed up on my own with my earplugs from the night before back in my ears. Get your game face on. Be stern. Look like you mean business. Back then it was something I had to force a little.

The nerves were particularly bad that day and my legs felt like lead. Some people get hyperactive with nerves but I was always at the other end of the spectrum – heavy legged and always blanketed by a general feeling of sluggishness. I would blast tunes as upbeat as I could find on my CD player to inject some energy into my body and focus my mind. Nothing worked. I trudged onto that court with expectation draped over me like a heavy blanket weighing me down. The gallery behind the court was busy with people but I felt very alone. It was the most important day of my career to date, I had a good chance and I should have been bouncing with competitiveness and optimism. Instead it was like I was walking to the gallows.

I shouted at myself, got angry at the referee and tried anything to find a way to get some energy in my legs. I looked out and, perhaps because it was a reflection of what I was feeling, I immediately saw the worry on the coaches' faces. They had expected so much more from me and I was letting them down. That feeling crushed me, emotionally and almost physically. My legs got heavier, my reactions slower.

The rallies were going too quickly and Zehnder soon had the match on her racket. I looked out at Dad, the anger and disappointment was written all over his face. The match ended and, with it, my best opportunity to win a British Junior Open title. My eyes were stinging with tears as I ran off to be on my own. I hid, tucked away on a far away court, too embarrassed and ashamed of my performance to face anyone. My coach came to find me. Dad went back to his car.

As often happened following my matches, I went to have a shower and get changed, and then came out to find Dad sitting in the car on the phone or doing paperwork. As I approached I could see him waiting for me. I put my bag in the boot and slid into the passenger seat. He didn't look at me and carried on with whatever he was writing. My stomach plummeted, thinking, 'Oh God, he's really mad this time.' I waited for him to look at me.

'Sorry I lost, Dad.'

'It's a bit late for that now. What sort of a performance was that?'

'I tried my best but I just couldn't move properly today, I was really nervous.'

'We have this all the time …' his voice was getting louder as I edged further into my seat. 'What have you got to be nervous about?

'I don't know,' I whispered. But that wasn't true. Deep down this was the moment I had been so nervous about.

'Well, you better ring your mum to tell her you lost and that we are leaving now.'

'OK.'

Phoning Mum was never something I worried about. She wanted me to win but she always just felt sorry for me when it didn't turn out the way that I wanted. I knew she would be upset for me because she knew I always wanted to do well. She would have been dreading the phone call coming because she knew that Dad would be in a foul mood.

As we left the outskirts of Sheffield, the mood darkened and the radio wasn't doing quite enough to break the atmosphere. As the drive went on, so the tension built. I could feel it. Maybe it was Dad's face every time I looked over; maybe it was the silence itself. I felt hollow and empty inside. As happened so often in my future career, the hurt of the loss was so much lower than the high that the win might have brought.

The tension snapped somewhere on the M1 Northbound.

'Ring your mother and tell her to pick you up at the services.' It was the venom in his voice that hurt the most.

I just looked at him. 'What?'

He repeated what he'd said, but louder.

'Why, where are you going?'

'I'm not driving you all the way back to Chorley to get up early and drive to work in the morning. I've done enough ferrying you around. She can come and get you and deal with you.'

'But Dad I didn't mean to lose. Can't we just go home?'

'No, I've had enough of you. Just ring her.'

I was shocked. Was he really going to get Mum to drive an hour down the M62 with my brother, and then drive back in the opposite direction back to Sheffield? Was I really that bad? That horrible to be around? How can I make it right? I didn't know.

I made the call. Mum sounded shocked but she knew better than to argue or discuss it, so off she went and got in her car. I just sat and stared out of the car window as the bright lights of the M1 passed by. Having not spoken another word, Dad and I pulled up at Hartshead Moor motorway services, where Mum was to meet us. I opened the car door, got out without looking or saying anything to Dad and stomped off to Mum's car. I have no idea what was said between my parents. I was in my own little world.

Mum put her hand on my knee. 'Are you alright, love?'

I burst into tears. 'I didn't mean to lose,' I blurted out.

'I know,' she said. 'He's just angry. It will all calm down.'

Once we got home I went straight to my room and threw myself on my bed. I was utterly inconsolable. Mum came up later, cuddled me and stroked my hair.

'I'm quitting,' I said. 'I don't want to play anyone, I make everyone unhappy. I only want to win. Why can't I win?' All the anxiety seemed so stupid now, so what was the point? Maybe if I'd stayed calm I would have won. I was upset and frustrated all in one go. I had a huge weeping cut on my knee from throwing myself around and it was stinging like hell. Good punishment, I thought.

I've often thought about how hard that moment was for me, how maybe over the years I've made what happened worse in my mind. Or maybe not. Before sitting down to write this book, I asked my dad about that day and what was going through his head. What he told me surprised me and really helped me understand what had happened and why from his point of view.

He remembered seeing me upset and seeing my then coach really giving me a hard time, so he deliberately walked away and went to sit in the car so he didn't make that worse for me. While he was angry and disappointed, that was made far worse by the fact that he was completely exhausted and almost at the end of his rope after a long, hard week. He was working 16-hour days at that point, between his work and my squash tournaments, and everything was a struggle. Thinking back, I now remember looking at him on that horrible car journey home and seeing his eyes dropping as he drove because he was struggling to stay awake. He just couldn't face driving all the way home to Chorley only to have to turn around after a few hours' sleep and drive back to Sheffield for work. So he decided to stay there instead and get my Mum to collect me – anything for a few precious extra hours of sleep.

The 17-year-old me had logged that whole experience completely from my own perspective, oblivious to how things were for Dad. Was he upset and disappointed? Absolutely. Could he have handled things differently? Sure. The 37-year-old me can empathise with him being a human being and, at that moment, just having had enough. He ran himself into the ground for me and my squash, and sometimes it showed.

I also know that the success I had later in my career would not have been possible without him.

—

Some time later, after a lot of grovelling to Dad to get him to take me to events again, we were back on the road. I was winning, putting in the training and doing what I could to make sure that British Junior Open loss didn't happen again. Perseverance paid off and in July 2001 I got selected for the World Junior Championships in Penang, Malaysia – a hotbed of squash even then. Little did I know that I would have to draw on every little bit of resilience I had inside me.

After some early national success, I started to be noticed by England Squash and had been invited to some national squads, which I relished every second of. Everything was new for me and there was so much information and knowledge to absorb. National squads at Lilleshall were amazing – a full weekend away from my parents and time with fellow players, all of us immersed in squash. There was also a lot of hard work and the introduction of the dreaded fitness testing.

We were starting to see the benefits of National Lottery funding from UK Sport, which had first started in around 1997. Even as an up-and-coming junior you felt that money was flush and there was enough to spread around. That's not to say that my parents didn't invest a lot of their own money into my squash at an early age but it was nice to not be constantly asking and expecting more money from them. Just to put it into perspective, at the height of funding in my mid teens I was receiving £200 per month plus travel expenses towards my squash and was able to access free coaching on top. I can only imagine what the top players in the world were receiving at this point. The number of UK-funded players was through the roof back then.

As one national newspaper put it, England Squash had an almost 'Formula One style' pitlane team, a coterie of coaching, psychologists and physiologists, on top of free kit, frequent squads and paid trips to European events.

England also had its first female world champion in a decade when Cassie Campion won the 1999 world title, momentarily breaking the Australian stranglehold on women's squash – they had held a majority of British and world titles since the 80s. In turn, England's funding then controversially thrust squash to the front of the national newspapers when Scotland's Peter Nicol, who was men's World No.1 at the time, announced that he was to switch allegiances across the border to take advantage of our world-class programme. He was 28, an age where most British players started to peak.

The UK Sport funding also meant that the England Squash credit card was well used.

The now national head coach David 'Camps' Campion even had the nickname of 'No Budget Camps' back then. It got to a point where the women were getting more funding per month, the idea being that the men earned more on tour in terms of prize money. I can hardly imagine that happening now in squash or any other sport, for that matter. I certainly benefitted from funding in the sport and was a firm believer that all the monetary help I received should go back into my squash and performance. My longevity, the fact I was still a world top 10 player at 35 years old, was down to looking after my body correctly.

I was far from thinking about this when I turned the key to my hotel room when we arrived in Penang. England Squash funding saw five players travel for a three-strong team at the World Juniors – plus five staff, including coaches and physios. Best of all, we all had suites.

It was a fun trip compared to the set up now, where everything is more serious and geared around sports science and a lot of training. The Penang trip was all about the squash and camaraderie, even though we were seeded fifth and knew we were contenders. We bonded with trips to the bowling alley and fooling around with water pistols after practice. We all felt part of the team. We had a special embroidered kit and I had 'Long Legs' as my nickname – which has stuck to this day – written on the back.

The Malaysian press coverage was incredible. The event was back page news; we had never known anything like it. Even though our faces were all over the media, the hosts were probably more conscious of the pressure on them, with a certain young Penang-born player called Nicol David at the forefront.

How different this was to the UK. Despite our funding and participation levels ranking high, we were small fry compared to major sports being broadcast live on TV. Image, marketing and sponsorship was everything and sports editors, it seemed, had little time to give exposure to sports like squash. Not so in Malaysia.

We had reached the team final at the Penang International Sports Arena, where days earlier Nicol, then aged 17, had won the singles title in just 19 minutes and in front of several thousand passionate spectators. That was considered one of the biggest squash audiences ever, eclipsing the days when the Wembley Conference Centre would be packed out to watch Jahangir Khan win another British Open.

The hosts were going for a double and I remember Alison Waters going on to play her match in the first rubber. She won 3-0. It hit us all afterwards how we had just expected her to win easily, yet no one had considered the amount of expectation that put on her as a player. When she broke down at the end of the match, it showed how much pressure she was under. She had to go on and do a job, and she played brilliantly first up.

Nicol levelled things in the second match by beating Jenny Duncalf. Jenny had beaten me in the quarter-finals of the singles, so it was all left down to me to get the team victory in the deciding match. Things could not have started worse and my opponent was soon two games to the good and 7-2 up in the third. Sometimes it can be simple determination that can enforce change. I could be so far down in a match or so disappointed that I have just told myself: 'This is pathetic and I'm not having it.' It's not always as simple as that, of course. Sometimes it comes down to how you got to that point and how you deal with the disappointment of what's gone before. This was one of those matches. I felt there was more inside me and I needed to find it. On the cusp of defeat, I gave my team something to shout about and didn't lose another point in that third game.

When you dig out a victory like that in a team event, and your teammates see how much you're willing to fight to get the win for them, it's an incredible feeling for all of you. It gives you a feeling of being loved, appreciated and accepted that you don't often get in an individual sport.

The German team focussed their video camera on our team and, for some time after that, they used the footage in coaching sessions to underline team bonding. Team England was going bonkers after every rally and half of them ended up with sore throats after all the screaming. I came back to win 3-2, the first time I had beaten an international opponent from two games down. The Malaysian team manager was so stunned that he stayed rooted in his seat for around half an hour before the prize ceremony began.

I still have the press cuttings. 'The Empire Strikes Back' rang out the headline in the *Malaysian Sun* newspaper. In one of the other reports I had been asked how I was able to come back from the brink in the third. 'It all boiled down to who wanted the championship more,' I said.

When you win a team event like that you want to madly celebrate with everyone, even though you really don't have the energy. I left the festivities after an hour with a banging headache, feeling emotionally and physically drained. The satisfaction for me was not losing, which was far more important to me than winning. That's what gave me the warm, fuzzy feeling because it meant that I hadn't let the team down. At home if I won, I would buy the family a curry on a Sunday with my prize money. I was always happy that others were happy.

(Above) With Dad and my brother Christopher

(Right) The first time I walked onto a squash court

(Next page) With Captain Croc (Pontins mascot)

See my full photo gallery at lauramassaro.co.uk/photos

2. INVISIBLE PECKING ORDER

I had bridges to build. As I started out as a rookie senior player, travelling alone, I needed to make some friends. The squash tour, which involves travelling the world, is lonely enough as it is.

Our behaviour as a family unit had isolated us and created a few issues – I can now see how we might have come across to others. I think it's hard for competitive people, especially young women, to balance competing hard against your peers with getting on OK with them off the court. It's something I try to talk to young female players about at my girls' workshops. How can you understand that you are sometimes part of the problem? How can you adapt between competing hard and having social relationships? Most importantly, how can you perform at your best by understanding your personality and the personalities of those around you?

In those days young players weren't surrounded by the support systems that are in place for them now as they turn professional. Most elite athletes, even the younger ones, have a coach or physio you can call on and I know from training with sports like GB Taekwondo that they bring their athletes to events as a team. As a junior turning pro in squash at that time, I was on my own. I also had to prove my worth after it was plainly evident that many of the people in power in English squash didn't see me as anything special or as a threat in the women's game.

Being able to play squash for a living wasn't something I had really dared to think about as a junior, but as my early career progressed and the coaches then thought I was good enough for senior funding, it seemed worth a shot. When I deferred my university place – I had applied to study sports psychology at Cardiff University – it was with the intention of living life as a pro on the Women's International Squash Players' Association (WISPA for short) Tour for one year. I didn't want to have any regrets but I can't say that I was thinking that big. I just wanted to see how highly ranked I could get in one year.

I set about saving some money. I needed to be more self-sufficient. By then I had graduated from the chicken farm to working on reception at the local David Lloyd Chorley, which had opened its doors in 2000 and where I still train and coach to this day. I was on the rota for Wednesdays and Sundays, which meant never having a Saturday night out because I was up at 5am. While I didn't enjoy it, I knew it was good for me. I understood the structure and discipline of getting up and going to work, but it also made me realise that what I really wanted was to be a professional squash player on tour and not be sat behind reception, booking courts and handing out towels.

There were many, many times during my squash career that I got fed up with everything. When that happened I would stop and remind myself of that time and how lucky I was to be competing at sport for a living when most people never get that opportunity. At least I wasn't working on an egg farm, packing and boxing eggs for a few pounds an hour.

Working at the David Lloyd Club gave me a support system and meant I always had people rooting for me, which really helped me emotionally. Club members also got together and gave me financial support, which was absolutely vital at that stage. To help give me a start when I turned pro, members at the club put together a launch party for me. We had a brilliant night which included music, food, an auction and a general celebration that raised crucial funds. It was the brainchild of Adrienne Morris, helped along by Kim White and Sue Ashrafi – who I knew from those Lanchester Ladies League days – and others, and I will forever be in their debt for the time, effort and passion everyone put in for me that night. Just like when I used to play in the Lancashire and Cheshire Ladies League, when the older players took 16-year-old me under their wing, I had a group of women supporting me and wanting me to do well.

My squash was improving and I was getting more invitations to train with the crop of highly-ranked England pros. I found myself on court with some of the best women in the world, which included Cassie Jackman (who also competed as Cassie Campion), who won the World Open (later called the World Championships) in 1999 and was the best female squash player in the country at the time. It was a wonderful experience but I was always so anxious and awkward around Cassie and players like her. I wanted so much to impress them but, at the same time, I was so shy and starstruck that I could barely look at these women who I had so much respect for.

It wasn't just players I was in awe of; it was the coaches too. I will never forget my first experience on court with David Pearson – or DP as he's universally known. DP was national coach for 15 years and is the most successful coach England has ever had. He also worked with three-time world champion Nick Matthew for many years. At that time DP coached Cassie Jackman privately as well, so having a session with him was a massive deal for me.

I can't exactly recall our first session but DP told me later that I didn't look him in the eye for the first 30 minutes of coaching. He really had to work hard to get me to engage with him and take in the lesson. It was the same whenever I was around top players and coaches. To this day I can't shake the nickname of 'Pie Face' that the then assistant national coach Paul Carter gave me at the time. It probably gives you an insight as to how my face looked most of the time throughout my late junior and early senior career!

Those early awkward, anxious encounters with players and coaches I respected didn't help my fragile self-confidence. I carried so much of the internal pressure from juniors into my senior career. It seems silly now. I was travelling and playing only for myself now but I so wanted to win – and so didn't want to lose – that I got really nervous before every match. It felt like my feet were stuck to the floor. DP would often say: 'Oh no, it's one of those days where she's moving like she's stuck in treacle.'

What I had in my favour was that even when I had been crippled with nerves and lost matches because of being unable to control them, there was always an effort and determination to win that ran through me. I was, and always will be, a stubborn person. I hated to lose more than anything. Nerves were one thing but I would never have forgiven myself if a loss came because of a lack of effort.

My early insecurities probably weren't helped by getting my head around a life of international travel and the travelling circus of the pro tour, which is part and parcel of being a professional squash player. I got to go to some incredible places at a really early age but it is a lot to deal with when you first start out; missed flights, lost baggage, billeting in strange people's houses because you couldn't always afford hotels, not to mention trying to fit in with the other established players off the court and losing to them on it. This is all especially hard if you aren't very self-confident or outgoing. It was all a learning curve. At the Swiss Open in Zurich, I ended up with a billet at a single guy's flat with two other female competitors – all of us still in our teens. There was nothing in the fridge and there was a spare bedroom where two could sleep but you had to go through this strange guy's living quarters to get to the second bedroom. It was a very odd situation and we tossed a coin to see who had to basically move in with a strange man none of us had ever met before. I think they changed the rules after that so single men couldn't host.

I had my fair share of small prize money success in my first year on tour, at least enough to keep me going and top up the support I was getting from England Squash and the fundraising at the David Lloyd Club. I also had a few tough losses. Getting so-called 'good draws' and not being able to take advantage of it was always frustrating and took me back to those unexpected losses as a junior. My coach at the time, Annette Pilling, was great at helping me deal with those defeats and find a way to stop them happening again. Annette was my coach for seven years up until I was 21 and she used to say that I had created a winning habit as a junior and it was important to keep that going. What she meant was that she wasn't about to throw me into big events where I would come across players who would hammer me. Instead, she had me play a mix of small and medium events to start with and as my level improved we increased the size of the events I played.

Within my first year as a professional I had risen to 47 in the world and after two years on tour was up to a world ranking of 26. It was certainly enough progress to justify deferring my university place again – perhaps indefinitely.

In those early days I was flying to events and getting several matches under my belt – keeping myself in the winning habit while also gaining valuable experience on tour. I started to understand how to put matches, rounds and events together. Of course, I wanted to be in the big events and playing against the 'big guns' but Annette wanted me to hold back. It was brave advice to give and a risk because it wouldn't suit every player. It worked for me though, because I learned my trade and kept winning. Sometimes I saw players dive straight into the big events and I was jealous. On reflection, I am grateful to Annette for holding firm. When I was finally let loose, I was ready to draw on my experiences, that maybe others didn't have, of battling away the lower tiers of the sport. Having been away from the big events and not seen many of the top girls play also gave me an advantage in a weird way. I don't want to say I didn't have any respect but just didn't know what players had achieved and so I went into those early matches without fear. I wanted to win and at the time I'm sure that came across as arrogance and overconfidence but really I was just a bit clueless.

Later in my career, I would recognise myself in some young players when I watched them turn up without any scars because they hadn't yet endured the tough losses. They hadn't had match balls and lost; they hadn't got on a 12-hour flight only to lose in the first round and then had that happen to them again a few weeks later. They are fresh, hungry and fearless. It's an attitude that will always make you dangerous against well-established professionals. I would sometimes hear the other older players commenting and laughing on how the so-called 'newcomer' should have respect or bitching about a youngster's on-court behaviour. I've been part of that kind of talk; I don't mind admitting that. Sport is hierarchical; there's a pecking order and players don't like it when some upstart comes along and upsets it.

There is a cliché about women's sport being bitchy and I'd love to dispute that but in all honesty I can't. I have never been on the men's tour but having spoken to some of the guys and, from playing mixed events, I am absolutely sure that there is more whispering and gossiping amongst the female players. Not many of the women will admit to the invisible pecking order but it's there, like a shadow ranking system based on a calculation of a player's number of years on tour, actual ranking, up-to-date gossip, close friends' ranking and, of course, banter level. Young players are often oblivious to all of this. It's like a secret club that they have yet to break into. As the scars start to form on them and the pressure builds, they will usually unknowingly find their place in that pecking order and become one of the 'in crowd'.

From 2002 to 2004, I was just riding the high of being on the tour circuit, winning some great matches – like when I beat Madeleine Perry, who was then ranked in the top 20, to score the first really big win of my career. Needless to say I was also taking my fair share of tough losses and there were periods where I felt I was stagnating. Having started January 2002 as

World No.75, I was in the twenties by 2004 but I then hit a plateau, as lots of players do, and it started to grate on me.

In retrospect, I wasn't fit enough and I was probably carrying a bit too much weight. Several coaches had given me a hard time about my movement. DP even accused me once of moving like an elephant. He says he can still remember the surly look I gave him when he said it.

I was also still struggling to assert myself off the court among the people who made decisions about funding within England Squash. For more than two years in my early twenties, I was told repeatedly that I didn't have a bright future in the sport. Then, one day, I was in the England Squash offices in Manchester and a staff member had left a file which showed all our individual funding. It was purely fluke and I shouldn't have seen it but I did. There in front of me was the confirmation that some players were on more lottery money than me, even though I was in the same ranking bracket. I was achieving as much but receiving less funding because they just didn't rate me.

I was so pissed off. I rang the Performance Director, Peter Hirst, and asked for a meeting. He told me directly that he didn't believe that I had the same potential as my tour peers, Jenny Duncalf or Alison Waters. I'm not sure how he reached this conclusion; both had started life well as senior players but then so had I.

It's hard to put into words how dispiriting it was. As players we had all come through the junior system together and, in my mind, we all had an equal chance of progressing, yet for some reason I was the one who wasn't good enough. I couldn't believe it and I was devastated by what Peter was telling me. The people in charge of my sport in my country did not see me as a real contender to be the world's best. So, on top of my own self doubt, I had to deal with their doubt as well. It went on for months.

As much as this upset me, as so often happened throughout my career, it was more the anger which fuelled me. It got to the point where I would think about that conversation with Peter during a really tough gym session and I'd go harder for another 30 minutes almost just to spite him. And yet, if I had the chance to sit down with Peter now, I'd probably say thank you and I might even buy him a beer. All that extra effort I put into proving him wrong turned me into a much better player than I might otherwise have been.

Going from a junior to senior also came at the time when my parents had split up in my late teens. Mum had moved out of the family house and our home was broken.

My parents split not long after our victory in Penang at the World Juniors. I was oblivious at the time but my brother will say even now how unenjoyable that trip was for him. It should have been the holiday of a lifetime for my parents and brother – instead it was far from ideal.

I always had this vision that my parents would be together forever. Doesn't everyone? So, when my parents sat my brother and me down to tell us they were separating it hit us both pretty hard. I mean, I think we knew things weren't great but I guess I never thought past that really.

I remember saying: 'So, what happens now?' The answer I got was: 'Well, nothing really, we aren't sure.' That surprised me and, from that point on, I think things went from bad to worse. I was lucky that I could get out of the house a little more than my brother and I think it hit him a little harder than me, being around the tension a lot more.

Things finally came to a bit of a head and couldn't go on the way they were. My mum left the family home and moved in with a friend. It was absolutely the right thing for her to do – something needed to change to save the household from arguments and further breakdown. Honestly, it didn't really get any easier over the following months. It was a long process that took a long time to work through. Eventually, I actually left and moved in with Danny at 18 years old. Looking back, making that move made me mature and grow up quick. I had to be self-sufficient and learn very quickly how to look after myself. It was really tough leaving my brother, who was also under a lot of tension and also three years younger than me but, I guess selfishly, at that age I did what I needed to do to keep myself sane. I can honestly say none of the four of us were happy. It took a long time for the separation to be finalised and for us all to be in a situation where we could move on.

On reflection, everyone is better off for the split. No one wants to be in an unhappy marriage or household. As kids it was tough, really tough for my brother, but you learn from it, try to forgive and then move on with life. No point in hanging onto bitterness. Having said that, it's taken a lot of talking and working through those thoughts to get to this point. If I hadn't worked through those issues I am pretty sure I would still be struggling with parts of it. Like all issues in our childhood, they have an effect on our adult life. For me, this included my squash. If I had any hope of being the best player I could be on court, I needed to work through and past what happened in my childhood. Even though that was extremely tough.

Dad and I weren't getting along after the split and Danny became my rock. He proposed in a local village near Club La Santa in Lanzarote and we got married in 2007.

I will admit, the boyfriend/husband-coach relationship wasn't always rosy. It was a learning curve for both of us in the early days on tour. Danny says he was like a 'bull in china shop' during our first coaching sessions together. He had been a coach and studied sports psychology, so he thought he knew all the elements – technique, fitness, learning, tactics – but he admits now that he had yet to learn just how tough professional squash was and what it took to win. We also both had to navigate being husband and wife, as well as coach and player, and sometimes we both got it wrong.

We had our moments in those early days. Sometimes when I lost, Danny would even blame me – you can imagine how that went down. He hadn't travelled with me when I lost to Madeline Perry at the Australian Open and right after the match, he sent a brutally honest email. The gist was that it wasn't good enough; I wasn't being myself, my movement was poor and I couldn't play a drop shot. I was devastated at losing and the man I loved was on the other side of the world and sending me emails like that. At that moment I needed comfort from my husband, not criticism from my coach.

I was starting to develop a worrying habit of losing matches from winning positions, which, as any athlete will tell you, is a horrible feeling that can really stay with you.

I played Vanessa Atkinson, born in England, raised in the Netherlands, who is now the partner of top English squash player James Willstrop. At the time, Vanessa was second in the world and someone I massively looked up to. She was one of the first top pros I played when I started out (she once hammered me for just four points) and even though I'm sure I made a complete fool of myself when I tried to speak to her, Vanessa was always lovely to me. So, when I found myself in a winning position against her at the 2006 Hong Kong Open, I couldn't believe it. Not that long before, I had almost beaten Australian Rachael Grinham – another great player – in the British Open having had a match ball and lost. That was fresh in my mind, so, even at two games up, I was full of anxiety, nerves and doubt. When that happens, it becomes a self-fulfilling prophecy and I went on to lose the match from a winning position again, which in turn gave me more anxiety. Something had to change.

Danny started to realise that how he was talking to me – with feedback straight after a defeat – was sometimes counterproductive. He thought that was the way you could speak to a player as a coach but it wasn't always what I needed to hear or the right time for me to hear it. We realised that he, and the whole coaching team around me, needed to find a different approach.

That was the start of the thought process to leaving Annette, my coach, which was never going to be an easy conversation for either of us. As a young player, parting with a coach, especially one who's been such a huge influence on your career up to that point, is an incredibly difficult decision to make.

Annette had invested so much time in me over 10 years and had such a massive impact; she had moulded and shaped me as a player. I know she felt she had more to give, but I felt it was the right decision for me. I handled it as well as I could but it was a horrible conversation for both of us.

I started to work part-time with Nigel Willis, who had been working in the Lancashire squash scene for years and he helped to implement more creativity and deception into my game. He instilled court sprints, new movement exercises and made me work harder. He wasn't a strictly technical coach but had a great understanding of the game, his fresh approach gave me a new impetus. It worked and I had my breakthrough by beating some good players at the British National Championships. It was quite an original coaching relationship because we were friends and I never paid him because the sessions were more supportive than formal. It was another coach, Nick Taylor, who then introduced pressure sessions and got me to use my strings more. It was the perfect knock-on effect after working with Nigel because Nick had just retired from the professional game and had 'tour knowledge' combined with excellent technical understanding. Nick was then handed a role in Jersey and the partnership couldn't continue.

By 2010, I was just inside the world's top 10 and without a coach again. However, Nick suggested working with Welsh-based coach Phil Whitlock, who told it how it was and who I knew would get me working hard to improve my physical conditioning. Phil was 'all in'.

The decision to change to Phil paid dividends almost immediately, before a stroke of bad luck stopped us in our tracks. I was match point up against Jenny Duncalf at the KL Open in Malaysia before losing in the quarter-finals and I rolled my ankle for good measure. I then got food poisoning hours later. I was out for three months with the ankle but the most frustrating part was forging a relationship with a new coach while unable to get on court. When I was finally back, things became a lot more intense. I drove to Colwyn Bay to work with him once a week and he was on the phone all the time. He continually wanted to know practice match results, what I was doing and where I was.

He was able to watch me live for the first time at the Irish Open in the autumn of 2010, where I lost in the semi-finals and he told me directly afterwards that I wasn't fit enough, that I needed to get fitness tested. I was too heavy as far as Phil was concerned. It was difficult to hear because nobody is happy to have their body criticised, but deep down I knew that he was right.

That was probably still in my head at my next tournament two weeks later, the World Championships in Sharm El Sheikh. The tournament could not have gone any worse and me losing in the second round was only the start of it. After I lost to a talented young French player, Camille Serme (who went on to become one of the best players in the world), Danny and I went out for a meal to chew over the defeat. Neither of us was in a very good mood. Sitting outside in the cool Egyptian night, the conversation turned to how badly Danny thought I'd played.

'You blew it even before you went on today,' started Danny. 'I could tell before the match. That's why you lost.'

'No, you're reading into it too much. I was fine.'

'Come off it, Laura. You were quiet all day and moody. You weren't excited enough to play.'

'I was fine, Danny. You don't know what it's like out there, you don't understand. I didn't mean to not play well. I don't want to let you down and I don't want to let myself down. It's causing me pressure.'

I'm sure the rest of the people in the restaurant were shifting awkwardly in their seats by now. Was it just a young couple having an argument or was it a coach giving his player some hard truths? We didn't really know either.

'I'm not causing you pressure; you want me to be here. I could be off doing something else. Don't push that onto me.'

'I know but I just don't want to lose. It means we have wasted money and your time to come here and I know how gutted you are when I lose.'

'It's the World Championship! Of course I'm gutted. Do you expect me to be happy?'

'No, of course not, just some understanding or a bit of sympathy or something, since you're my husband.'

I could feel my voice wobbling a bit. Danny was adamant.

'Well, it's just not in my nature, this is business. Besides, why can't you just see me as inspiration? I can't believe you see me as pressure when all I am trying to do is help you? You need to sort your head out. You're just soft and if you carry on being soft you will end up getting worse and worse until you hate playing!'

'If I am so bad, I will stop coming. Will that satisfy you?'

I couldn't hold back the tears. Dinner was served in silence, with tears dripping down my face.

'Why are you crying?' he continued. 'This is what I was talking about. You've gone soft.'

'Just leave me alone, Danny. It's making it worse, just stop …'

By the time we went to bed that night, we were barely on speaking terms.

Danny admitted later, when we looked back on that horrible conversation, that it wasn't so much an argument as a one-way assault. There were accusations, threats and doom-laden prophecies about how my career would turn out if I carried on how I was going. Danny cringed about it afterwards but he was open enough to recall the episode in his book 'The Winning Parent'. Looking back, he admitted, it was clear to see that he was a big part of the problem.

The emotion of sport had clouded Danny's perspective and he'd allowed his own disappointment to influence the way he spoke to me as a coach. It was one of the most difficult experiences I'd ever had after a loss, and it brought back some memories of how I had sometimes felt as a junior, travelling with my dad and feeling that I'd let him down. Losing hurts enough without someone you love having a go at you about it afterwards.

Needless to say, after reflecting on things, Danny felt really bad about his reaction and was trying to work out how best to apologise to me.

At the time, he was coaching a highly ranked men's player, Jon Kemp. He trusted Jon's opinions on pro squash and personal relationships, and he also had a perspective on what happens when squash becomes part of your home life, since he was engaged to a top female squash player at the time.

Danny asked Jon whether he was being too intense with me.

'Yes, you are,' Jon told him, almost instantly. 'When you coach me, it's fine to be straight talking and go for a reaction from me. You're my coach and I know it isn't personal. With your wife, you just can't be so brutal. Now, when she has lost, she needs to know you are there for her. It's the same with parents and their kids.'

It was a huge reality check for Danny and he began to feel very guilty.

'It's not your job to make her play well or win,' Jon told Danny. 'That is her job. You're here as a husband to support her through the good times and the bad.'

Jon then said something that changed Danny's whole perspective and our professional relationship forever.

'What would you feel like if Laura came to work with you every day and told you what you were doing wrong, and how every time you had a bad day it was all your fault?'

Guilt immediately turned to embarrassment and Danny felt ashamed of his self-centeredness. As he wrote in his book: 'How had I become so nasty and unsympathetic to my wife's needs? I loved her very much, yet I had behaved like I didn't care for her. All I saw was a player, not a person.'

Both Danny and I are plain-spoken people so it's not as if I ever wanted him to shy away from saying what he thought as a coach. It was something I wanted from everyone who coached me. In fact, that honesty was why it worked so well between us professionally and personally. At the same time, however, Danny going too far that night caused him to think differently about how he coached me and it really strengthened our relationship as coach and player, and as husband and wife.

19th September 2010 (diary entry the night after that infamous argument between Danny and me)

Where do I go now? So many mixed results. The World Champs in Sharm El Sheikh I lost to Camille Serme 3-2. Another last 16 loss. More nerves, more tightness, no drops, no fight, feeling sorry for myself, no toughness. Where has all the grit gone? Have you really changed that much? Another loss, you must be getting used to them by now. You love to win so why not take it to them. Why are you so soft? Where has all your belief gone? Pressure is a privilege. No failure, just feedback. If you always play like you've always played, you'll always perform the way you've always performed. Negative, no enjoyment. When will you learn to change? Your life must revolve around squash. Enjoy it and be gritty. There's only one way from here and THAT IS UP.

It's funny to me that my diary entry from the following morning doesn't mention our fight, even though it turned out to be a huge turning point for Danny and me and for my career. At that moment I was more concerned about what I could do to stop losing at big tournaments. I still couldn't seem to quell my nerves before matches and it was becoming debilitating.

I also thought more about what Phil had said about me being too heavy.

I knew that Phil could be tough but I didn't hide away from that; I asked for it. When people give you advice, they are giving you responsibility. I was ready to do what he told me to do. Phil wasn't going to be able to help me otherwise. There is sometimes a perception with female athletes that they need or want a gentler, more sensitive approach and male coaches who are quite harsh can be perceived as bullying. I don't think it's as simple as that. There are definitely different ways to coach men and women, and there is no question that women's bodies are very different to men's, but every athlete's personality is different, irrespective of their gender. I was used to toughness and I responded well to it.

Weight gets talked about a lot in women's sport. I know there have been many examples across different sports of coaches – often men – obsessing about a female athlete's weight and shape and making remarks about it. I have no doubt that this could be incredibly hurtful for young women who might already be struggling with their self-image. It's one of the reasons why all sports need more female coaches and more understanding of how women's and girls' bodies differ from men's and boys' because female weight fluctuates more, especially during puberty.

Phil was not a man to sugarcoat things and I'd be lying if I said that him saying I was too heavy didn't get to me; it did. At the same time I wanted to be the best that I could be and the way Phil put it made sense to me. He was into his cars and he said I needed to be like a Porsche, with a light body frame and a big engine. It de-personalised it somehow.

It was time to take action and that meant educating myself about nutrition. I read a book called *The Calorie Carb & Fat Bible*, which was a bit of a revelation and ended up having a huge impact on me and my career. The book helped me work out how active I was and how many calories I should be eating per day for my body weight. It made me realise that I could eat an apple or a Mars Bar, set myself a target for the day and understand how that affected my overall calorie intake. If it was a hard training day I was on about 2,300 calories to maintain my body weight. If I wanted to lose half a pound per week, I needed to cut down by around 500 calories per day. For the first time, I was matching my calories to my training, measuring my food and writing everything down.

I became very strict with myself and I took care over exactly what I ate and when I ate it, as well as my portions. I ate porridge for breakfast, then salad, a sandwich, fruit or a cereal bar for lunch, and either fish or a stir fry plus fruit or yoghurt for dinner. Junk food was ruled out because it wasn't energy-efficient. I cut down on tea and coffee, and I gave myself a treat at weekends if the week had gone well, just like I had done at junior tournaments with those family curries we'd celebrate with if I'd won the trophy.

Phil never spoke to me in an emotional way and his directives were always factual. His direct approach meant I sometimes had to take deep breaths but his words cut through and I began to get better. I soon recorded my first victory in over a year, which turned out to be the first of three tournament wins in a row – the first time in my career that I'd done that.

Having improved my body and got myself fitter, now it was time to get my mind into shape as well.

In the lead up to the final event of 2010, the Sharm El Sheikh Open at the Laguna Vista Hotel, I had a session with Peter McNab, a Neuro-Linguistics Programming (NLP) coach, who had been brilliant in a course I had briefly attended with Danny. I thought he could help me in my squash. I've never been afraid to try new ways of improving, even those that didn't fit into people's idea of traditional squash coaching. Danny is also an avid reader and has an amazing thirst for knowledge and self-improvement, which has also influenced me to think 'outside the box'.

NLP essentially aims to give practical ways to improve self-awareness and confidence, and where you can change the way that you think, view past events and approach your life. I really enjoyed the course; it expanded my mind and I started to realise that I could actually take control of the way I thought. I wanted further help with my mind and Peter seemed a great choice. I actually felt it was a bonus that he wasn't involved in the sport because he came with a new perspective.

We talked about my squash and my family, about learning to play a lot more for myself and taking each match as it comes a bit more. Peter introduced me to the Enneagram, a personality system that gave me a perspective, not only on what I am like as a person but the reason behind why I behave the way I do. I started to understand why I act in a certain way and why I am the way I am. It liberated me and helped me understand myself and throw off some of the previous behaviours that had been shackling me – like getting nervous and allowing those nerves to affect me when I was in winning positions. It was a big breakthrough.

My squash had started to turn around and I didn't realise how the things we were talking about in my sessions with Peter were really helping me, albeit in a very subtle way. I was giving it my all in matches. When I went to Sharm for an event full of mainly Egyptians, who were all very accomplished players, Peter and I had created a trigger, which is an NLP technique whereby you do a small ritual which immediately triggers a certain feeling or behaviour. I see athletes using these triggers in other sports, for example a tennis player bouncing the ball a certain number of times before they serve or a rugby player having a certain ritual before taking a kick. Our trigger was me putting my thumb to my strings, which instantly calmed me down, relaxed me and made me feel light and nimble in my movement.

I spent a lot of time on my own in Sharm, being one of just a few English players in the draw, and I had a room to myself. It meant that, for the first time in my life, I felt like I was playing more for myself than anyone else.

I was returning to the same city as my world championship meltdown two months previously, but this time the venue was the tournament hotel, which had two of the dustiest squash courts I have ever seen. I spent the first three days mopping the courts myself every few hours to clear the dirt and desert sand and stop the floor slipping. I felt as if I wouldn't be able to move at all in my first round and people seemed to be laughing at the fact that I had taken to mopping it myself. Perhaps this should have been a job for the organisers at this early stage but I felt more comfortable doing it myself, that way I knew I wouldn't slip. It put me in control, even if at that moment, I was only in charge of a mop.

Being in the desert, every cleaning session was one step forward and two back. I would go back in the morning with my mop and there would be a new level of dirt on the court, plus the remaining dirt from previous weeks. Every day I would mop and it would get a little bit cleaner and less slippery. By the time I played the semi-final, the courts were as good as perfect and I won the event, beating Raneem El Welily, a rising Egyptian with bundles of natural skill, to the title. It made all that mopping feel worthwhile.

I had a proper break that Christmas and before I started training again I chatted with my coach Phil, my fitness trainer Matt Cooke, and Peter about where my squash should go. It felt great to have a team around me who could lead me in the direction we all knew I wanted to go.

———

I worked with Peter on a number of techniques and processes, one of which is called The Organic Belief Process, an NLP technique that we discuss in greater detail further into the book. The effect was immediate.

At the Cleveland Classic, I beat Jenny Duncalf for the first time in five years and then faced Nicol David in the final – the first time I had made it to the last day in a Gold event.

Nicol had dropped just one game in the entire Cleveland tournament. We also knew that 'the Malaysian queen of squash', the World No.1 for just shy of 60 months, hadn't been beaten since November 2009, a 14-month run. She'd also beaten me nine times in a row.

But despite all that, perhaps for the first time, I had belief.

When you played Nicol you had to consistently hit quality targets in the front and back corners, where the aim was to try to force weak returns. If you hit a good length, you could set up volleying opportunities, apply pressure and, crucially, win rallies. Phil always used to say to me that Nicol isn't as fit as everybody thinks. Her speed covers this up but, the problem was, I had to get her to the point where she couldn't rely on her speed anymore to expose the fitness side. On the other hand, if she got a head start on you, even if you could fight back you'd be so knackered that she'd still win in the end.

I had real focus that day though. One of the things that stood out was that I didn't care if I won or lost. I was focussed on each rally, the next rally. It felt like I had never played a match like it. I was two games up and in a battle to win the third and close out the match. It was tight and turning physical, as matches against Nicol always were. I narrowly lost the next and came off a little deflated. During the break I had Latasha Khan in my corner, who was one of the best players tactically at the time.

'I needed that game,' I said to Latasha, breathing hard. After all, I was knackered and I was playing one of sport's fittest players.

Latasha looked me in the eyes. 'No. You need the next one.'

I served for the match and I remember it being far from a big deal.

Strangely so. It was Championship ball but I just knew I needed to play a good rally, just like I had been doing through the match. I had a good team around me and I'd worked hard but in the past that hadn't been enough because I hadn't believed. Now, thanks to all the work I'd done with Peter, beating the greatest player of all time to win the biggest title of my career felt very normal.

What's interesting now is that I always thought I'd played amazingly in that match but when I watched it back a few years later, my memory wasn't quite as perfect as I thought, nor was the squash. It's not always about how you play but how you feel when you play.

When I came off court after winning that match, I rang Danny straight away. We had agreed beforehand that he wasn't going to watch. It was the middle of the night back home and he had work the next day. In our last conversation before the match he had said to me: 'You've played great all week, you don't need me, I trust you.' It gave me a lift hearing that from him.

When I rang at close to 2am, he was asleep but he knew I wouldn't have rung at that time if I had lost. He was over the moon. He couldn't believe it. I told him how well I'd played, that I had believed and felt calm the whole match, even at the end. I was still gabbling down to the phone to him excitedly when I had to rush off for the presentation and it made everyone laugh when I went down the steps to collect my trophy still saying goodbye to Danny.

I took that confidence into the British National Championships straight away when I got back to England. I then won the national title for the first time and became the first Lancastrian – male or female – to do so.

I was now beginning to accept who I was as a player. Coach Phil had a lot to do with that. He made me look at my game in a different way, to play to my strengths, and he taught me that there was always more I could do to get better, even when I thought I was being professional enough.

Within a few weeks I won my first major title at the US Open, beating Aussie Kasey Brown in the final. That victory, on a glass court, was my biggest achievement to date. I was now a top five player and my form continued into 2012 where I won the Carol Weymuller Open in New York and reached the last four of the British and US Opens. But I knew I could get more out of myself.

Phil hadn't changed much about my technique and he was fixed on wanting me to play straight rather than looking to adapt my play so I could hammer an opponent's weakness in a creative way to take control. We clashed about this more than anything. The bottom line is that it's no fun to play straight all the time. I was starting to develop my own ideas about how I wanted to play.

It was a massive part of realising that the best way for me to play was not to try to open up the court too much, to protect my movement, to be accurate and to play the way I was good at, which was to bang the ball to the back of the court. I was beginning to get to grips with what my strengths were, to solve problems based on what I did best.

The Hong Kong Open was where I finally decided to leave Phil. He had done a great job in getting me to World No.2 but it was clear that we had very different ideas about what was best for my squash. It all came to a head when I played Egypt's Omneya Abdel Kawy in the first round, a tough, highly-skilled opponent who was usually a top eight player. Phil told me she wasn't fit, to just play straight, volley and make her move. In my head I didn't really want to play like that. I knew it needed more than that, I needed to not let her get into patterned play. I had this internal battle going on during the match and, unsurprisingly, it spiralled away from me.

In squash a match can slip from your hands in the blink of an eye when you aren't 100 per cent focussed. I started to melt down and I even stooped so low as to call Omneya a cheat – something which, to this day, I really regret. She went crazy at me, which is completely understandable.

Omneya clearly wasn't a cheat. I was just a mess at that point and furious with myself and I lashed out at my opponent. At least, despite that, I had the sense to apologise to her.

I phoned Danny afterwards. We agreed it was time for a change. It was one of the only times I can remember coming off court, not showering and calling to change my flight within 15 minutes. I headed straight for the airport. I called Danny again, bawling my eyes out as I sat on the floor at the flight gate with my phone plugged into the wall. I was a mess, on my own and faced with this huge decision about my professional future and what was then one of the most important relationships in my life. Thoughts turned to my first coach, Annette, and how the parting of ways had affected my off-court relationship with her for a good decade afterwards. Now, with Phil, I was going to have to have another horrible conversation.

As I sat there on the floor, tears streaming, I suddenly felt a tap on my shoulder. A woman I had never seen before quietly placed a bar of chocolate in my hand and spoke to me, in a quiet, calm voice. 'I know that whatever is bothering you this won't make it better, but I hope it helps.' Then she turned and walked off. It's up there with one of the kindest things anyone has ever done for me.

After my semi-final loss in 2012 at the US Open, I had done a session on court with DP on a side court at Drexel University in Philadelphia. I remember I was strangely nervous. I was World No.2 but I really wanted to impress him, just as I had when I'd had coaching sessions with him in juniors. I certainly didn't want him thinking that I was the same player I was then. He had coached our last English World Champion, Cassie Jackman. I wanted him to think I was as good as her.

I had had a few coaching sessions with DP previously and he'd taught me that there was a way of being able to take control of my own thoughts and tactical ideas. Ideally I would have liked for Phil and DP to work together.

In my call to Phil, I told him that DP looks at the game differently, has some creative ideas, and that I needed some fresh input and technical work which would unlock other aspects of my game. I wanted Phil to work with me, build it all into the plan and perhaps bring his daughter, Emily, who was an emerging player.

Phil told me to ring back once he had thought about it. When I called back he made it clear it was all in with him or nothing; just as it had done with Annette, the relationship effectively ended at that moment. I played Emily a few years later at the British National Championships, where she played really well and I had to come back from two games down. In my post-match speech, I praised Emily's play and the work she had done with her dad. I said that I was partly the player I was that day because of Phil and that I never had the chance to properly thank him for the work he did with me.

In the changing room afterwards, Emily told me that her parents were gobsmacked at what I had said because they never thought I was appreciative of what Phil had done for me. It made me sad to hear that. I meant every word of what I said on court that day. The coaching relationship with Phil might have broken down in the end but I'll always be grateful to him.

After splitting with Phil I had one last tournament in 2012, the World Championships in the Cayman Islands. Without a full-time coach, Danny and I headed over to the event together. I worried about the pressure of Danny travelling with me and the financial cost for us because it meant an extra flight, hotel and food. I broached the subject mid-flight and we had a great chat about his role. I explained I was feeling nervous about him travelling with me and the expectation that might come with that. Looking back, it was another big moment when we clarified our professional roles with each other. He asked what I needed from him while we were away. I asked him to help me set a plan for my matches, be there to hit with me if I needed it before my matches and then watch me play. That was it. I was happy with that but Danny said: 'Can I say what I would like then?'

I laughed because I selfishly hadn't factored that in. He said in return he would like me to say 'thank you' when he gave his time, to try my best in matches and then let him have a holiday around our commitments. It was brilliant and I instantly felt more relaxed to have an agreement we could both stick to.

We arrived in Cayman after a long journey via New York and Miami. I had some good hits and was getting used to the temperature, the court and the humidity. After my second hit, I did some court sprints which was a normal routine for me to blow my lungs out and give me confidence in my fitness and speed. I felt good immediately afterwards but that soon began to change.

By the time we got back to the hotel, my legs were aching and tired. I thought it was the aftermath of the sprints but the achiness got worse and I soon had a fever. I woke up the next morning feeling awful, with a bad case of the runs and feeling sick. That night Danny suggested we go to a local restaurant to get out of the hotel room and get some fuel back into me. The only thing on the menu that felt plain enough to eat was chicken and chips – not the best meal for the night before a major first round or for recovering from a gastric bug! Danny eventually nagged me into forcing it down, because he knew I needed to have some fuel in me to have any chance on court the next day. It lasted about 10 minutes before I quickly had to leave the restaurant to be sick. Danny found me bent over a bush outside the restaurant. Classy. It's fair to say he felt bad about nagging me to eat after that!

I hadn't had much luck in Cayman. I think I had withdrawn from only three tournaments in my whole career, two of them being back-to-back years in Cayman when I first rolled my ankle, followed by a back injury where the family had booked a holiday and ended up going without me. Now, here I was, back in Cayman and throwing up in a bush the night before my first round match at the World Championships.

I was playing a Colombian girl called Catalina Peláez. I still hadn't hit in two days. I spoke to Peter McNab about my feelings because I wasn't sure if I should even try to play, yet I was a third seed and this was the sport's biggest tournament. Peter suggested that I make a mental deal with myself: I was allowed to rest, sleep and feel rubbish until the match and then I would ask myself to raise it for one hour. Meanwhile, Danny suggested that I get some makeup because he didn't want my opponent to see me looking so pale and he knew it would help get my game face on.

I managed to get off court after a 20-minute win and recover for the next 36 hours. That deal I made with myself paid off.

After two less eventful matches I was through to face Egypt's Raneem El Welily, the second seed. Despite feeling so rubbish early on, all the matches I had played had real focus and clarity. I had been reading Tyler Hamilton's award-winning Tour de France book The Secret Race that week and I was loving it. It was all about the pain cyclists go through and the will they need to find to overcome it and climb those mountains. I took lessons from it into my matches. I had a 'go get it' attitude that meant I was going to be aggressive and go after every point; playing to win not just to avoid losing.

That semi-final against Raneem was incredibly tough. At two games all, as I sat in my chair trying to prepare for the decider, my heart was beating fast, I was pouring with sweat. My mind was suddenly very clear, though. I turned to Danny.

'I am not losing this match. I have been here before and I am taking it to her. If I lose then I'm losing on my terms.'

I won 12-10 in the fifth and I was through to my first World Championship final. Suddenly the holiday we promised ourselves afterwards felt a long way away.

By now, the business end of the tournament had been moved to the picturesque all-glass court housed at an open air venue at Camana Bay, which had been voted one of the world's top 10 most beautiful beaches. This is where the sport can excel. Find a stunning backdrop, rig up a glass court with arena seating and the periphery makeup and it becomes a heck of a spectacle. Think of some of those iconic photos of glass courts set up before the pyramids or in Grand Central Station for the annual Tournament of Champions.

Predictably, if I was going to win this World Championship title, I was going to have to beat Nicol David. By then she was already widely regarded as the greatest female squash player of all time, she'd been ranked No.1 for nearly seven years and she was now going for her seventh World Championship win in a row.

Nicol, then 30, was under her own pressure after a couple of unexpected losses (at the peak of her career, all of Nicol's losses were unexpected). She'd even lost at home in the Malaysian Open final, prompting a few headlines back home that were a tiny bit critical. In the pre-tournament media previews, it was written that I 'might manage an ambush' and looking back maybe I'd got too caught up in that big win over Raneem and the magnitude of playing Nicol for a world title. It was a new experience for me to come back off such a huge win and recalibrate before playing such a huge match.

I lost in straight games. She kept it tight, was better than me on the volley and her timing was exceptional, especially in taking the ball short. She was significantly quicker than me too. I was proud of my performance though and it was a breakthrough week from which I learned a lot. Playing Nicol in a major final was a big step up.

In a week I'd gone from feeling like death's door to taking home the biggest prize-money cheque I had ever received, £10,393, and playing the World No.1 in a major final. She'd beaten me handily but, not for the first time, she'd shown me where I needed to get to. There were now a few of us pecking at Nicol's heels but there was a lot of work to do. I got voted Player of the Year in 2012. That World No.1 spot still felt very far away but somehow also within reach.

(Above) With Nicol David after my
first win against her in Cleveland

(Above) Phil giving me some coaching tips on
my way to winning my first British National title

See my full photo gallery at lauramassaro.co.uk/photos

3. FEAR OF LOSING

One of the real positive attributes of having a big fear of failure was that it never made me underestimate opponents or have inflated expectations where I assumed I was going to beat the person I was playing. I wanted to win, sure, but I was actually driven much more by a fear of losing.

I was always worried or full of nerves before a match. I used to be worse and I would often feel physically sick hours before matches. As I got older the sickness evaporated and the nerves tended to come later in the day but they always came, every time. It's hard to describe but it was uncertainty of what was going to unfold – a fear of the unknown. Without fail, I was always a bit of a mess emotionally before matches and I just hoped I would be okay come the start of the match.

Nerves are part of being an elite sportsperson. Everyone gets them to some degree and in many ways they can be useful in firing you up, but at their worst nerves can be a nightmare because they can scramble your brain and also stop your body working the way it should; your legs can suddenly feel heavy or wobbly, your arm can feel shaky. As time went on, how nervous I was had less and less effect on how I played. I could be nervous and play great or I could be less nervous and play terribly.

As these diary entries show, life in sport doesn't always run in a straight line.

22nd June 2009

Had a breakthrough with Danny yesterday. I realised that I care about what people think of me. What I do, what I wear and what I say. What I didn't realise is that this affects how I play, feel and improve amongst other things. It's my main reason for wanting to achieve a high ranking and win titles. Because of this, I am never fully relaxed and more likely to follow the script of what is supposed to happen. Anyway, after the chat yesterday I have become more aware of who I am and also aware that I don't have to be this way. I have started reading Eckhart Tolle's A New Earth and I will see how it goes. Awareness is the first thing.

14th September 2009

Day after my British Open loss to Rachael Grinham, 3-1. It's all bull****. I was 2-0 down in my first round and won 3-2 and then a poor performance against Rachael. I played great and then, as she pushed back, I got more defensive. It's a pattern. Alison in KL (1-0, 4-0 up – lost 3-1). Nicol in Singapore (game ball up, won second and then lost 3-1). My brother (1-0 up, 8-4 up, lose second and third and lose 3-2). It's the same all the time. There's a lack of confidence in my own game when someone pushes back. Not fully knowing what my game is. Not being present when my concentration goes or not present enough to get back in the moment. Maybe I am a wimp and don't have enough oomph about me. Gut feelings this week – work out and be clear of what I am trying to do on court. Be present and work on it going into the Worlds. You are top 10 in the world so prove it and get some bloody results. It's your time now. You're holding yourself back, no one else. Dig deep, dig hard and take the leap of faith.

———

I generally knew how well I would play in my later career in the lead up to a match. I could feel it in my head on how focussed or prepared I was. I accepted the nerves but I also tried to get my pre-match routine down so it was planned and regimented because that got me focussed and gave me the best possible chance to play well. The pre-routine was key, whether that started the day before or the morning of a match.

There were a lot of days where I played poorly but still won. Because not losing was so important to me, I used to worry in the morning as a junior about how the day would pan out and how the family dynamic would go. It started with those early morning breakfasts with Dad where I couldn't eat anything. Away from squash, when I started a new school year I could barely sleep, the exact same way I would be before a major match. I would lie there trying to quieten my mind.

When Danny started to think about how he could avoid playing the blame game after defeats, he went to work on himself. He read and then qualified in Neuro-Linguistic Programming. I did a short qualification myself but Danny went all the way to Master Practitioner level. It struck him how you could use images in your head, how you could change them and alter your belief in what you could see, together with the language used.

Traditional sports psychology has always used mental imagery and visualisation but NLP seemed more specific and advanced in how you could apply it to yourself. It gives you structured processes to use your imagination to examine your fears, beliefs and negative thoughts and to deconstruct them. The 'fast phobia cure' is one such NLP technique, which is designed to get rid of unwanted and irrational fear, for example, flying or spiders. It's a process that Danny adapted to conquer what he called my 'Oh my God, I've got to the World Championship final!' fear.

We know that when people are affected by phobias, seeing a spider or a snake, for example, can make them freak out and make their heart rate go up. In sport, the phobic feelings can be prompted by an athlete returning from an injury and feeling fearful of those first tentative steps back into the area, or simply being scared to play a squash match.

With Danny, we did the 'fast phobia' process to help me get rid of negative images in my head of what was to come in a match. It was all about getting me to put myself into situations in my head through visualisation. He would ask me to imagine a favourite cinema, to pick some popcorn or sweets, to sit down on my own and look at the screen. On the imaginary screen there is a backwards black and white clip of me running.

At least I can handle that. It's black and white, the film is going backwards to the beginning so you know what's going to happen. But, if that feels too much, you imagine yourself in a separate room where you are disassociated with the film. If you can't stand that, in extreme cases, you imagine yourself in the projection room of the cinema, where you can watch yourself watching it. And, in extreme, extreme cases, you go down the corridor and watch yourself watching yourself watch it. That's how deep the phobias go and you keep going until you don't have any fear. This process, which could basically be done with the two of us in a quiet room with my eyes shut and him talking me through it, was to help immeasurably in the coming seasons.

Working on my mental strength certainly helped me become more aware of the need to be focussed on my own performance and not on my opponent. I remember thinking countless times things like 'what would it mean to beat her?' or 'I really don't want to lose to that player'. It's not a healthy place to be in and it often gave me a negative attitude, which was never going to help matters.

Playing a friend, an enemy, a team-mate or someone who just gets under your skin can be really distracting, so getting into a place where I had performance goals for a match was really important for me – even basic things like 'I want to volley as much as possible' or 'I want to attack the front forehand'. I made a deal with myself that if I came off court and I had achieved those goals then, win or lose, I will be happy. I knew deep down that if I got my performance goals right then I would usually be on the right road to victory, but a win isn't always in your hands and that depended on how your opponent plays and feels on the day. It meant I was concentrating on what I could control and accepting the things I couldn't control.

—

October 30th, 2009

Worlds went fine. I lost to Natalie Grinham in the last 16 which was my seeding. DP said I needed to change my technique a little so I could get the edge through the ball quicker, meaning I can finish the ball more often. I lost to Sam Wildman in league and couldn't play a drop shot. I had a chat with Danny on the way home. He said: 'Are you willing to live your squash? You can't keep moaning about results if you're not willing to change. You need to decide how much you want to get better and how much are you willing to dedicate to it.'

It sounds silly but I actually had to ask myself, which shows I certainly wasn't already living my squash. I decided I have the rest of my life to live when squash is done so I decided to GO FOR IT. That was two weeks ago and since then I have been training differently. More purpose and I am much more open to learn and change. I have been reading more and watching more matches which I didn't do as much before. I went to Hong Kong and had some great solos. Then had a good run and lost in the semis to Nicol. Things had started to click, I wanted to learn and practice. I have started to relax and it's made a massive difference. Therefore I am playing the ball short more.

—

In general this is around the time when I realised that I needed to give myself a break and loosen the reins a little. In the past, before matches I would almost start to create tension from the night before by going to bed saying I HAD to sleep well to play well, because I HAD to feel good when I got up. I HAD to have a good practice; I HAD to have a nap before I played. And definitely, under no circumstances, could I do anything too strenuous on match day, which included walking too far for lunch. Looking back, that was especially ridiculous. I was a professional athlete; a walk was never going to affect how I played squash five hours later.

I learnt, as I got older, to relax a little. If I didn't sleep well I would just have a nap later. I had realised how you get out of bed impacts your mood and energy for the hours to come. When I got up I would tell myself, as my feet hit the floor, that I was taking that energy into the rest of the day. If nothing else it was something to think about as I came round from my sleep. Of course, it was forced to start with but I felt a huge difference in my body and mental energy. If I have a bad practice I would tell myself it was all out of my system for the match. If I had a great practice then I was on fire for later. What's the truth? None of it. It's all in the mind and what we choose to believe and listen to. I certainly chose to interpret things more positively, convinced that it was one of the reasons for improvements in my game.

Having worked hard to manage my mind and my emotions, I also needed to make sure that I got everything else right as well. I needed to become more professional in every aspect.

As professionals on tour, we all saw the way Nicol David approached tournaments. She would have a coach, a psychologist and a physio. We had no idea what she did away from the courts because she was so private. Here was everyone else all going for dinner together, going to functions together and sharing a room. Nicol kept to her team, apart from tournament requirements where she was the face of the sport (a responsibility that she took very seriously and gave a lot of time to) and allowed no one else into her inner sanctum. She was setting an example of professionalism for the rest of us. I started to think how I could get an edge on opponents. Counting on psychology around tournaments, coupled with having Danny by my side and a full-time coach in DP, my team was beginning to take shape.

DP had told Danny that it was time to create an aura and get a team around me at tournaments. It was time for us to stop worrying about everybody else. At events, it meant that DP and Danny could be saying hello and be fairly jovial, while I remained in the background and it was hard to know what I was like as a person.

———

Danny read something to me recently from a German philosopher called Martin Heidegger that made complete sense. Stick with me here! Heidegger came up with a strange phrase – *'Das Man'*, translated as 'the they', which basically means the 'others'. On tour, that would be everyone who made up 'the squash scene' week in week out: other players, coaches, organisers, reporters, referees etc. It is all too easy for these people ('the they') to influence you so much that you are unknowingly dragged towards a state of 'averageness'. It is a subtle, normal thing and everyone is dragged in to some degree. Fashion, hairstyles, things like the sudden emergence of tattoos, technology trends, opinions and so on. An example on tour that crept in was the sudden trend of hugging each other after match point instead of the traditional handshake. Almost an unwritten code that 'the they' collectively decided was the new normal. No single person started it or wrote the code, it just kind of becomes the way things are done. Very much like when I was at school, the 'in girls' set the tone and the rest must follow or be judged mockingly in the playground and corridors.

It is easy to fall into this pattern and hard to escape. It starts by knowing everyone else's business, the gossip and idle chit chat going around, the in-jokes. This is, as Heidegger said, 'extremely tempting' because it gives you the feeling of comfort, acceptance and a bit of temporary power over those who are not joining in. Now Heidegger said that the problem with this was that you are overcome with 'contentment' which in turn 'washes away one's restlessness to act'. In other words, you get comfy and complacent. I know that feeling. I had it in those times I had nothing to prove and many suddenly wanted to be friendly, especially after a big win. It felt nice to be popular, a relief maybe from the focus. The downside: I lost my 'edge'. I suddenly knew too much gossip and I had been seduced by 'fitting in'. I was no longer keeping my distance, forgetting my drive to prove myself with action. What Heidegger said happens last struck such a chord with me the most. He said we become 'alienated' from our true selves and rather than recover our true deep desires, we instead stay content by following the pack. More a sheep than a lion, according to another famous philosopher Friedrich Nietzsche.

Not only have I felt this in myself, I have seen it in the very best players who I competed against. I could easily name 10 champions, lionesses, who resisted the full magnetism of the others and mostly kept a vital independence. I also noticed many who despite their talents and big efforts just got too sucked into the tour soap opera which almost became a social life for them. This was what DP meant by creating an aura. You want to remain a mystery and do what you need to do without, of course, being overly rude or serious. I had my own friends at home, I did not need to follow 'the they' on tour for fear of not 'fitting in' or desiring popularity. Of course, having a team around me made this much easier for me. It was a vital part of having Danny about, who in many ways was similarly single-minded and, although naturally more friendly, does not suffer fools easily. Maybe being a woman there are different pressures when it comes to tour life and that 'in crowd' but, for me, I was certainly at my best when I stayed true to myself, my natural personality and my own desires. Maybe this was why 'they' nicknamed me the Ice Queen – cold, frosty, strong.

Since retiring I have had so many people say things along the lines of, 'Oh, you're really nice, I didn't realise you were like this.' It has shocked me to be honest because those close to me know I am just myself, in many ways just a normal person who really likes people. I now understand more how important it was for me to be able to be strong enough to separate myself 'at work' especially from potential competitors. It can give you so much power and save so many needless headaches. It helps you accept yourself more fully, all your faults and all your strengths. You don't give in to them and their opinions and judgements of you only prickle, they don't cut. A lot has been made of my mental strength over the years, and what Heidegger explained back in 1927 was the foundation of it for me. I learned how to keep my own fire burning. I only listened to those I totally trusted. I put personality over popularity. And, above all, I was there to WIN.

It suited my personality much more this way and maybe it was comfortable because it was reminiscent of when I used to travel with Dad as a junior and we kept to ourselves. I have always felt that being a professional squash player is a job. You have colleagues but my friends were at home; they were the people I could count on no matter what and the people I had grown up with. They knew me better than anyone and were friends because they were my sort of people, not because we played squash together. DP was good at putting this into perspective. It was ok to be friendly but he knew my strength was my competitiveness. I didn't want to be playing my 'friends', I was playing colleagues. Of course, they were people I liked but not who I would choose to spend time with over my friends at home.

DP saw me as a stubborn character and he knew that I felt there had been favouritism towards Jenny Duncalf and Alison Waters. The situation with performance director Peter Hirst had shown that. And I now know Peter's opinion had come from DP. In DP's eyes I worked hard, wasn't a great mover and that I had played a basic game throughout the majority of my career, without much of a power game. He thought I was a good player but simply didn't believe I really had what it took to make it to the very top.

However, when Danny went up to DP at the British National Championships to ask if he would put more input into my game and that I wasn't getting what I deserved, I think that as national coach he felt that I may have had a point and he began to take more interest.

When our relationship formed, DP was communicating with Danny, who he thought was a bit intense but was nonetheless also willing me on. A three-way partnership blossomed as DP started to make the changes that he felt were needed to win the big titles.

We tended to work on transfer of weight and make my movement more 'electric'. I liked the sound of that. This would help me move quicker and become more efficient. Transferring my weight made my breathing easier during rallies; my breathing became steadier and more controlled rather than a series of short gasping breaths that usually come with quick movements in long rallies.

When I put in my last lunge, I was always thinking about getting out of the shot. I would strike the ball and then almost try to snap back. This helped my recovery back to the T to make it a single, clean movement if I got it right. Therefore, unless I got involved in a brutal match, DP's method meant that I would hopefully never get to the stage where I was totally and utterly exhausted as I was in rhythm throughout the match.

I was encouraged to take big, bounding strides to get to a short ball at the front rather than merely scampering for it, which would also enable me to get my breathing rhythmical during rallies. It made everything flow. I kept closer to the T in the middle of the court, so over the course of a full match I did significantly less running and produced many more energy-efficient movements. DP was also working with Nick Matthew, who had already won world and British Open titles. There would be certain matches where Nick was barely breathing at the end. In the 2013 World Championship final against Gregory Gaultier, Nick won after 111 minutes to become world champion for a third time. DP says that Nick could have played another 90 minutes that day because his movement was so good.

One day, I asked DP at the end of one session if we had anything else to work on. 'Well…,' he began to speak, his voice deliberately gentle. 'You are World No.3 and unless you make a slight grip change you won't get much better.'

I looked at him wide-eyed, almost in disbelief and I asked him what he meant.

To most people, this might sound like a very small thing – moving your hand a couple of millimetres on the handle of your squash racket – but to a professional squash player at the height of their career in a sport that relied on coordination and accuracy, this was potentially a huge change.

DP admitted to me later that he took a few big gulps at that moment. After two years working with me, he feared that he might be delivering a fatal blow to our working relationship. I'm sure that the look on my face at that moment didn't do much to lessen his fear. DP was a bit better at hiding what was going on inside than I was.

Calmly, he told me that by turning the grip slightly around and over, it would enable me to take the ball out in front of me a bit more.

'It will open up your short game and give you more of an attacking presence,' he said.

I swallowed my shock. I trusted DP and I was ready to do whatever it took to win big events, having moved up and down between No.2 and No.3 in the world recently. 'Okay, let's do it.'

I was on court doing a solo session a few days later and was still struggling a little with the new grip adjustment. So much so, I was starting to doubt if I even had it in the position DP wanted me to. I went home and tried to ask Danny, who had watched the original session with DP, if I was doing it correctly. He said it looked right but told me to just call DP. 'You two have to own this.'

I called DP and he was out shopping so he told me to Facetime him and show him. There he was, standing in the queue for the till at Marks & Spencers, showing me how to open my racket face and telling me to draw on my grip the position of the new 'V' between my thumb and forefinger, and making sure that the grip sat in the right place in my palm. God only knows what the other shoppers in Marks & Spencers were thinking as DP tried to tell the then World No.3 squash player how to hold her racket!

It took time but I started to feel more comfortable practising it away from DP. It was all about having more shape on the ball and being able to take shots out in front of me with a more open grip.

Life with most professional athletes is a bit of an emotional rollercoaster, where seemingly little things can really throw you off. The grip change was one of those moments for me. How you hold your racket is such a basic principle in squash and I was struggling to comprehend the fact I might have been playing it wrong. I needed to find a way of mentally processing it so it didn't become something that I might fret over.

I was always interested in different ways to develop and understand myself better and one of the next NLP techniques I took on board from Peter was the Fishbone diagram (shown later in the book, in 'Notebook'). It was used by the Japanese car company, Honda, as they tried to tackle the seemingly overwhelming task of rebuilding after the Second World War, when something called the Ishikawa diagram helped organisations work out what it is they were trying to achieve. A friend of Peter's had adapted it for individuals and so he started trying it with me.

Essentially, the diagram looks like a fishbone, with a head, a spine and then ribs which come off it. I would start to write down on the diagram the things I needed in order to get where I wanted to in my squash. At the head of the fish is the goal: To win major events. From the head comes a straight line representing the spine and from the spine there are lines representing the bones. Each bone of the fish represents different parts of my training that I need to get right to reach my goal, such as nutrition, training, physical work, psychology and even my social life. Off each bone are smaller bones where I add specific goals for, say, my diet goals. Whereas other NLP processes, like the Organic Belief Process were used sparingly, the fishbone was in action most days as I would fill it out and stick it on the fridge or have it in my pocket travelling to events.

Amid all the worry, stress and pressure of the game, I still took a huge amount of pride in doing things correctly, in being authentic and holding up to those values in training and at tournaments.

There was a long time during my career where I wasn't achieving anywhere close to what I wanted. Many, many times I would be getting on to flights the day after a loss with red eyes and that dark well of disappointment in my stomach. Once I got the right team in place and I started to have a clear idea of who I was and what I needed to do in every area of my professional life, the highs started to come a lot more often.

It took a lot to get to that point and looking back at my diaries shows just how difficult that journey was.

7th December 2009

The lead up to Monaco hadn't gone that well but, now I am finally here, I feel better. In the lead up I forgot about my enjoyment again, I had a couple of niggles and I had got back to being result-focussed. I wasn't enjoying any of my matches. I was getting angry and upset. Danny sent me a harsh text saying: 'You're not enjoying your job like millions of other people. How many times do you have to feel sorry for yourself before it's enough. Sort your feet out and get quicker or stay as you are!'

6th September 2010

Got home from the Irish Open and Phil told me to get fitness tested. I knew deep down I wasn't as fit as before I did my ankle earlier in the year and the results proved it. Down on all of them and no hiding from the numbers. I was disappointed but also happy in a way because it explained the way I was feeling on court. Now, I just have to put the hard work in again.

28th November 2011

So off I went to Rotterdam to the World Champs. I was excited but nervous because of how I had been playing. I spoke to Peter McNab from the airport and I told him I was nervous and worried. He asked me to ask the worried voice what it was trying to tell me. The answer was it was warning me not to be complacent. Wake up and take it seriously! Peter asked me to thank the voice for being there and for me to be aware of what it wants. It helped me so much. I couldn't believe it. I left for the airport feeling happier about everything.

23rd February 2012

Nationals! I had two easy 3-0 matches. Then, in the semi-final, I played Madeline Perry. I text coach Phil beforehand and wrote that I was nervous. He replied, 'We are not having this conversation. Sort your head out.' Rightly so I guess! I had my plan. I won 3-0! I played Alison in the final. I was nervous before but when the match came around I told myself to stop getting wrapped up in the result. I kept the ball really straight, especially down the backhand and I took the drop in whenever I could get in front. It was tough but mentally I was good. I tried not to boast or flick but stayed solid. I won 3-1. A second national title and a brilliant celebration afterwards.

(Above) Working with DP to change my grip on the
racket. A seemingly small but hugely impactful change

See my full photo gallery at lauramassaro.co.uk/photos

4. THE PSYCHOLOGIST

By Peter McNab

I had never worked with a sportsperson prior to meeting Laura and the last time I had played squash was in the Seventies. As a rule, I much prefer working with groups to one-to-one but I had a feeling that working with Laura would be really interesting.

NLP is all about the process and the way in which people are doing things – the 'how', if you like, rather than the 'what', so it was better that I didn't play squash and could come at it naively and just explore the process with her. When I first started teaching NLP in the late 80s, we didn't know why it worked. With the advances in neuroscience, we are building a better understanding of what is happening: By creating these processes we are building a new neural pathway in the brain.

Laura's husband Danny had attended our Neuro-Linguistic Programming (NLP) Practitioner and Master Practitioner courses in the North West. He persuaded Laura to come on a two-day introductory meeting and, while I think that she wanted to continue training with us, her tournament schedule got in the way. I didn't see Danny for a while after he'd finished our course and then, out of the blue, he phoned up and asked if I would coach Laura. I was surprised because I knew that she already had other coaches in her team. Danny pressed and told me that Laura had got to World No.10 and had got 'stuck' around that ranking.

At the time, I thought that tenth in the world was fantastic but, to Laura and Danny, it was a limitation. They sensed that they could make a shift and she could move up in the rankings not by changing her squash but by using NLP to change the way she thought and felt.

It's really important to remember that this was just one piece of the jigsaw. I was one part of a team which was working on squash technique, strength, resilience and diet and all the other pieces. She needed all of the pieces of the jigsaw to fit together to be at her best.

Laura had to work through some personal issues relating to her childhood in our first sessions, as we also worked out which behaviours she had to change. To start with, I just kept asking her questions. When you meet people who are really good at what they do, very often they can't explain why or how they do things like, what constitutes a good match or how they felt. I wanted her to explore her inner voices, become more aware of what she was saying to herself and whether it was helpful or not.

We started off using something called the Enneagram, which classifies personality types like The Perfectionist, The Reformer, The Helper and The Individualist. These types are designed to help you understand your behaviours and why you behave the way you do. As we worked together, we realised that Laura is a Type One, which is known as The Perfectionist but is really about being and doing things 'right' rather seeking perfection.

This 'being right' affects all aspects of her life although we predominantly explored how it affected her squash. Being right or wrong is so important for her and we started to play around with it – when it is useful to be right, and when it is limiting to be right.

One huge advantage of this was when her coaches asked her to, for example, train for three hours every day; she would do it as it is the right thing to do. The other side to this was that by doing the right thing she ended up doing only one thing. This led to Laura having a certain way of playing that other players could pick up on and then being 'right' became a disadvantage. Using the Enneagram, we played with the idea of being more flexible.

The process was all part of her trying to reel in Nicol David. Whenever I spoke to Laura about Nicol, I sensed a shift in her body language – and the other girls were the same. There was diffidence because Nicol was unbeatable as World No.1 for so long.

I once went round to Laura's house and we watched a video of Nicol and Laura playing. It is hard to describe but there is a point in that match, just before Nicol serves, where Laura 'steps into her body'; it is a small movement but looks very significant. At that moment, Laura 'stepped up' and, at the same time, Nicol takes half a step back. Reviewing it, it was almost as though Laura wasn't inside her own body when she played Nicol; she was what we call 'dissociated', almost like an observer. During this particular rally, she literally takes a really small step, a minimal shift, but for Nicol as it was like she had almost been blasted; someone had stepped up and into her territory and that hadn't happened before.

At some level, Laura had a belief that she didn't deserve to be World No.1, but there was a shift in Laura's psyche in that moment she stepped into Nicol's space and it was something we worked on a lot as a positive. From the outside, I saw all these other women going on court knowing they wouldn't win, and this acted as a self-fulfilling prophecy. At the same time, there are many examples in sport – for example, running a mile in under four minutes and the Fosbury Flop – where once one person has broken a record, it busts the belief wide open.

From that moment, Laura started to believe that she could be World No.1.

Another important process is called Self-Anchoring, which works by linking an emotion with a physical action. I would ask her how she felt going into a tournament – just as I would with a business client ahead of a really important presentation. You want the 'negative' emotion and then you ask the person how they would rather feel. It's the latter feeling that's probably the better emotion to take into the situation. All of us use past experiences and the feelings around them and then take these feelings into our future experiences. Most of us unconsciously use negative experiences and the negative feelings about them. It seems to be purely accidental whether we are remembering a positive or a negative experience and emotion. This is not right or wrong, but it is a choice; we can decide how we want to feel.

Like most of us, Laura would often head into tournaments or matches with negative feeling emotions such as fear, nervousness or low self esteem, because she was subconsciously recalling negative experiences and disappointments. What we needed to do was to find times when Laura was really successful. She would remember times when she won a junior tournament and we would 'anchor' it. You will see lots of sportspeople using these when they bounce a tennis ball in a particular way or chalk a cue when it is already chalked, or have a very specific way to address a golf ball, or even doing a little dance before kicking a rugby ball. Consciously, or often unconsciously, they have associated positive feelings to this 'tic' or 'ritual'.

I got Laura to tell me what was useful for her. One was the way she held her racket and the way she squeezed her racket, those helped her to remember the winning feeling. Another was the way she stood in the serving box when she was about to receive and she bounced on her feet slightly. To resettle her, the third anchor was to associate that feeling of being more grounded with wiping her hand on the wall, a common trait for players, except that they do it just to get rid of the moisture; Laura was doing it to get rid of the moisture and to ready herself for the next shot.

Laura was always willing to put in the work, even if it was sometimes quite confronting and hard. When she was World No.2 and working with DP, I remember he plucked up the courage to tell her that she was holding the racket in the wrong way. I saw her a few days later and she was furious with him but she soon started holding the grip slightly differently, marking the racket to make sure she was holding it correctly. It was a subtle change but it almost made the racket bigger and she got a lot more balls back because of it.

She had to really practise that for several months for it to become the norm. For some athletes, they would likely fall back to the old habits. The grip change told me that she had the grit and determination, which stood her apart from the others. The important note here is that changing habits is not easy and takes stamina and consistency; things that Laura has in abundance.

There was one final shift with Laura that really made the difference and it was her thinking around her goal to become number one. This might seem admirable but the problem with it is that she wanted to achieve something she didn't have full control of. After all, she couldn't make herself become number one with so many other people wanting the same. She had to let go of that. Instead she changed it to being 'the best squash player she could be' and then she was right back in control.

Her childhood was absolutely crucial in how her career panned out. She kept on coming back to it so much in our working together. She needed independence and to let go of her bond with her father. I've seen it so much in the sports world where it seems to be the parent's goal, not the child's.

That important pattern was repeated later in her career, like the first time she travelled to an event without Danny. She would call me quite often during events but she didn't for that one. It was another shift in her career, letting go and growing up herself.

One direction that we took early on in my working with Laura was to undergo the Organic Belief Process, an NLP mental belief technique designed to break down the barriers which had been holding back her belief. In our sessions, we would have a chat and she would answer my questions and, before she knew it, she would be off down a path where she would start to feel uncomfortable about what we were talking about. It was almost a physical reaction, as though I had literally hit a nerve. Then we would try and get to the root cause of why Laura felt like that.

We discussed heading off to the next group of tournaments, which included the 2011 Cleveland Classic in Ohio. I asked her whether she could win these big events. At the time she had never got to the final of a Gold event like the Cleveland Classic, let alone won one. We questioned whether she could go to these events and win them, and it soon dawned on her that she believed she could beat each player individually but doing it back-to-back to take a title wasn't something Laura thought that she was capable of.

The belief technique consists of six pieces of paper with a heading on each one: Current Belief, Open to Doubt, Museum of Old Beliefs, Preferred Belief, Open to Belief and Identity. The idea is to imagine yourself actually walking onto the six pieces of A4 paper, getting into the physical emotion of each thought.

Let's get into Laura's head as we go through this process:

I'm standing facing forwards and directly in front of me is the first of them, with 'Current Belief' written out in big letters. As Peter leads me through the line of questioning and I confront the truth of what I really believe – that I can't beat enough good players in a row to win a title – I feel my body language start to change. I feel myself shrink, my shoulders droop and my face becomes sad. It makes me realise what this inner belief is actually doing to me.

So much of what you see of top sportspeople is based on what they think they can achieve, which is why you get those who are in a position to win but never quite get over the line because the other player believes that little bit more. Because Laura felt she could win matches but not back-to-back in those higher level events, she got nervous before playing, almost anticipating the disappointment. She told me how hard that was to admit to herself and how it made her sad. But she needed to know.

Each time we examined one of the six beliefs, I would prompt Laura's thoughts. She'd be silent with her eyes closed and when she was in the emotional state associated with that belief, she would nod her head and move forward to the next bit of paper.

We got to 'Open to Doubt'.

I asked Laura to think of an example before we start the process, something in her life that she was adamant that was true. For Laura, that example was the recollection of the conversation at home as a teenager when her parents sat both Laura and her brother down to tell them they were splitting up. Before that conversation, Laura's belief was that she had a family, parents who were together. Almost in an instant, that belief was broken.

We move to the piece of paper marked: 'Museum of Old Belief'. Laura has in her head a wooden ottoman box she had in the family home when she was younger. I ask her to imagine herself placing the belief of not being able to win back-to-back matches and the 'broken belief' of her parents' marriage breakdown into this 'Museum of Old Belief' and shut the lid of the wooden box. She nods her head and moves forwards.

Then I would ask Laura to turn around with the final three bits of paper in a line facing her in the other direction. Stepping into the fourth – 'Preferred Belief' – I encouraged her to dig deep and find the deep well of confidence that had been hidden by the other, negative beliefs. Laura said out loud that she was playing for herself and that she could win Gold events, whether she was at her best or not. I would always say there was a body language change whenever this happened – you could see the emotion coursing through Laura when she got into that specific emotional state. Perhaps I was witnessing Laura growing in confidence, standing taller with her shoulders back.

In 'Open to Belief', I would ask Laura to think of a situation that could be true that maybe she didn't think was true. Here, the scenario could be Laura's technique, where she would think a certain way of playing a shot was nailed but then would get this new information. She would struggle with it for a bit but then it would click and would be completely natural and she became a better player for making the change.

The sixth and final piece of paper is the new 'Identity'. The big thing here is that it is all about Laura – Laura is winning Gold events, believing she deserves to be there, with the number one goal in every match to get a new level of squash. Identity should be just a complete change of emotional state, body shape and posture so that you are saying: 'I am now this person.'

I would then say something unrelated at the end, like how many lights are in the room. Laura would then have to count them and it would make her snap out of the previous, almost trance-like state of concentration and I would always then ask her how she felt.

Sometimes we would go through the whole process two or three times to make sure that Laura really delved into the emotional state. The natural progression would be to get into them quicker and the 'identity' would be stronger each time.

This technique is so simple and effective, I can be done anywhere at any time. Laura would often tell me that sometimes on the road she would feel her belief and confidence waning so she always had the pieces of paper in her travel bag and either Danny would help her through the process or she would do the technique on her own. A huge part of the process with Laura was that knowledge that realising a belief was half the battle.

On reflection, Laura realised that there are sometimes invisible barriers deep inside that stop you really believing that you can do it, when in fact there are hundreds of opportunities through our lives where you think something is true and it isn't.

It was such an important realisation for her and it changed her mentality not just as a competitor but in lots of areas of her life.

5. CHASING NICOL

I wonder what would have happened if Malaysia hadn't won the right to stage the 1998 Commonwealth Games. Would the emergence of one of squash's most successful men's or women's athletes of all time ever have happened? Nicol David has been such an important figure in squash, especially in the women's game, and there's no getting away from the fact that her presence loomed over much of my career.

Squash was one of the 17 sports on the programme for the first time when Malaysia was awarded the 1998 Commonwealth Games. With the Malaysian government spending around $600 million on the Games, officials were clearly on a mission to find the nation's future darlings with six years to go before the opening ceremony in Kuala Lumpur. The story goes that a scout was sent off to spot talent and soon heard of an eight-year-old who was regularly playing with her two older sisters at a local squash complex in the region of Penang.

Several years later, Nicol lost in the second round of those 1998 Games but I remember her being touted in *Squash Player Magazine* as a future great after she won the Asian Games title and then beat world top 20 player,

Vanessa Atkinson, to reach the KL Open final in Malaysia as a qualifier aged just 17. She was still quite short then but there was a buzz around her. Four years later, she teamed up with Ong Beng Hee, a top 10 Malaysian men's player, as they took silver at the 2002 Commonwealth Games and it was then that Malaysia's sport council began to invest in the sport and its rising star.

A year before, I had watched Nicol beat Jenny Duncalf easily before England defeated Malaysia in the 2001 World Junior Championships. The Khan dynasty had been a huge force for Asian squash for a couple of decades but Asia had never produced a particularly strong women's player. At that stage, nobody was tipping Nicol for world domination, certainly not me, even though she'd won the Asian Games title aged 14. By the time she'd lost the 2002 Asian Games title, Nicol seemed to be disillusioned with the game as she dipped out of the squash scene for a few years. I read later that she had said that this was the lowest time of her life, which just shows you that you never know what players are going through on the inside. To get herself out of the rut, Nicol travelled to Amsterdam where she began to be coached by Liz Irving, an Australian who had been a runner-up at the World Championships and a three-time British Open finalist during the 80s and 90s.

It proved to be a huge move for her and, in the end, might have changed the course of history of women's squash. If Nicol hadn't made that move, who knows whether she would have made it, let alone become the greatest female player of all time. Would that have changed my destiny too? We'll never know.

Still only 20 and living more than 7,000 miles away from her native Malaysia, Nicol allowed her game to be totally broken down as Liz worked with her strengths. Apparently Nicol could do a 400m sprint that rivalled all the Malaysian guys but she just had no body weight. Irving used her speed to make her game more efficient and made her more structured in rallies.

Nicol was ranked 53 when she started to play on the tour circuit more in 2003 – I was ranked in the thirties by this stage – but she had broken into the world's top five by January 2005. That year, she became the first Malaysian player to win the British Open and the first Asian player to do so. Nicol, who was three months older than me, ended it by becoming the youngest world champion after winning in Hong Kong as she was elevated to World No.1. If people hadn't been tipping her for greatness before, they were now.

Apparently, it took Nicol two hours to finish her media interviews after landing back from Hong Kong. She's been sponsored by major banks, been the face of many billboards in her home country, trumpeted by successive Malaysian prime ministers and she seldom won a big trophy without one of them calling her to congratulate her. She was even made an honorary major by the Royal Malaysian Air Force. And she is definitely Malaysia's most famous athlete and the youngest person ever to receive a Datukship – Malaysia's Order of Merit, the equivalent of a knighthood.

I often wonder how she dealt with the pressure of being such a big focus of attention. It must be lovely to get the adulation but every missed shot or, God forbid, lost match would be treated like a national tragedy. Don't get me wrong, I would have loved to have achieved what Nicol achieved – and the sponsorship income wouldn't have hurt – but I'm not sure how I would have dealt with everything else that came with her position.

There were only a handful of players who were close to Nicol, and they all trained with Liz Irving at Squash City. Importantly, they were all ranked much lower than Nicol, which bears out a piece of advice once given to me by Sarah Fitz-Gerald, who had also helped out Nicol for a short time. As a top player in the weird bubble of the squash tour the whole time, it was much better to surround yourself with players with a lower world ranking than you. That way you never have the complications of being rivals while trying to be friends, which I think is probably impossible.

I learned a lot from Nicol and how she did things. There is no question that trying to emulate her made me a better squash player. Reading interviews with her, I also knew that she liked to take the best attributes of each top athlete she admired, from Olympic sports to F1, and sought how they kept in the zone, how their body reacted and how they kept their minds clear. This was something I could certainly relate to.

Even though Nicol is only 5ft 3in tall, there was always an air of mystery about her. She and her team were so self-contained that they seemed to function in their own little bubble. We never even got to practice on court with her as she had Liz to spar with. No one was ever able to get even the most basic information out of her because she didn't really chat. It sent a message to the rest of us that she was almost untouchable, and I was certainly a touch jealous of Nicol's set up. As well as Liz constantly by her side at tournaments, she also had a specialist physio, the late Ronald Fauvel, a Canadian who looked more like Nicol's personal bodyguard than what Nicol called her personal 'body mender'.

This is where Nicol's ability to generate sponsorship money really had an impact, because it allowed her to put together an amazing support team of coach, physio and sometimes a psychologist as well. That created a high professional standard for the rest of us to aspire to.

Nick Matthew also saw gains when he created a 'team'. His psychologist was Mark Bawden, who worked with the England cricket team – he got Nick to focus on his super strengths: volleying, fitness and the mental side. Then he had the Kiwi Mark Campbell, who trained out of the English Institute of Sport in Sheffield, and he put Nick through the infamous 'rumble' fitness circuits – a continuous block of exercises consisting of bench dips, bodyweight squats, side planks, leg rowers, a row and a cycle lasting up to an hour. At the heart of Nick's setup, was DP as coach. The pair's relationship was as strong as any, with DP able to get Nick to be level-headed, humble, and get his mind and tactics ready for the next tournament. DP coached Nick to win three world titles in his thirties and this was a real inspiration for me. Nick himself has always been really supportive of me and my career.

Seeing and hearing about the players who had built a team, I tried to copy Nicol as soon as I could afford to. When I took Danny away to tournaments, I separated myself from the girls on tour, creating that bubble. I had tried to do it early on but it was very lonely to isolate yourself when you don't have your team with you. I remember going to one tournament in Kuala Lumpur and I didn't want to socialise so I went to the cinema on my own, got a takeaway and went back to my shared room. It felt so lonely. You want to be able to talk to people, to express feelings and thoughts or even just chat about nothing to take your mind off things. After that, I tried to create a balance of finding time on my own and being with the group on tour but it was never easy.

Once Danny started travelling, there was no need for me to get into the tour grind or ask what everyone was doing for dinner. I guess that is what Nicol David had for so long. She must have looked at the rest of us and thought, 'How are you going to beat me when you are all such cliquey mates with each other?'

Trying to copy Nicol's set up cost a small fortune. While DP was usually at events as he also had other athletes on his books, including Nick, having Danny with me meant double the cost of flights, food and extras. It meant that at the US Open in Philadelphia, a trip could total £2,000, so there was a fair bit of pressure if I lost in the first round. It was a price worth paying if I won the tournament, which I did with a brace of US Open titles in 2011 and 2015. I am a worrier when it comes to money and the need to bring home prize money often raised the stakes and the pressure.

Some of my best times on tour came at the US Open in Philadelphia. Apart from usually doing well on court there, Danny and I shared an apartment with DP and Nick. Danny found a brilliant block of apartments in uptown Philadelphia right in the centre of all the best shops, restaurants and bars. The rooms were always high spec and it felt like a home from home. The only snag was that DP didn't have a room of his own but he was more than happy to stay on one of the new electronic airbeds we bought for him. It sounds harsh but all the other elements made up for it and, after testing it the first year, we went with the same set up for five years.

My main memory of those stays in 'Roost' apartments is a feeling of fun and togetherness. We would arrive and get straight in a cab to Whole Foods (it had to be organic at that stage!) and pile up the trolley with the week's supplies. Oats, berries, yoghurts, various milks, sourdough, beers, veg, rice and bananas all spring to mind as the main purchases and, of course, almonds. One morning, almonds became a topic of conversation that pushed DP over the edge.

Now, in DP's defence, Nick usually got up early and entered the main living area, which was all nicely open plan with the kitchen. Not one to be too gentle in the kitchen, Nick would be banging cupboard doors and pots and pans, even emptying the dishwasher whilst DP was still snoozing away. I could always hear him from our room so DP had to have been able to hear it. DP had a tendency to listen to music on his laptop into the early hours, so he probably needed that extra hour's sleep that Nick pierced with his 'clanging about' as DP comically complained. Nick, being obsessed with routine just like myself, had to get his morning smoothie in along with his bowl of porridge and berries. All nicely timed to fit in with his morning practice, which included a full warm up and precise cool down. DP could simply stumble out of bed, grab a coffee and somehow find his way to the courts just in time and deliver a perfect session for us.

This particular morning, Nick went for it with the NutriBullet machine for his smoothie. I looked at Danny and said: 'What's he doing?' Danny laughed visualising DP being woken up so loudly.

'What's that?' we heard. 'Nick, Nicholas, turn it off,' DP muffled. Nick pressed it on again, 15 seconds.

'It's like a bloody pneumatic drill, turn it off!'

Of course, this had us all laughing. Mainly because there were actual drills going on outside the building for the construction of a huge skyscraper and, each night, we had passed them blasting in our ears. The obvious over-exaggeration made us laugh but to poor DP, trying to sleep, the noise probably did sound deafening. About 30 minutes later, me and Nick were chatting about food and almonds came up. We started to talk in depth about them and which were better and how they helped us as players – recovery or digestion perhaps. Well, DP had had enough.

'Danny, how do you cope with this? Bloody almonds. Look you two, what type of bloody almond you eat or don't eat ain't gonna make you win or lose a game of squash. Or a smoothie either. It's rather boring and just shows how you can get up your own backside being a pro.'

He said it in a way that we knew he hadn't had his morning coffee and was still agitated by being woken up. As always with DP, he wasn't angry, just more exasperated. He could see the humour in it even though he was the butt of the joke.

'Anyway, I'll see you at the courts. Make sure you have your almonds for practice. Are you coming with me Danny? Come on, let these two prepare properly. Bye darlings, be good!'

As they left – Danny still laughing, DP with his hair stuck up and one sock tucked into his tracksuit bottoms – me and Nick looked at each other not knowing if we had been told off or not. We did feel a bit sorry for him though and kind of realised that maybe we do get a bit over serious at times. We agreed to get him some beers for the evening. He did put up with a lot on those trips but I know he loved them. We remarked a few times how we were a bit like a family for the week and DP was the father figure, the rest of us teasing him whilst looking after him at the same time.

The airbed we bought for DP was the best $150 we spent, although by the fifth trip it had seen better days. It started to deflate through the night. I walked out one morning to see DP sleeping at a 45 degree angle, head on the floor, feet up. My first reaction was, 'Aah, poor DP.' My second reaction was to rush back to my room for my phone so I could take a picture, my third to go and tell Nick. DP was fast asleep, laptop still on top of him, headphones connected, hair dangling.

'Oh dear, what's happened? My head.'

'The mattress has deflated DP,' I said. 'Be careful all the blood might have rushed to your head.'

'Oh, I can't get up. Help. I'm stuck.'

Well you can imagine the giggles now, especially from Danny and Nick.

'Help! Stop laughing, you two. This isn't funny. I'm stuck.'

He looked just like a bat sleeping! It was funny.

I re-inflated the bed and all was well.

'I bet Serena Williams' coach Patrick whatever-his-name-is, doesn't go through this, ha. What's going on, eh?'

That was a great start to the day – a day in which we both had quarter-final matches. Laughter really is priceless. There is a lot to a coach-player relationship and these memories. There are so many more moments that are just as cherished as the squash side of things. I have realised that even more recently. Some things can seem so overly important to some players, especially someone with my personality and habits. I think wise coaches sense this and, rather than adding weight to those situations, they help you to feel lighter. DP was a master at this and those weeks in Philadelphia are some of my most loved. Nick was great too and it was very reassuring to have him around, watching how he navigated tournaments and all the extras around it. It was nice to get to know him better, even if he was loud in the kitchen too early.

———

I think, sometimes, people outside of sport assume that all professional athletes are all earning lots of money but the vast majority aren't, especially in an individual sport where you have to cover expenses for several people. Squash, a bit like tennis, is a sport with a circuit that goes around the world but the prize money at our top events is not as big as it is in tennis. The outgoings can be huge.

Even the most promising young female players often don't trust themselves to win a first round match outside of the domestic squash leagues. You are putting your livelihood and your ranking on the line by missing a league match and flying off to play on the professional tour. If you lose, you are in trouble. You have paid the money to be at an international tournament, you are on your own in a foreign country and you have missed out on the league money. Yet, you have to go all in to have any chance of succeeding.

It was the same having a team with me at tournaments; I had to back myself and go all in. The investment made the wins all the more satisfactory. Having a team there meant being able to watch the opponent and wake up in the morning with a plan. If we lost, we could still have three or four days in a competitive environment with no distraction, training, spending time on court and working on tactics. Having Danny there meant he could watch other opponents and take notes for future events. With DP, we could work on tactical or technical points he had seen, and share new ideas. Whatever the situation, we could view it as a win-win. In women's squash, this was a big luxury.

While this was going on, Nicol was accruing more and more ranking points. No one was near her. Up until the midpoint of 2013, my countrywoman Jenny Duncalf had spent 28 successive months as World No.2 behind her, but there was never a hint of Nicol being toppled.

I was always looking for inspiration and I often got it from reading books by other female athletes. Taking tips from sports books helped in certain times of my career. Tim Grover was trainer to basketball great Michael Jordan and his book *Relentless: From Good to Great to Unstoppable* helped me through to three tournament victories. I needed that extra little part to my game. Getting inspiration and learning from other athletes and coaches made me step up, sharpened me and made me be accountable and to believe in myself. There are so many books by men, and I read those too, but there are distinct differences in how male and female athletes think and feel, and how their bodies work, so I tend to find books by women in sport particularly engaging.

One book turned out to be especially significant for me. On a trip to Malaysia where I went for the KL Open in April 2013, I started reading former Ironman world champion Chrissie Wellington's autobiography on the flight over. Although I was blown away by her discipline and how hard she trained and worked for her success, I could also relate to it. In Kuala Lumpur, I had reached the last eight and was playing some good squash before I picked up a slight sore throat before the quarter-finals. I thought of Chrissie's book.

Against Ireland's Madeline Perry in the quarters, I had lost my length and totally lost my focus. I brought to mind excerpts from Chrissie's book, like when she describes being in the final few kilometres of the Ironman, when she couldn't feel her legs through tiredness. She found a way and so could I. I scraped through, was wiped out after the win and I missed the next morning's practice session, but I was through and I knew I could find the belief and strength to keep pushing until I got to the finish line, just as Chrissie had done.

My diary at the time, as I set up a semi-final against Nicol, tells the story.

29th March 2013

Thinking back to Chrissie Wellington's book, with all she went through and all she raced with, surely I could give it a big effort when the time came? A semi-final against Nicol. Even though I was trying to stay positive and have belief in myself, I did have a lot of negative thoughts before the match. Things like: How am I going to perform well when I don't feel well? I struggle to beat Nicol when I am feeling my best. Am I just going out there to fulfil the fixture? I just didn't think I could win if I wasn't at my best. I think Danny sensed it and when we went for lunch he said: 'How are you going to approach the match today?' My first thought was 'What's the point!?' It's hard enough to win when I'm at my best. How am I ever going to do that when I feel rubbish?

We started talking it through and it sounded like Danny really thought I could do it. It was a real lift and so we discussed the plan. All I had to do was enjoy sticking to it and even if it was hard and if I could do that then it would be a success win or lose. We could honestly review what happened. We discussed that I am training to beat Nicol and Raneem, and to win a World Series event. Surely those goals start right here, right now with a big effort. Win or lose! Only then can we review it and learn from it. We can't learn anything if I don't give it my best.

I knew I needed to be aggressive and Danny asked if I could handle that. Could I stand up for myself and show her I really believed I could beat her? I left feeling like a different person than when I entered. Those are the moments that massively help having Danny with me. Questions answered, focus clear, new beliefs and targets. To give it everything I have for the entire match.

———

Despite the lift I'd got from that conversation with Danny, in the warm-up I was spraying it all over the place and it felt terrible. I was aware of trying not to let Nicol get into her groove before we had even started and so I took the decision to under hit or over hit every shot I sent back, as I tried to focus on getting out to the ball and reaching for it so I could volley.

The one thing Nicol made you realise before stepping on court was how hard it was going to be, how deep you were going to have to push and dig from the first serve. Before you hit a shot, you had to make sure that her aura and her reputation didn't give her a head start over you. You almost had to have a word with yourself and ask whether you really were in the position to go there. Once you were on court, you had to be crystal clear about what you were doing or you could forget it. Your strategy had to involve a plan of what to do the moment it started to get tough, because you knew that was coming. You needed to stay strong and survive the constant ride.

When you stepped on court with Nicol her physical attributes were immense. She had ridiculous speed in both attack and defence, and her raw speed and turning were phenomenal. She seemed to recover aerobically very quickly and you knew you were in trouble when she was running to the service box to serve. She volleyed well and kept you pinned back in the court, making the distance to the front feel huge. Every time you made a big push physically and mentally, she was able to take all of the wind out of the attack by battening down the hatches and making it as hard for me in return. She seemed to wait for my flurry to pass and I was left wondering about what I should do next.

Squash is like boxing in this respect, just you and your opponent in the middle of this maelstrom of tension between you. In boxing parlance, Nicol held all the championship belts while I was just full of anxieties of whether I could perform in the ring.

Although squash is a physically brutal sport, you can have an 'out' at any moment during a rally. For example, you could play a boast shot – which hits the side wall before the front – to get a breather, rather than stay in a particularly long and leg-weary rally but you can't succumb to the temptation to get the point over with unless it's the right play. That's what is so sadistic about the sport. You have to keep wanting to have the pain if you want to win. If you keep choosing to end the rally early, even if you hit the odd winner, you are succumbing to weakness. Against Nicol, this was especially true. You needed to show that you could deal with your legs and lungs burning and the effect that can have on your decision-making.

There is no hiding place inside the glass box.

When Egypt's young teen talent Nour El Sherbini came onto the scene, the tin height for women was lowered (in 2015), and she didn't have the scars of the senior professionals against Nicol. It was almost as if she was saying, 'Why would you keep the rallies going?' Bang, into the nick (the intersection between the wall and floor where you can hit spectacular winners). But it wasn't as simple as that. From our perspective, it was the legacy of the pain, the amount of beatings over the years Nicol had handed out to all of us. You can stay present, knowing you can only play this match, this rally, this shot but it's not realistic. It's there with you: past matches, past results, past pain.

All these thoughts were the conversations Nicol made you have with yourself before the spin of the racket – that worry of the pain and how difficult the next hour was going to be on the glass court, and that you simply didn't want to be embarrassed by another one-sided performance.

On this particular day in Kuala Lumpur, Nicol and I did the spin for the serve before our semi-final. Everyone knew Nicol had to spin the racket. Every now and again a player attempted to throw Nicol off-kilter by insisting on spinning it themselves and it always became incredibly awkward. I remember Jenny Duncalf trying it when she was World No.2, and there was this very painful stand-off until one of them wilted. Nicol did cave in eventually but she still won the match.

Although a strange superstition, it didn't normally make a difference to the match outcome, so I decided not to bother fighting her for it. Instead, when time was called and she turned quickly to say 'P' or 'D' – Nicol used a Prince racket, so the bottom handle had 'P' for up and the upside down 'D', instead of the usual 'up' and 'down' – I looked her straight in the eye and said: 'P.' I was now trying to carve my own mental belief and stamping my own presence.

For me it started with the spin.

I didn't look at the racket, I just looked directly into her eyes. When she broke eye contact I turned and walked off the court, not waiting to see the outcome. It doesn't sound like a lot but it showed how normally submissive I was to her because this felt so massive. Because it felt so big, I knew it wasn't something I would normally have done.

It felt rude of me not to say 'please' or not to wait for the spin of the racket. It was a major move at the time for me to do that, to think, 'You might be spinning the racket but you're not dominating me.' Of course, once I got back on court I awkwardly had to wait for her to take her position as I didn't know who had won the serve. Yet, it felt like a small win and a tiny step towards more dominance. Of course, none of that matters if you don't believe you can win. But I did.

It was a small step of dominance. The aim was to try to not let her do something which would settle her down, which I guess is what Jenny and other players were attempting with the racket spin. I tried to do it in another way, which would not have been construed as outwardly awkward for the spectators.

The preliminaries over, now I had to keep it straight, to kill her speed, get on the volley and take her time away by getting out to the ball. It was a close game and I lost it 12-10. It was tough going but I was playing well. I had memories of Cleveland (my first win over her in 2011) where I was so focussed on the plan that winning or losing didn't matter. I just had to execute. During the match, I really stood up for myself and started to ask Nicol questions to her face. I had a huge amount of focus and I knew it would be a physical push. At one point, when there was a bit of player interference, Nicol had asked the referees: 'Can you see what she's doing with her movement?'

I took a couple of steps towards her, which must have been quite intimidating for Nicol because I am a good six inches taller than her.

'What did you say? What am I doing?'

I stared at her. Inside, I remember thinking that I had never said anything like that to anyone on court before. No one spoke to Nicol during matches. For all Nicol's mild-mannered, ever-smiling public face, she had absolute authority and an unmistakable aura when you were in a competitive environment with her. Yet, she had backed down as soon as I stood up to her. I couldn't believe that was her reaction.

Funnily enough, a few years later I read Ronda Rousey's *My Fight Your Fight* and I found it resonated, even if the story of her Ultimate Fighting Championship (UFC) career was remarkably different to the life of a pro squash player – after all Rousey was a complete animal, a vicious fighter and she talks about breaking her opponent's noses. But, in some ways, I could still relate to some of her experiences. If Rousey could handle someone trying to smash her face in, then I could handle someone having a whinge to the referee. It meant that I was doing something right.

People don't realise how much using your body to steal an opponent's space is a big part of the sport. For a non-contact sport there is so much contact in squash. You have to be able to handle the moments when someone is almost screaming in your face. It's not like tennis, where the opponent is down the far end of the court and you don't interact much with them. In squash, you are so close that you are breathing and sweating on each other and that means that you can be heavily swayed and influenced by the opponent's behaviour. If you get someone who isn't on your wavelength or you don't get on with, it can easily spill over into confrontation on court.

But there was no confrontation from Nicol. As soon as I stood up for myself and asked her to repeat what she had accused me of, her body language changed instantly.

'No, nothing,' she said. Her voice was small.

For the first time ever, I realised how much mental control she'd had over me in the past. That moment changed everything. It seemed like her body language wilted but maybe it was just that I grew in confidence. I knew I had shown her that I believed I was ready to do something I had never done before. There was still work to do but, crucially, I felt like I was going to win if I kept up playing the right way.

Danny kept telling me to take my space, hit my targets. It meant that Nicol was now doing a lot of extra work running around me. She began making errors and over-thinking. After points, you sometimes catch Nicol replaying shots two or three times in slow motion, as if she was becoming over-analytical and second guessing herself. This was a telltale sign that she was thinking too much, something Peter McNab and I had seen and analysed when watching her. He pointed out that she rarely did it when winning and, if she did, it was perhaps one replay or shadow stroke. Now, she was doing it almost every rally and each time with two or three repeats. I knew her 'tell' and I knew what it meant. I was getting to her.

And, all the while, I was telling myself to enjoy executing my game plan, even though it was incredibly hard work. After playing her countless times, I was always searching for little signs of Nicol physically waning during matches. I really started to notice it in her body and as soon as I saw the first forehand where her head or stomach collapsed and she lost her shape, I knew she was going. I used these little nuggets to boost my mental morale. You had to get past thinking of her as a machine. She was a human being with weaknesses to be exploited.

In the third game, I was really getting out to the ball and reaching for it. This meant that I was taking the ball a little bit earlier than normal and although it was hard, I stuck with it and I started to feel her fading. My straight target hitting was getting to her, I could feel it. Now it was about staying calm. I was one game from the winning line.

I was solid. I could see she was starting to repeat her swing on mistakes. At times when I got tired, I thought of Chrissie Wellington running when she couldn't feel her legs. I came through the final three games 11-6, 11-8, 11-5, winning the match with a tight backhand kill that stuck to the wall.

It was my first World Series win over Nicol and it also meant that I was the first player to beat Nicol four times since Vanessa Atkinson had recorded the mark. But it felt much more significant than the other times I'd beaten her. With Danny in my corner, and Liz Irving watching on from Nicol's corner, I had taken on the greatest female squash player of all time and beaten her on my own terms.

Danny's after-match notes

Nicol got frustrated with her straight game and got technically analytical.

Laura stood up to her and directed comments towards her.

She was pinned behind constantly by Laura volleying and getting out to the ball.

Laura is taller so why is Nicol volleying more?

Stayed in the rallies and didn't mind Nicol getting balls back. Just reset and restart the rally instead of panicking.

———

There was still work to do in KL. I was in the World Series final against my long-time English rival, Alison Waters. Physically, I wasn't one 100 per cent and I made a deal with myself to give it everything against Alison. There were also self-doubts again, even though I knew that I should now win the tournament after beating Nicol. As top seed, I had lost to Alison the previous month over five games at the nationals. It was a different challenge to playing Nicol but it was another mountain to climb.

31st March 2013

Could I back up the day before but with more pressure? I didn't want to be flat after my win. It didn't feel as exciting to win against Nicol like it had in the past so I thought I would be okay. Could I focus and stick to the plan against Alison where I really wanted to win after the nationals loss and prove I deserved to be England No.1?

I told Danny I wasn't sure I could raise it and that I felt drained. I had hit in the morning and felt wiped out after. He told me to control what I could and just stick to that deal one more time. Win or lose it was just one more match.

I read a quote from British boxer Chris Eubank and it hit home:

'It's the fights where you are asked the most questions and come through. You didn't want to go through it but by doing so you came out proud of yourself and gained massive self respect, which, at the end of the day, is all that matters. The easy fights had to be won but they don't really give you anything new, it's only when you hadn't much left but found a way through to stand up and fight and win.'

This is amazing to read, particularly where I was positioned at the time. So, we get the plan clear and speak about being performance focussed. Get in front of her, hit with pace to her backhand and believe in myself. My legs felt heavy and it was so hot and draining on the court and I thought of Chrissie. She ran in 80°F heat for eight hours and this was all a matter of focus. It's just in your mind, I kept telling myself. Your mind wants you to stop but I knew, like the Eubank quote, this was all about being proud until the end. It will hurt but try to enjoy it. Don't come off knowing you went soft and stopped doing the plan when it all got hard. So, I dug in and I forced the pace. I hit my targets, peppered her backhand and I grew in strength. I won it 11-9.

I came off and Danny said: 'Well done, how do you feel?' I said: 'Not great, can you tell?' I had pushed hard in that game and I was desperately trying to hide it from everyone. Ignore everything and stick to the plan was all he said! I went back on and my legs were a little wobbly. I thought, well at least I can still feel them. Chrissie won an Ironman not being able to feel her legs so I'm still okay. I had never realised how much this was all in the mind before.

Big push in the second, get the face on and do the plan! I got a lift because I could tell she was struggling. The third was the hardest. I became more and more result focussed and it was a battle of mind. I had done enough though and I managed to close it out. She was tired physically, I could tell, but she also had a sore ankle I think, but it felt so good to come out on top in a major final. This was my first individual title on Malaysian soil, my second World Series title and I did it after my biggest win over Nicol. This feels amazing!

(Previous page) With DP, Nick and Danny (l to r) in Philly

(Above) After winning the KL Open

See my full photo gallery at lauramassaro.co.uk/photos

6. A HULL OF A VICTORY

My first coach Annette Pilling told me when I was a junior that one day I could win a British Open title. For Annette, the British Open was always the prize, not the World Championships. In her mind, and in the minds of so many in the sport in England and around the world, it was 'the Wimbledon of Squash'.

During the 80s and early 90s heyday of the sport, the British Open, which then had a great sponsorship with shoe and clothing brand Hi-Tec behind it, had been staged at Wembley Conference Centre and enjoyed record crowds. Apparently, it even had ticket touts standing outside its doors as people clamoured to see the squash superstars of the era, like men's unbeaten champion Jahangir Khan.

By the time I broke into the world's top 10, the British Open had lost some of its glow. The superstars had long since retired, the sponsors had moved on to other sports and squash had gone from being one of the most popular sports in the country to being more and more niche.

On the women's side it didn't help that there had only been one British female winner since 1961. In 2001, a few of the women got together to brainstorm ideas around building publicity because no-one else seemed to be doing anything. One of those ideas was a photoshoot with my close friend Vicky Botwright. She was to pose in a bra and thong on court with her racket.

The whole PR stunt was based around Vicky saying that conventional clothing could be quite restrictive and the WISPA women's tour was open to players wearing what they liked. Vicky had a great figure, still does, and the subsequent publicity and photoshoot sparked a media frenzy and made newspapers all over the world. Vicky briefly became the world's most popular squash player and had all sorts of interview requests. Her website attracted more hits than tennis player Anna Kournikova's and one newspaper even called her the 'Lancashire Hot Bot'. She also got a few marriage proposals.

When the global media coverage subsided, it didn't bring a home winner or lift the tournament in any way. Over the following years, the British Open was staged in Birmingham, Aberdeen, Nottingham, Liverpool and Manchester, before another promoter failed to take the tournament forward after making a lot of promises. That left the tournament in a pickle and it wasn't staged at all in 2010 and 2011. Imagine that, supposedly the biggest and most prestigious tournament in our sport just not being held for two years.

It was a disaster for us English players, especially as England was enjoying a bit of a golden era of players. We had the World No.1 and 2 in Nick Matthew and James Willstrop, while myself and Jenny Duncalf were in the world's top five women's players. The history and prestige was supposed to be special, and winning one was meant to be on everyone's bucket list, but the British Open became a sad shadow of its former self.

But then came salvation.

After a five-year break, England Squash took back control of the tournament's rights and set about signing a sponsorship contract with Dr Assem Allam, a wealthy Egyptian businessman and philanthropist who had fled the country of his birth in the 50s, settled in East Yorkshire and grew a very successful manufacturing business. Dr Allam and his family had thrown their support behind Hull City Football Club and he loved squash with a passion. He gave the British Open a lifeline when it looked like it might disappear forever.

Dr Allam signed a sponsorship deal of around £1 million and he was still backing the tournament up until the 2020 British Open, which showed his love and commitment to squash. In his first year of sponsorship, the tournament was taken back to London where the glass court was erected in the atrium at London's O2 Arena. Jenny and I did some exciting publicity around the event that year, including a photoshoot on the London Eye and outside Parliament. The event itself was a success for me. I had a great run making my first semi-final and I got a taste of what it was like to play in a British Open in front of an excited home crowd.

Nicol won again, where she beat Nour El Sherbini, then a very quick and clever 16-year-old who became the first Egyptian woman to reach the final. Meanwhile Nick Matthew beat Ramy Ashour in the final to give us a home champion on the men's side. I felt the energy, the vibe and the magnitude of winning the British Open as I watched him. I saw how much it meant to Nick, his team and the crowd and in that moment I knew for sure that I wanted to feel what Nick was feeling.

There was still uncertainty over where the British Open would be held the following year, 2013, before Dr Allam and England Squash took the bold decision to stage a squash event outdoors in May at a football stadium in Hull. They built a glass court under a tarpaulin roof and put it at one end of the football pitch at the KC Stadium, home of Hull City FC, where Dr Allam was owner of the club.

My own preparations for the British Open weren't going well. I had struggled to recover from an ankle injury, training wasn't going well and I had played several training matches against men, which I tended to do before a big tournament, and got roundly chopped. I was desperate to do well in Hull but my confidence was pretty low.

I was still taping my ankle after that injury and, even though I felt back to full strength and had been training well, something wasn't clicking with my movement. I didn't want to risk injuring my ankle again but I honestly didn't believe I had any chance of doing well at the British Open with it taped. I arranged a match with Wales' Tesni Evans just before the Open and drove to Manchester to play on the glass court. Jade, the England team physio, and the English Institute of Sport doctor both looked at my ankle and agreed it was strong enough. I was scared and worried. If I injured my ankle again in this moment, then any hopes of competing, let alone winning, in Hull were gone. I voiced my worries and finally it came down to a single question: Do you think you can win the British playing with a taped ankle? The answer was no. Simple as that, the decision was made. I would play without tape and hope that my ankle held up.

So, off I went to prepare against Tesni with no tape. Jade gave me a load of warmup exercises and then stayed and watched me play. It was certainly calming to have her there. I felt good on court; I felt like I had been let free. Finally I could feel all my strength in my legs. I could push off quickly and hunt the ball. I felt excited for the first time in weeks and off we went to Hull.

The opening round was actually held at Pontefract Squash Club, where I came through easily against Joey Chan. We stayed locally and then drove the rest of the way to Hull on my rest day. I was due on court on the football pitch for an 8pm start against India's Dipika Pallikal. Watching other matches during the day, I could see that the conditions were getting worse and that Hull's weather was proving to be very wintry, even though it was May. The players were competing in long-sleeved tops, the crowd sat huddled together, looking frozen in huge coats and blankets. Before the match started, we were given hand warmers and blankets which, I have to admit, was a first and freaked me out a little bit.

Once I got on court, in a flash I found myself one game down. The freezing conditions meant the ball felt heavy like a stone. Dipika was firing the ball in short at every opportunity, making it hard for me to retrieve it. Panic set in. When that happens time can speed up on you and I found myself close to going two games down. I had to do something. I gave it a massive 'COME ON' roar and it sparked me up. I got angry and the situation I was in, the scoreline and the conditions. All the work that had gone into making sure that my ankle was ok and it was all slipping away. I played a few good points, Dipika's shots went lower with a couple hitting the tin, while I began thumping the ball to give it extra heat and pace in a bid to retrieve better.

I was back in the game and somehow had done a Houdini act and levelled at 1-1. Meanwhile Danny was sitting with DP, his first event as my official coach, both were shivering in the cold, despite the blankets. In these situations, sometimes it's the little details that matter. Here, two friends from my club, Dave Abberley and Andy Wyn-Jones, had stayed to watch me in the cold. Danny told them to shout at every rally and they did a great job of keeping the energy up. It really helped me stay up emotionally.

I somehow came through it. I was closer to losing than the 3-1 score might have suggested and I felt it was my mental strength that saved me that day. Drama happened on the final point as Dipika smashed her head on the side wall after tripping over my foot. She couldn't catch her weight and went flying into the backhand side wall, smashing her head so hard you could visibly see the wall panel move. She got a 'no let' as my shot was deemed too good and we shook hands with her crying. It was a bad way for a match to end but it seemed I had a bit of luck that day. I later found out she had a concussion from the bang. I can't imagine how hard she must have hit the wall to make it move the way it did.

Danny said it was the coldest conditions he had ever experienced watching squash. James Willstrop said after his early round match that the conditions were like 'playing on court eight at Pontefract in December'.

Then, the next day, the rain, wind and hail started. The court was leaking water through the roof of the tarpaulin and, in a classic squash moment, a call was hastily put in to the local Hull and East Riding Squash Club to see if they could host some matches.

When I found out that we were playing on a traditional plaster court at East Riding, I was relieved. Facing a shotmaker in Egypt's Omneya Abdel Kawy, I was aware that if we had played on the glass I was in for a tough draw. I had really struggled with Omneya through the junior ranks and although I'd started to get my belief up against her, I knew that if you played poorly she had the skill and confidence to beat me. The plan was not to open the court up and not to wind her up. Unlike other players, when Omneya got angry, she played better. My job was to refrain from being argumentative, stay calm and keep quiet.

DP had spoken to me about showing my level as World No.2 and stepping up to the plate against these other girls. My attitude could help get me through and I had to have intensity from the start. I felt I got it right. Sometimes a stressful match can release the pressure and that seemed to be the case. I picked up a lot of balls from the start, which meant that I could get work into Omneya and make her play one more ball. I closed it out in four games. Luck had been on my side that we played inside.

Finals weekend saw a welcome change in the weather, with bright sun and warm conditions for my semi-final clash against Raneem El Welily, who by now was proving herself to be the most naturally talented player on tour. We were back to the glass court, with 1,500 spectators set to watch from the stand behind the goal. Again, I made it through in four tough games; I had secured a place in the final for the first time. Now it was time to learn from my previous mistakes in big finals, like the World Championships final in 2012, when I spent too much time reading congratulatory text messages instead of preparing. I was still reading them on the morning of the final.

That night, we had a function at the KC Stadium organised by Dr Allam. The men's final was between Greg Gaultier and Ramy Ashour, two of the most charismatic players on tour, while I was due to face Nicol who was then the defending, four-time champion. With the final due early afternoon the following day, attending a large function the evening before such a big match wasn't really where I wanted to be but it actually turned out to be quite a good way to spend the eve of the final. We heard past champions talk about how the British Open was the most prestigious event in a series of really interesting interviews. As I listened to these players talk, the magnitude of the event and what I was playing for really hit home.

All four of us current finalists were then invited up on stage. The introvert inside me hated every second. I felt completely out of my comfort zone; I didn't feel like I deserved to be up there with the company I was with. The way the interview went and the way people were speaking to me, it was like reaching the final was the end of the road; winning the trophy was never going to be a possibility and that I deserved a big pat on the back. Nicol was favourite and no one expected me to beat her the next day. Maybe I hadn't yet earned the right for it to be any different but it did annoy me.

Yet, I had beaten Nicol before and I knew she was probably more worried about playing me than anyone else at that time. Even though you never sensed emotions from Nicol, you could sense when she was feeling a bit edgy on court and because she used to go for shots which weren't really on, rather than just be happy to rally it out and make it extremely tough for her opponent. She'd also do those shadow strokes that Peter McNab had noticed.

Everyone has their vulnerabilities. God knows, I did.

I remember playing a tournament in a convention centre in Kowloon, Hong Kong. It was the first time I made the business end of the event and, with that, the chance to play on the glass court in the shopping mall. It was a hugely unexpected result and I should have been thrilled. Instead I freaked out. I remember being out in front of the mall with under an hour to go before the match, with tears streaming down my face. My mind was all over the place and the emotional stress began to take effect. It was just too big a venue for me. I was going to let everyone down and I didn't deserve to be there. All I wanted to do was please people. It's ironic that I'm known for being mentally strong given what I mess I was inside during some of the most successful times in my career. If only people knew what was actually going on in my head and how much I doubted myself and worried over things.

This generally happened before I played Nicol, the fear that it may be completely one-sided. Realistically, as an athlete you shouldn't really be worried about a match where you might not live up to a crowd's expectations. On top of that doubt, when I was under stress or playing Nicol, the way I looked on court had a huge impact, especially considering the way Nicol looked on court – she was always in amazing shape and wore really great, pristine kits. You could easily end up feeling like you were some kind of second-rate athlete. It always looked like someone had also stuck a massive lump of muscle on top of both Nicol's thigh bones. It was as if they were looking at you when she briefly twisted her body to serve. When you were absolutely knackered and looked over at someone serving, and your rival didn't have an ounce of fat? That was intimidating. Quite often Nicol wore colours where you couldn't see she was sweating. Even if sweat did appear on her arms it made her look better, almost like she was glistening and in mint condition, while opponents would be sweaty, feel dishevelled and simply be hanging on for dear life.

What I did know on this Sunday in May was that Nicol was going to be fresh for the final, after beating Alison Waters in just 27 minutes the previous day. Usually, I was almost always in a foul mood on a big match day. It wasn't at anyone or anything in particular; I was sick with worry, which would come across as grumpiness. I would internalise and spin everything in my head. The question I often had swirling in the back of my mind would be, 'What if I lose this?' For all the work and psychology I had done over the years, I never knew if this was from my childhood or not. It was relentless and, unfortunately, it was something I could never break until the end of my career.

But, on that day, on that court, against Nicol of all people, in what was the biggest match of my career up to that point, I actually didn't have any of those pre-match worries. I knew I had to stand up for myself and get stuck into her but there were no thoughts of winning, losing or of the occasion. From the off, I was aggressive and took the opener before I got a little bit carried away and Nicol got things back level. DP had always ingrained into me how crucial the third game is in a best-of-five. I dug in, my body language picked up and I was able to give myself some 'Come ons' which began to ignite the crowd.

There is sometimes too much politeness in England as far as the squash crowds go. Most of the time it's gentle applause at best. It's the opposite of Egypt, where you win a rally and there is complete silence but lose a rally and the crowd starts screaming at you. Yet every so often, an English crowd will really get into it – that was what happened that day at the British Open final in Hull. I was never one to look for energy from the crowd but when it happened unexpectedly, like it did from the fans at the KC Stadium that day, it felt like the atmosphere was getting louder and louder. You win a rally and it kind of shocks you. Am I playing well? Wow, I must be doing something right here. You can feel the energy and the passion, and you almost want to win a rally just so you can hear the crowd again. It is intoxicating. And it is a thrill to be in that moment.

I was on a high in that third game and I pushed as hard as I could, but Nicol pulled away and suddenly I was 10-7 down. Right there and then, I just told myself that if I am losing this game then I am losing it volleying – on my terms. I played great for the next four points and, game ball up, Nicol hit her return down the middle. The refs gave me a let.

'LET?! I had my thumb up her nose!'

I was already opening the glass door as I yelled.

'Review!'

'Decision overruled, stroke to Massaro. Game to Massaro, she leads two games to one.'

I wasn't getting too excited between games, despite the atmosphere and the scoreline. I knew it would be hard and I expected Nicol to come back. I made a great start in the fourth and I started to see her 'tell' reveal itself, just as it had done before. She was becoming over-analytical, replaying her swing and I knew she was thinking too much. She even hit a few errors, which was so rare that you knew you were getting to her when that happened.

At 8-3 up I was thinking 'don't mess this up now', which seems like a negative thought when I think back on it now, but in that moment it pushed me on and made me focus.

I had to keep quiet any thoughts that this was a British Open final or what it would mean if I won. When I was 9-4 up, Nicol won two rallies – now my edginess started to reveal itself. I was focussed but I was still really nervous. I got a lucky let and, when she retook her serve, I knew straight away that it was going to go too high above the cut line. I actually smiled. 'Oh my God, that's going out!' She'd just handed me a Championship ball.

Stop smiling. Don't be an idiot, it's not done. Concentrate.

Suddenly, my brain began to get in the way. Should I be quick and get it over with, go for a shot? Or play it out and wait for the right time? The next rally started and, in a flash, it was over, I'd lost it. A soft and pathetic rally, neither attacking nor biding my time. A rally played by someone thinking too much.

Come on, get your head back now before this turns really nervy.

I returned the serve down the backhand wall and, when Nicol put a simple putaway attempt into the tin, I couldn't quite believe it.

I'd never really thought before about what I would do if I won a major title. I didn't know where to go or what to do, so I just jumped up and down in a blur and found myself at the front wall where the photographers are housed, at tin-height level, and I rested my head on the glass in disbelief. Nicol was there to shake hands.

The media later labelled it Nicol's most surprising defeat at a major tournament in four years.

I looked at Danny and my family all watching. I dropped down to the floor and it hit me at what had just happened. I stayed squatted down. As I stood, Nicol was still graciously waiting for me to exit the court. I was soon met by a huge hug from Danny. It was my third win in four against Nicol and I had become the first British Open home champion since 1991. Lisa Opie, who'd won it in 1991, was there watching somewhere in the crowd. My entire family came down to where I was. It was just a sea of tears and smiles and hugs and pure joy.

Sometime later, I found myself sitting alone in the stadium changing rooms. My phone had blown up with so many messages to read but just at that moment I enjoyed the solitude as I tried to process what had just happened. After the trophy pictures with Ramy Ashour, the men's champion, Danny and I drove home reliving the day and speaking to friends and family. We also stopped for a sneaky McDonald's on the way home. We invited a few people round to our house for when we got home. It was great to see everyone and celebrate with them all. I had watched my first professional match live at the 2001 British Open. Now, here I was a champion of one, only the second home winner in over 50 years. It meant everything.

Even after everyone had gone home, Danny and I were still giddy, enjoying the night. At 4am we finished watching the replay of the match, reliving every ball, only with none of the stress and sweat, and loving every second.

(Opposite page) With Danny
and the British Open Trophy

(Next page) Playing Nicol
in the 2013 British Open

See my full photo gallery at
lauramassaro.co.uk/photos

7. LIFE ON THE ROAD

Diaries

8th September 2013

I read a great extract from a book Danny is reading about fear. The general points of what I read were – worry repeats itself and the repetition makes the response stick. I feel bad when I worry. I need to stop at this moment. The future is unknown and worrying is pointless. Fear is convincing when you believe it. For me, it was good to remember that nothing bad is actually happening. It's unlikely that worst-case scenarios will happen and I'm really okay right now.

18th October 2013

Into the US Open semi-finals and I didn't play a drop the entire first game. Danny said: 'Do you want to be sat later wishing you'd played some or take the risk it might work?' I struggled my way through an 85-minute battle against Low Wee Wern winning 3-2. I was in the final to play Nicol. I was so worried I was going to get pummelled. I was tired, my ankle was a bit niggly. I felt the pressure that organisers had made the event equal prize money and I felt I was going to get hammered. I was worried about my tiredness and spoke to Peter McNab. I got upset on the phone when he said I had nothing to prove – it hit home the pressure I put on myself. The match was on a knife edge but tiredness set in and I lost out in four games. I will learn that I didn't push hard enough at 7-4 in the fourth and didn't stay positive enough. Next time, I need to go for the throat but I am happy that I did the women's game proud.

29th October 2013, Monte Carlo

At the Women's Monte Carlo Classic, I won my first round in 16 minutes against Kylie Lyndsay. Danny said I looked weak in the front two corners, which didn't go down well as I had won so easily and I didn't want to seem disrespectful. But he was right and it wasn't about winning now but about the rest of the event. We went to the hotel gym and I did some Bulgarians off the side of the treadmill with the heaviest weight they had – 12kgs! It was the same in my next match. More nerves and edginess. Danny asked if I was here to win the event or was I happy with reaching a point where it wasn't a failure anymore? The hunger had gone ever so slightly since the British Open victory and it was adding more pressure. I had always worried my career would be a failure with all my effort if I hadn't won a Worlds, British Open or become World No.1. It sounds stupid but after that British title maybe I have just settled in my own mind that I can no longer fail in my career. Do I want more?

31st October 2013, Monte Carlo

I played Nouran Gohar in the semis. This young Egyptian player was causing a stir. Not only with her squash. We felt I needed to keep her calm. Gohar's opponents had both got angry, shouted at her and themselves, and argued with the ref. Nouran played better. I had watched and knew I needed to be clever and mature. The plan was to keep her calm. Compliment her shots, enjoy the match and respect her. I did everything I wanted to and I won 3-0. After, I remember Line Hansen saying: 'I was watching, thinking how and why are you keeping so calm. We all thought you would tell her straight and put her in her place. As the match went on I could see what was happening and I realised it's what I should have done.' She was right but I had learned from watching her match and learning that Nouran plays well when she's angry.

26th January 2014, New York

Tournament of Champions at New York's Grand Central. It isn't always match info that's needed by a coach and, in certain situations, paying and investing in having Danny there won me matches. The one I played against Kiwi Joelle King in the quarters was one of them. That one extra round paid for three flights regardless of all the other benefits. I wasn't moving well and I came off ranting at the end of the second. Never a good sign for me! I was saying: 'Here we go again, the roller coaster starts again.' Danny calmed me down and gave me a great talk. While I sat in my chair he put his hands on my thighs and told me to look at him. I looked up and he said: 'You're doing fine.' I'm not, I thought! He said to play for you, enjoy it. You're not letting anyone down. Just go on there, have fun and entertain the crowd. I went back on a different player. He had freed me up and let me be me. He gave me permission in a moment of stress to play how I want to play. I won the next two games and I honestly don't think I would have won that match without the talk. I lost to Nicol in the final but a great start to the year.

8. BECOMING WORLD CHAMPION

Before I began to make my body leaner and get in better shape, I always had the thought of going on court and thinking, 'How do I look here?' I wanted to look like an athlete, to represent squash and to show how athletically demanding it was just by the way I looked. For me personally, it was another part of being 'all in' and committed in every possible way to being the best squash player I could be. I guess this is a lesson I took from watching Nicol, with her pristine kit and muscular, athletic look.

I mean, I always wanted to look smart but I also wanted to look in good shape. If I didn't feel as if I was in the best shape possible, it would knock my confidence a little, or I would pick up a vibe that I was being judged by the people watching me, that maybe they were thinking I looked overweight or I had a little bit of fat round the belly. I know that women talk about 'fat days', where for whatever reason you just don't have body confidence. Even being a professional athlete doesn't make you immune to those so-called 'fat days', if anything it makes them worse.

It was important to me to wear a kit that was smart enough to be intimidating or to wear something that stood out, especially against a player who was a different body shape to me or who looked different.

This was in my head before the 2013 World Championships, which had been delayed until March 2014 due to the women's world tour being unable to make a deal with a host city until Penang stepped in. The main draw of the event was to be played on the all-glass court at the Penang International Sports Arena. I knew the venue very well because it was the exact same place I had played the deciding rubber for England in 2001 at the World Junior Championships when we became champions. Having good or bad memories of a particular venue can definitely get in your head when you go back to play there again. Fortunately, this time I could tell myself that it was a good omen.

The women's tour had played on Nicol's status as a superstar in her home country and managed to strike a deal with the Penang state government to host the Championships at short notice, plus the event would sponsored by Malaysian bank CIMB, who had also backed Nicol since her rise on tour back in 2005. I can't imagine the pressure Nicol must have felt in the lead up to this event, where she would be playing for an eighth world title in front of what was likely to be the biggest crowd ever for a women's squash event.

I hadn't understood the level of adulation Nicol gets in Malaysia until I saw it with my own eyes. I knew that she had moved to Amsterdam to train for a bit more privacy but the penny didn't really drop until Danny and I went shopping in a supermarket during the KL Open and suddenly started seeing her face on loads of different products. There was Nicol staring out and me from the shelves, a household name like Roger Federer, Serena Williams or Cristiano Ronaldo.

Nicol withdrew from the Windy City Open in Chicago, a big event in its own right, which was due to take place right before the Worlds in Penang.

It was understandable. After all, it was on the other side of the world and close timing but, whether deliberate or not, it did also send a message to her rivals that the upcoming World Championships meant everything to her.

I remember thinking I couldn't have done that because it would add so much pressure to me mentally but I guessed that Nicol and I were very different people. She had certainly done an incredible job over many years of handling being the focus of attention and player everyone wanted to beat.

This meant that I was top seed for Chicago and, thankfully, I lived up to seeding by winning the event. I had travelled with DP but without Danny, and enjoyed having him with me. I beat some really good players that week and it gave me a lot of confidence, not least because it was also my first title win since the 2013 British Open, nearly 10 months earlier. Before I won in Hull, I worried that I would be seen as some kind of failure if I didn't win a British or World Championship title, so that first British Open title did take some pressure off. Deep down, though, I still had this nagging sense that it was some kind of fluke.

Danny and DP put their head in their hands when I suggested this. You don't win a British Open by fluke, they said!

I had nine days of training after Chicago to build up to Penang. Sitting at David Lloyd Chorley, in between training sessions, I had idly picked up a copy of Squash Player magazine and read an interview with Liz Irving, Nicol's coach. Liz was asked to predict if there were any rivals for the undisputed World No.1 spot and she listed several players but didn't mention me. She also stated that she couldn't see anyone overtaking Nicol in the next five years – so, she basically thought that Nicol would reign as World No.1 for an unbroken 13 years. I can still remember the quotes. They still rankle a bit, even now. 'I don't see any other player on tour as professional as Nicol in any aspect. They might think they are, but they aren't. Hopefully they strive for that, you need the No.1 to lead the pack and show how it should be done and Nicol does that really well. This is what the girls need to aspire to.'

I decided to use Liz's words as extra motivation. I was playing well, the flight over to Malaysia was great and I was really happy to be back in Penang. It's a great city and because of my happy times there in the juniors, I immediately felt at home. Danny and I were both big fans of the pool, where we spent a lot of time in between matches and training sessions. Never too much time to drain me or have too much sun but enough time to relax and chill a little. Things were good on the court as well. Like I said, it helped that I'd played well in that venue before and I knew the surroundings, but I also felt a lot of confidence from the way I'd played in the lead-up.

Winning the title was a long way off – and it definitely felt that way – but I was starting in a good place.

I played local girl Vanessa Raj in my opening round and tried to find some footage of her online beforehand. I won the opening game and Danny came over in the break. He was all set to give me a serious talking to because he thought I was too relaxed and not intense enough. Unfortunately, he tried to deliver this important coaching insight while wearing a tiny girls' brightly coloured tracksuit top that came nowhere near fitting him. I later found out that he had been cold and didn't have a top of his own with him, so he quickly borrowed one from Lisa Aitken, another player that he coached at the time and who was also courtside that day. Lisa loves wearing eye-catching colours so, let's just say, it wasn't a very manly look. I burst out laughing at the sight of him. Danny wasn't impressed and we ended up having a mini-argument.

'Get your head on it, it's the World Champs!'

I won the next two games comfortably and Danny never forgot his hoodie again.

I needed to be on guard in my last 16 match against my old friend and rival, Jenny Duncalf. Friend or not, Jenny was often a very difficult opponent for me and she'd got the better of me plenty of times, going all the way back to when we played together as juniors. I knew she was struggling with her achilles and she showed her frustration by breaking a racket on her shoe mid-match. I just remember mentally noting that whatever I was doing was working, and to make sure I kept on doing it. I was relieved to get through because I knew that it could have been a match that could have gone the other way if Jenny had been on her game.

I was now in the last eight playing Low Wee Wern, who was from Penang. I knew it had the potential to be a really difficult match – I had seen her name in my section of the draw (I know some players say they don't look ahead in the draw but I could never help myself!) but I felt ready.

It's a good thing that I was prepared for a battle because that's exactly what I got.

———

Diary

She was in good form and it was the match that had worried me in the lead up to the event when the draw came out. She was at home, being from Penang, and they were expecting about 2,000 people in the stadium. The biggest crowd I had played in front of. They wouldn't be shouting for me! The match was close the whole way. The crowd was loud! I was patchy in my play and not able to force the pace as I wanted against Wee Wern, who is so good at soaking and playing at a medium pace. The conditions were hot, which made it so hard to volley but I needed to do that to make the court big. It was a tight match and at 2-1 down I found myself facing three match balls. I don't know how but I clawed my way back to 10-10 to face another at 11-10. I looked out at Danny when down in the fourth and he just looked back at me deflated. I managed somehow to sneak it and when I came off, I said to him: 'Don't give up on me.' He said he was trying to calm me down, but I didn't believe him. I won the fifth more

comfortably and was so happy with turning that around. It was the turning point of the
whole event. To win major titles, they say you need a bit of luck. Big recovery needed
after that and I swam down in the hotel pool, good stretch, saw Jade and got ready to
play Raneem in the S/F. Repeat of Cayman the year before!

It's a cliché but coming through a match like that gives you a really deep well of confidence that you know you can dip into later. You've been at the edge of defeat and survived and it can make you feel almost bombproof the next time you get down in a match. Looking back, a handful of points against Low Wee Wern changed the destiny of my career and my life. I tried not to think it that way at the time, however proud and pleased I was to come through the match, but it added to the little voice inside that told me that maybe, just maybe, this could be my year.

I was now one match away from making the World Championship finals two years in a row. It seemed like Raneem El Welily, the World No.3, stood in the way of another likely showdown with Nicol, this time on her home court. I needed to focus on Raneem, an incredibly difficult opponent in her own right, but it was hard to avoid Nicol's presence at that tournament. It felt like she was everywhere.

Raneem has amazing hands and so much skill. The opener was fast and furious as she kept chopping the ball short. I was soon 9-3 down. I began to adjust, relax and set myself up for the second game but somehow or another I came back and won that first game – I'm still not quite sure how. It's as if somehow letting myself let go of the fear of losing that game somehow allowed me to win it. Her head then went down in the second game and I could sense she was angry once she found herself 0-2 down despite playing well. She fired herself up and took the third game 11-6. I told myself that the fourth was the decider and to really go for it. It worked and I won through 11-7. After 48 minutes I was through to another final.

I was just coming out of the shower in our hotel room when it happened. I was drying myself and I idly refreshed the feed on the laptop to keep an eye on what was going on in the second semi-final between Nicol and Nour El Sherbini. I almost did a double take when I saw the result – Nour had come through 11-9 in the fifth. Nicol was out. Nour hadn't won a game off Nicol in their three previous matches and she was still playing junior squash at that point and even though she was already competing beyond her years on the main tour, nobody – except perhaps Nour herself – saw that coming. Nicol losing was always big news but getting beaten by a junior in her home city, when everything about the tournament to that point had made it seem pre-ordained that she was going to be in the final? The unthinkable had happened.

My heart sank. It caught me completely off guard, so much so that I had to sit down, as if my body knew before my mind did what I was thinking. I was now favourite to become world champion.

OH SH*T.

In my head, all the pressure that had been on Nicol's shoulders was immediately heaped onto mine and from that moment I had an awful feeling in the pit of my stomach, knowing I was going to walk out there with the match mine to lose. I was playing an 18-year-old, the youngest ever finalist, and this could be my last chance – my only chance – to be World Champion. I wasn't prepared for this. Within seconds of realising that I was going to play Nour and not Nicol, my mind began reeling with competing anxieties: The lack of sleep, the nerves, the expectation, the feeling of not knowing.

I was worrying about worrying.

That night, as Danny slept, I woke up several times during the night and tortured myself with all permutations. Would I rather be playing Nicol? That was crazy – I had a much better chance against an 18-year-old playing in her first final. I knew Nour had some big wins in Penang and was a deserved finalist, beating three top-ten players along the way, but she wasn't anywhere near as experienced or as accomplished as Nicol – or as me for that matter.

I told myself it was just another match. I told myself that she was young, that I had never lost to her and that I had the experience from last year's final under my belt. I tried, and failed, not to think about it as I lay there in the darkness, staring at the light fitting on the hotel room ceiling for what felt like hour after hour. To this day, I have never had a worse night's sleep.

In the morning, Nick Matthew, who knew a bit about winning World Championships having won his third one the previous year, sent me a text message to tell me that it was just another match and the final was about who hits their areas better. He was right, of course, but as much as I tried to think about my tactics and focus on the match itself and not the occasion, I was a nervous wreck. I began to feel sick from about an hour out from the final starting. My heart was beating loudly in my ears and I had anxiety coursing through my body. It was about the worst I had felt before any squash match, ever.

I set off to warm up for what felt like the sixth time. It was freezing with the air conditioning on in my little warmup room and I didn't know if it was the cold or the nerves that were making my teeth chatter. Danny came into the room and I just looked at him. 'How am I going to play if I can't even warm up without feeling sick?' He put his arm around me and I felt myself relax a little. 'I've tried every trick in the book to try to settle down. It's just another match, I have more experience to draw on, I've never lost to her. I am the higher seed …'

I know what you must be thinking. How could I, with all that experience, be feeling like that before any match, let alone the World Championship final? It was as much as a shock for me too, believe me. I had endured my share of nerves and self-doubt but nothing like this. I had heard of athletes throwing up before matches with nerves and I couldn't believe anyone would get that nervous.

Danny squeezed my shoulder.

'All you can do is your best. You deserve to be playing in this match. You have trained hard, you have played brilliantly all week and you are a winner. You always have been, and always will be, whatever happens today.'

He's always said that to me. He always saw it in me when I never did. I had always just been me: Laura from Chorley. And right then, Laura from Chorley needed some convincing that she could be World Champion.

Danny asked me if I wanted to do one of the NLP processes, the belief process, to get myself into the right headspace. Normally, I wouldn't have wanted to do something like that right before a match. The processes were sometimes hard as they made you look in places you didn't want to look. But, at that moment, I was prepared to do anything that made me feel a little bit better.

These are Danny's memories:

We were outside the courts at the venue. Nour was sitting down with her headphones on and looking chilled out. It seemed as though it was all a big laugh for her. She was causing havoc through the draw, beating Nicol in the semi-final, and now into her first senior world final as a junior. It looked fun and easy, as if to say 'what's so complicated about squash? Just play with a smile, what's the big deal?'

We went into a sideroom and I asked Laura whether she wanted to do the mental process. Immediately, she said: 'Yes, let's do that.' I could tell she was struggling mentally. She closed her eyes, looked at the 'screen' and played it through in her head. She was visualising herself being on court playing a rally in a movie, visualising what was going to happen. In the first, she saw herself not moving right, not playing well. So she played the movie back.

Of course, she had already been imagining herself in the match, whether she liked it or not. She would have been doing so since the semi-final. But what you end up doing when the nerves take hold is not seeing yourself playing well. Instead you start to see things that don't go so well or seeing yourself in negative situations. Images start popping up in your head: You playing badly, the opponent with the trophy.

With the belief process, at least you've run through it in your head and taken control of what you see. Hopefully, all being well, it would get the brain to see the positive image and you start to clock the associated feelings that come with those positive images. A tingle of excitement or the shoulders relaxing.

The first few times you visualise everything, it's like you are watching yourself in a movie, which you can stop, rewind and replay with more positive images. When you run through the visualisation the final time, you are starring in the movie and seeing things through your own eyes. You are really feeling it in your body and you are, hopefully, fully immersed. Watching Laura do it, you could sometimes see her twitching at this point, as if she's playing a shot.

Then, she was ready. Once she had the right feeling, it was time to anchor it to a trigger that she could use on court. She clenched her fist, she shut her eyes and started to feel it. When she was in the match and she clenched her fist, she would get that positive feeling again from doing the process.

Laura had now settled down, her warmup was better and, moreover, it had killed some time before the final started.

———

I stood up again, took some deep breaths and started jogging. The introductions, speeches and announcements seemed to go on forever and we were held back for about 15 minutes before we hit the first ball.

I made a good start but I can't remember anything about that first game, which probably means that I was locked in and not letting the nerves get to me. With a 2-1 lead in games, I strode back on to court with a bounce in my step and a buzz about me. I felt I had it now; the nerves were out of the way and I was ready to stamp my authority on the match. In hindsight I should have known this was not a good sign. Whenever I got too up for it or too emotional between games, it never turned out well. Sure enough, I bounced back onto court and immediately went 7-2 down. I managed to battle a few points back but lost the game.

I walked off knowing it had come down to a one game shoot-out to become World Champion.

At this point, part of you hopes that your opponent might bottle it or hand the match to you, but this is rarely the case at the very highest level. This was a World Championship final and I was going to have to work for it. I went 6-1 down in the fifth, but never felt out of it because I knew that I was in all the rallies and that my chance would come. Perhaps I also relaxed because I was getting behind in points but the stubbornness and experience also kicked in just when I needed it to. After all, I had saved match balls so far in this tournament and still won those matches. The memories of that fight back against Low Wee Wern were still fresh.

Dig in. Just make it hard for her.

I levelled at 8-8 and now both of us were within three points of winning. I told myself to string together four world-class points. I don't know why I said four rallies instead of three in that moment, but I guess the logic was that it was likely that I would lose one of the points at the very least, even if I put my best rallies together.

I was right. After hitting two cracking lengths to win two points, Nour hit a flat nick and it was 9-10. On my match ball, I hit a brilliant forehand length deep into the back corner and it rolled so tight that it almost seemed to stick to the wall. Nour had to scrape it off the side just to keep the ball in play. As she moved off the shot, the ball followed her. It ran loose down the middle and she ran into me as she followed the ball.

Stroke, Massaro.

Never had those two words from the referee sounded sweeter.

With a 11-7, 6-11, 11-9, 5-11, 11-9 scoreline, I was WORLD
CHAMPION!

I looked for Danny and he was somewhere dancing down the side of
the court, just jumping for joy. I went into the corner of the court, bent
over and put my hands on my knees with my eyes shut. I couldn't tell you
exactly what was going through my mind or what I was feeling in that
moment. I think it was a mixture of everything – pride, relief, joy and quite
a lot of 'thank God I didn't mess it up!'

I have no idea how long I was there because time almost stood still as I
tried to process what had just happened. The whole time, Nour waited
patiently at the back wall glass door so that I could come off first, which
was unbelievably classy for a teenager.

Outside the court were Danny, England Squash coach David Campion
(Camps), his wife Sarah (a former England team-mate) and Jade Leeder,
the England physio. I hugged Danny for the longest time and then there
was just this ecstatic scrum of us all celebrating and hugging each other.

Once we were back at the hotel, Camps told me to grab a shower and
meet us at the pool when I was ready. To my surprise, he'd ordered a bottle
of Moët champagne and popped the cork when I arrived. We all clinked
glasses and toasted the win, which still didn't really seem real. I was elated
and exhausted as we sat there, sipping champagne. It was a long way from
the curries the family used to celebrate our junior wins with, but it tasted
just as good.

We were supposed to fly back that night and it was the first time in my
career that we decided to delay our flight by a day rather than just rushing
home. I knew I had a lot of phone calls to make and my manager, Faye

Andrews, was organising some media interviews for me to do to make the most of this moment and raise my profile. It also gave me a chance to enjoy the feeling of achievement and come to terms with my win, rather than just getting on a plane and going back to training for the next tournament.

I went off to spend a £500 voucher in a local jewellery store, which I had received outside of my main prize money, and I was called up by *BBC Radio 5 Live* for a quick interview while I was shopping, which felt a bit strange but exciting. Meanwhile, at the David Lloyd Club in Chorley, Mum, my brother and a few other friends and supporters had watched the match, including Peter McNab.

I phoned Peter soon after the win. Peter later told me that for 10 minutes all I did was list all of the things that I had done wrong in the match. It was well into the conversation before Peter was able to say: 'Well, you've won haven't you?' I was reluctant to say yes because I was caught up in the fact that I hadn't played well. Not for the first time, Peter put me straight.

I then contacted DP, who was really emotional on the phone. He had been unable to travel to Penang as he already had a prior coaching trip scheduled in Kuala Lumpur. For DP, it was a huge recognition of his coaching capabilities that he was now coaching the current men's and women's world champions, both of whom were from England. People seemed to be continually writing DP and his teaching methods off as being old-fashioned or out-moded, and he'd been underrated for years. Fifteen years earlier, he'd coached Cassie to the World Championship and now he'd done it again with another Englishwoman.

The one thing I now realised was that being a world champion literally does what it says on the tin. When I won the British Open I kind of expected to receive more attention but what happened in the wake of the World Championship win was on a totally different level. Becoming world champion is the one thing that transcends squash because everyone knows what a world champion is. It's the one thing that resonates with the public and the media, much more so than a British Open or even being World No.1.

The two biggest accolades I have received in the sport have undoubtedly been the Penang win and the MBE I was awarded in the Queen's Honours List in 2019, which partly came, I imagine, because of winning that World Championship. I soon learned that Peter was right; it didn't matter how well you played, only that you had won. I even took the trophy back home on the flight to Manchester instead of getting it engraved from the organisers because that's how much it meant to me to be in touching distance of it.

Faye, my manager, had been brilliant in setting up a succession of media appearances and the profile was important to raise the coverage of the sport as well as my own profile in order to attract more sponsorship. Just to sum up how squash was perceived, the interview I did in *The Independent* was headlined 'Britain's Anonymous Squash World Champion Recognised At Last'. I had to lip sync Take That's 'Never Forget' on *Blue Peter*, there were *BBC Breakfast* slots and other national newspaper interviews with *The Telegraph* and *Guardian*. Faye took me to the BBC's headquarters at Media City in Salford and we spent a whole day meeting people and doing interviews. I brought the trophy with me and we attracted a lot of attention as we walked around between studios – at one point Robbie Savage asked me for a photo with the trophy!

This is where having a management team or someone helping with your media comes into its own, because if you're having to handle all that yourself, it could be totally overwhelming. I would have no idea what to say yes or no to and you could really miss the chance to make the most of this really big moment in your career. I've worked with Faye and her company, The Emilia Group, for years; she and her business partner Eleanor Preston have really helped me in lots of ways. Promoting yourself doesn't come naturally to everyone – it definitely didn't for me – so it's great to have someone to do that for you, to manage the interviews so that it doesn't become too much and to help you understand your value when it comes to sponsorship. They work in lots of other sports so they think beyond the squash audience (which is important if you want to grow the sport) and they've worked with a lot of other female athletes as well.

Working with an all-female management company is another example of where having strong, supportive women have really helped my career. I've worked with loads of brilliant men but, as a female athlete, you really need skilled, experienced women around you as well because they bring a different perspective and it starts different conversations. We need to get more women working in sport across the board.

I was invited on to *A Question of Sport* and to my local football club, Preston North End, where I took the trophy on the outside of the Deepdale pitch and got unbelievable applause at all four stands. I was invited to the middle Saturday 'Athletes' Saturday' at Wimbledon, where Danny and I got dressed up and sat in the Royal Box. That was completely surreal but we had the best day. It's traditional that they invite athletes that day and you get introduced to the crowd before play, so I can say I've had the crowd applauding me on Centre Court – not bad for a squash player. I met the likes of David Beckham and Anthony Joshua, as I sat where the Royals normally sit and watched matches and had tea. I was also nominated as Sunday Times Sportswoman of the Year alongside some amazing names.

Back home in Lancashire, I got tweets that people were standing behind me in a coffee queue, rather than the locals coming up to me. At the David Lloyd Club, where I had been training since 2000 and now had a court in my name, I genuinely didn't think there was anyone who really knew who I was, even though I had worked behind reception back in the day. For several weeks after my win in Penang, I couldn't leave the Club without being stopped by someone congratulating me. It felt great, as a sportswoman, to be able to represent my local area. Closer to home, when

I was out shopping one day, our postman even asked my husband if 'this really was where Laura Massaro, the squash player, lives?'

My World Championship win had come right before the Canary Wharf Classic men's event London, which is always a sell-out. I went along to watch Nick Matthew play and listened as he said that my win had inspired him. That was a huge compliment, seeing that I had tried to use Nick as motivation through my career. Part of both our personalities was trying to prove people wrong throughout our careers, even if we came at it from slightly different angles. For me, even if people weren't talking me down, I imagined that they were doing it half the time. Nick was much more confident in that respect; he just went out to prove that he was better than anyone else. Most of the time he was and he went on to win the Canary Wharf Classic again that year.

After his first round win, with me in the stands, Nick said that he hoped my achievement would inspire more girls to take up the sport and he got the packed crowd to join him in a round of applause. Nick had always been really supportive – remember his text before the World Championship final – but to hear him talking about women's sport was a huge boost. At the time, it wasn't uncommon for the top men and women in the sport to be playing different tournaments in different time zones, with vastly contrasting prize money to boot. But there was change in the air.

I had never thought of myself as a role model up until that point but my World Championship win changed that. I felt a lot more comfortable with the idea that young women and girls in particular might look up to me as someone who had made something of themselves, and gone about it their own way. One girl in Chicago even set up a Laura Massaro fan page. I began to realise that people liked my stubbornness and my resilience and even the way I played. I might have still felt like Laura from Chorley but other people now looked at me and saw Laura Massaro, World Champion.

(Previous page) Flying home as World Champion!

(Above) Camps with my surprise champagne after winning the Worlds

See my full photo gallery at lauramassaro.co.uk/photos

9. THE MANAGEMENT TEAM

By Faye Andrews

W e first met Laura when our company, The Emilia Group, was contracted to run media operations and PR at the World Series Finals at The Queen's Club at the start of 2013. My business partner, Eleanor Preston, and I had never worked in squash before (our background was in tennis, hence The Queen's Club connection) and it was eye-opener for us in all sorts of ways. In tennis, the players are celebrated and promoted as stars, particularly at their home tournaments. We were surprised at how little focus there was on the two best English players, Nick (Matthew) and Laura, both of whom were friendly, articulate and accessible. It was almost as if within the sport they were so familiar to everyone that they were taken for granted. It was just Nick and Laura.

Laura was very down to earth but also incredibly professional and to us, as one of the best squash players in the world, and a Brit, we saw so much potential for her. We ended up working with England Squash and got to know both her and Nick much better, which in turn led to us working with them both on an individual basis to increase their public profiles. Laura is a lovely person and she always wants to please people and do the right thing.

It's great to be accommodating as a professional athlete but we also wanted her to say no to things sometimes, to help other people learn that her time was precious. It's not about being a diva – it's hard to think of someone less diva-like than Laura – it's about understanding your value to others and other people appreciating that value too.

We were working on behalf of England Squash when Laura won the World Championships in March 2014. We have worked with and been around quite a few athletes when they have had big wins and we knew how important it was to maximise the moment and use it to raise her profile and promote squash. It's the job of a media manager to plan for success and be ready, so, as soon as she won, we were on the phone, setting up interviews, putting together press releases and looking at how we could gain as much coverage as possible. When you don't have experienced people in your corner, it's very easy to feel overwhelmed after a big win or be focussed on celebrating with your team and ignore messages and calls from journalists, who then move on to the next story because they can't reach you. We wanted as many people to know who she was and what she had achieved. We worked her hard and, being Laura, she never complained about doing so much media in the aftermath of the final or spending the day touring TV studios at Media City in Salford doing the broadcast interviews we'd set up for her.

From there, we began working more closely with her on both the PR and commercial side and we put together a plan to build on all the coverage around her becoming World Champion. Squash has a very enthusiastic core audience but our goal was to get her known and appreciated by people outside of squash and therefore also reach a wider pool of potential sponsors. We wanted people to see that she was a fantastic role model for young people and also to encourage her to talk more broadly about some of the issues in sport, particularly for women. Laura is very bright and incredibly articulate so we knew that media and sponsors would like her. We also had an eye on her post-playing career and knew it was important for her to develop the skill of being a pundit and speaking about a range of different subjects. She got more and more confident and comfortable with voicing opinions, which is something we really encouraged. She had so much knowledge and experience, particularly once she got more involved behind the scenes in the running of her sport, that it was very natural and authentic for her to speak about things like equal prize money.

Laura was often more worried about what people in squash would think or say than the rest of the world, perhaps because it is a small and very close-knit sport in England in particular, and also because she likes to please people. Working across so many different sports over such a long period has given us a broader perspective and we sometimes felt that her accomplishments were more appreciated by people outside the sport than inside it. She is one of the most successful sportswomen of her generation. Squash, especially in this country, is incredibly lucky to have her, especially as she's so committed to giving back to the sport she loves.

I'm fairly plain-spoken and I think one of the things I said to her most often is: 'Why do you care?' – particularly when she would get anxious about how people might react to things she'd said or done. I wanted to reinforce to her that as world champion and a seasoned, highly successful professional she arguably knew a lot more than many of the people who were all too happy to offer her their opinion. I think she found my frankness quite amusing, and hopefully helpful too. We have worked with a lot of female athletes and this has been a common theme because they spend a lot of their careers feeling judged in one way or another. If you aren't born with bullet-proof self-confidence (as some are) then it takes a while to acquire that armour.

I always knew that I could be honest with Laura because she trusted our judgement and, with Eleanor and I both being female, she could say things to us and we would understand. We've become really good friends over the years and now have a shared link with the North West, so whenever I visit my husband's family we meet for a walk on the beach in Lytham

St Annes. She is incredibly giving and kind, and I admire the way that she gives everything she does her total commitment, from her squash career to making a humble gin and tonic. She's still the only person I've ever met who has a custom-built gin cabinet in her house.

She can definitely add gin aficionado to her incredible list of achievements.

10. AT THE HEART OF CHANGE

While Nick Matthew was championing the women's game in front of a largely male audience at the Canary Wharf Classic, behind the scenes the WSA Tour itself was in a bit of a mess.

The tour had around 90 annual events (61 'full' tour events and 28 'challenger' events) around the world but a lot of these were dependent entirely on personal relationships without a sound commercial footing, plus we were losing tournaments. There didn't seem to be a long-term plan and there wasn't much leadership. By 2014, there had been a raft of significant departures in just three years – a president, chief executive, tour director, an acting tour director and an acting chief executive and chairman – which just added to the sense that we were on a rudderless ship, heading for the rocks.

More to the point, things were a long way from being equal between the men's and women's tours and the women's prize funds were being dwarfed by the standalone purses on offer for some of the men's events. It was no different at a national level, even with three English women inside the world's top 10. And so, Jenny Duncalf, Alison Waters and myself took matters into our hands and sought change after becoming disillusioned with how we were being treated. We confronted England Squash over the fact that they had held the men's World Championships in Manchester in 2013 as a standalone event, with investment from UK Sport, without trying to include the women.

We couldn't understand why, as a governing body, they didn't hold a combined Championships together. We emailed the board several times and they responded saying that they didn't have funding for both and had to pick. We had received no contact over the decision – all we wanted was communication over the matter and to be kept in the loop on their initial application.

We had a lunch meeting during one national squad session where we asked England Squash if they were planning anything to make up for a lack of a women's event and us missing out on playing a World Championships at home. As a compromise, Nick Rider, the then chief executive, committed to equal prize money at the British National Championships, which was a small but significant milestone.

I realised that my voice had started to now carry a bit of clout and weight.

Rather than asking, it felt as if I could be a bit more demanding. People were coming to me more and I was becoming confident that I could speak up for myself, my fellow players and my sport. It's easy to whinge about things and then sit back and wait for them to change, but sometimes you have to make the change happen yourself. I think that's especially true when you're fighting for equality.

I decided to speak my mind and be honest, whatever some players thought of me. I just hoped that players would trust in me that I would see things through.

In turn, I got approached by a few players to back a merger of the men's and women's tours, the Women's Squash Association and the Professional

Squash Association (PSA). I still wasn't sure of the route the women's game should take and whether it should be a separate entity or not.

At the time, we were being told that the women were holding the men's tour back; that Saudi Arabia could hold, say, a $300,000 event and the women could barely scrape together a $100,000 World Championship. So, as far as I saw it, the men's tour was flourishing and the worry was that, if we merged, the men would take all our tournaments and we would all be swallowed up.

Depressingly, the gulf in prize money between men and women was actually increasing. As an example, the winning purse for the 2013 men's World Championship, won by Nick Matthew, was £28,000, whereas I received £12,000 for my efforts in Penang. For the 2014 Championships, the men's prize money was upped a lot, to $325,000, while the women's purse for our standalone showpiece was less than half that, at $150,000. However, it wasn't all doom and gloom. In a squash first, the 2013 US Open provided equal prize money, with $115,000 prize money for both genders. It was heartily backed by Billie Jean King, the former tennis star and equal rights campaigner.

But this was a small victory and there were many other signs that things were going from bad to worse for the WSA Tour. It was clear that Nicol was the key cog in the women's game, so, when a three-year deal was signed in 2014 to bring the World Championships to Malaysia, nobody was especially surprised. With a supposed prize fund of $500,000, it all seemed too good to be true to us players and a few of us had doubts. The tour was struggling on but here the WSA were signing a three-year deal to host a massive World Championships?

I guess things started to look worrying when the promoters went quiet and it became clear that the Malaysian deal wasn't worth the paper it was written on. Remember that we'd already had to play our 2013 World Championship in March 2014 because of cancellation. Thankfully, a deal was hastily struck with Egypt to stage the 2014 Championships.

A small group of us finally decided to get more serious with the merger idea. We knew something had to change so we put a vote on the merger to the WSA's AGM. Roadblocks were then put in our way at every juncture by the WSA board – who were worried that this was some kind of coup – and so we took our worries privately and quietly to the PSA and asked what would happen if we joined the men's tour body.

We needed clear clarification and ideas of how a potential merger would play out. Many of the girls were still worried about the merger and there was talk of us being left behind and swallowed up by the men's tour. Some, Nicol included, were dead set against it and her opinion carried a lot of weight, and that influenced others. She wasn't alone and many of the men worried that the women joining would weaken their tour and take their growth and potential away from them. There were issues on both sides.

The PSA were adamant the women would not be left behind if we decided to join. The women's lack of profile and prize money reflected badly on the PSA, they told us. We were told that the PSA wouldn't be able to drive our sport on and be seen as a sport of equality until there was a merger. With this knowledge, we had to convince our fellow tour pros that this was a necessity and, whereas I had a few wobbles along the way, Jenny was one who stayed true to the vision when things got tough towards the end, along with three Aussie players, Kasey Brown and sisters Rachael and Natalie Grinham. There was constant communication between us as we set about convincing the other girls on tour that we needed to merge.

The WSA board was adamant that no vote would be forthcoming and, at times, it felt like we were being treated like rebellious teenagers, rather than experienced professionals. One of the emails we received from a WSA executive summed up the fractious relationship:

'To be honest I am done by this whole thing as you clearly have no regard for me and the absurd number of hours I have put in. I'm not sure why I have been paying such professional courtesy to everybody. Your proposal to the board is an absolute joke and I am beyond furious. If you want to make a difference, I would suggest you have conversations with people who actually know what is going on.'

In another email, sent in late 2013, we were told:

'... not to be so blinkered, hit the pause button and to come up with a decent list of people to propose as new board members – people with real skills, qualifications and experience that goes beyond sitting in a few meetings and bitching over breakfast. Start acting professionally or your names will be permanently attached to the biggest failing of an organisation since women's professional soccer.'

As players we were fighting a losing battle with the people who were running our sport. We had to keep believing that what we were doing was right but it was really hard at times and you doubt yourself and what you're trying to do. But we really believed it was the right thing for the women's game and that it would make squash, as a whole, a stronger, bigger and more commercially viable sport.

We talked to a huge number of players of all rankings. These were professionals who were naturally worried as to what a merger would mean. Girls had voices in both ears, from the WSA who were telling them that this was all a 'farce', and us, a small collective who were trying to convince them of the merits of moving away from the WSA. Behind the scenes, we were indebted to Dutchman Tommy Berden, who was married to Natalie Grinham. At the time he couldn't be totally associated with the move due to his work and links with the PSA but if anyone understood the women's game it was Tommy.

Tommy and Natalie both talked so much sense and we knew that the proposals had solid grounding, whereas there was an amateur feel to how the WSA was going about its business.

The PSA had taken out loans backed by its UK-based chairman Ziad Al-Turki, a Saudi businessman with an undoubted love for squash, in its bid to build the sport, the tour and create cashflow on the back of creating its high-definition streaming service *Squash TV*. The risk was paying off but we were constantly being told by the WSA hierarchy that by going down this route and borrowing money against the association, the PSA was putting too much at stake. It was always very clear that the WSA was not prepared to go down this path, even though the PSA loan was repaid in full within two years.

All the while, the women were looking in from the outside at the professionalism and growth of the men's game. We wanted to be part of it. We wanted to be on Squash TV and to be part of the excitement. It's easy now, in hindsight, to say that growing your sport via internet streaming was a no brainer but, back then, it was a risk. The PSA took it and reaped the rewards. The WSA did not have the same long-term vision.

To add to the problem, 2013 also saw squash lose yet another battle to be included in the Olympics. We have now lost four bids in a row, yet it remains one of the most asked questions: Why isn't squash an Olympic sport?

I still can't answer that one.

At an International Olympic Committee meeting in Singapore in 2005, it was one of two sports put forward for London 2012 after baseball and softball were ejected from the Games. But squash and karate failed to obtain the IOC's two-thirds majority vote. This was a hammer blow given that I would have been World No.3 heading into what could have been a first Olympics in 2012, while fellow Brit Nick Matthew was World No.2 in the men's game at the time.

The IOC amended its controversial charter for the Rio 2016 vote where only a single majority was deemed necessary – and golf and rugby sevens were given the nod. The IOC said at the time the two sports were more 'commercially viable'.

The hurdle facing squash for Tokyo 2020 inclusion came from wrestling. Despite the ancient Olympic sport being cut from the Games programme, it had been given a last-minute reprieve by the IOC. Wrestling's chief had spent a reported $8 million on its bid to get back in ahead of the vote in 2013 in Buenos Aires. Our sport, meanwhile, had a modest £1 million bid budget to work with, though we also had the help of bid guru Mike Lee and Vero Communications, which had a long track record in getting sports onto the Games programme, as well as cities winning hosting rights, like London for 2012.

Although this time we felt optimistic, squash always seemed to be swallowed up by the murky politics of the IOC. We never felt as if the IOC truly knew the sport, the obvious health benefits, the cost-effective measures in bringing the sport to the Olympics and the global stature of the game. All the while, Nicol David had said that she would swap all her world titles for the chance to compete for Olympic gold. Even Roger Federer had endorsed Nicol's words.

We had a great bid team out in Buenos Aires, including Sarah Fitz-Gerald and Ramy Ashour, one of the most gifted squash players of all. Before the vote, IOC member Dick Pound had even proposed to delay the 2020 sport procedure by five months. He said the whole thing was 'absurd' and had been 'politically botched' over the way wrestling was seen as a 'new sport' while we had campaigned for two years. Of course, Jacques Rogge, the then IOC president, waved away the idea, wrestling was voted in with a majority, and baseball/softball and squash were cast aside.

Our plight continued when we were thrown a faint lifeline after the IOC later decided that future Olympic host cities, in this case Tokyo, could select extra sports they wanted to see on the programme. Squash was among eight sports put forward but we failed to make the final five as recommended by Tokyo's organisers. The sports? Baseball/softball, karate, skateboard, sports climbing and surfing.

It was no different for our campaign to get into Paris 2024. Breaking, sport climbing, surfing and skateboarding were all voted in. With sports like three-on-three basketball and BMX freestyle now on the Olympic programme and the IOC always voicing their message of 'taking sport to the youth', there really isn't much more we can do to become an Olympic sport.

I will never know if we will get onto the Games programme. I kind of want the sport to stop trying now. We have a good enough product now to grow, despite what the coronavirus pandemic has thrown at our sport. Let's have some dignity as a sport and, if we do a good enough job, they will come to us. We need to stop worrying about what the Olympics can do for us and focus on making sure our sport will bring something extra to the Olympics.

As a sport, we will come through this stronger and together because we aren't fighting against each other. It was part of the reason for squash's merger – we needed to be an equal, dual-gender sport.

In 2010, Andrew Shelley left his role as WSA Chief Executive and took up the same role as part of the World Squash Federation. Over the course of the next three years, the WSA World Tour declined by 20 per cent and we collectively sensed the game needed a change of direction.

We called an Extraordinary General Meeting in Hong Kong, which had been seen by some as a really aggressive move to bring about a vote of no confidence. We genuinely didn't want that, to oust those who had done so much for the sport. We just wanted the chance to move with the times and give women's squash the chance to grow and survive. After a lot of talking, we compromised and agreed that we would integrate into the WSA hierarchy and make change from within. It was time to take control of our sport.

In December 2013, I was put forward as a board member to the WSA along with Jenny; Latasha Khan and Marjolein Houtsma, who had worked high up in Nike; Nathan Dugan, who worked on the well-organised Cleveland tournament; Ashley Bernhard, who was pushing for women's equality on all fronts and worked with the United Nations, and Kasey Brown as the tour's president. We were all officially voted onto the new board at the AGM at the Tournament of Champions, New York, in January 2014.

We had a great all-round board, mixed with invaluable experience in business, current players and an ex-player, and we set about developing a business plan and budget for the board to review, promoting a possible merger with the PSA and dealing with the current promoters.

Our fight for equality was also helped by Nicol when she criticised the decision by British Open organisers for the 2014 tournament, where I was defending champion, to have all the women's first round matches played on traditional plaster courts at the nearby University of Hull, a step down from the main glass court at the tournament venue where all the men's matches were being played.

Nicol was quoted as saying: 'Now you have a women's World Champion,' referring to my win, 'that has to be special. There are also so many English players in the top 10 or top 12 and they are all here – surely you want to display them? Why not put them all on the glass court? It's the showcase and that's what makes sense.'

Finally, an announcement was made that October, of the historic merger of the two bodies under one governing body, effective from 1st January 2015.

Finally, we had one voice.

Looking back, I'm proud of what we did and, more than ever, I know that we were right to fight for what we thought was right. There is no question that the sport is in much better shape now than it was in 2013. The 2018/19 PSA World Championships became squash's first $1 million tournament, with $500,000 split equally between the male and female athletes thanks to the backing of Mark Walter, the American billionaire who owned the Los Angeles Dodgers baseball team. Later in 2019, there was a bigger prize pot of $430,000 at the Women's World Championship, held in the shadow of the Great Pyramid of Giza in Egypt. The prize pot was bigger than the $335,000 on offer at the Men's World Championship the same year in Qatar.

I was asked to be president of the women's tour once the merger was agreed but, by then, I wanted to focus on playing and Jenny stepped in to become the first PSA women's president. I also realised that I was spreading myself a bit thin. I longed to return more into the background and get my own squash back on track because it hadn't been at the forefront.

The other women and I had essentially become sports administrators as well as players, and we were balancing our own playing careers with lengthy emails and discussions going back and forth. That took a lot of mental energy and, as an athlete, you can't afford to be giving up time like that. Perhaps I would have helped by being on the PSA board, but Jenny was the right choice and I had no regrets. Since winning the 2013 World Championship, I had yet to lift a trophy in a run that was to continue for 18 months. It was time to be selfish and get my form and my results back on track.

11. 'THAT'S IT, I'M DONE'

We were billed as the 'Golden Generation' for English squash. Nick Matthew, James Willstrop, Adrian Grant, Peter Barker and Daryl Selby on the England men's side; myself, Alison Waters and Jenny Duncalf flying the English flag in the women's game. Between us, we won numerous European team titles, Commonwealth and World Team Championship medals.

As a women's group, we had been surrounded by players we could look up to and model ourselves on, with the likes of Cassie Jackman, Linda Charman, Tania Bailey, Vicky Botwright, Fiona Geaves, Sue Wright and Stephanie Brind. When I was coming up it was a big deal to be invited on squads with these players, on a world-class programme at England Squash.

It was these players who helped us find our way into the senior game. Alison was on court with Tania, I was on with Vicky growing up in Manchester, and Jenny had an array of players to spar with because DP was her coach as well as her stepfather.

We had heard stories about how nasty the team ethos could be before lottery funding existed, especially for those on the periphery and trying to break into the quite closed England set-up. My generation was lottery funded from an early age and I have ended up being one of the players who has been the beneficiary of the most lottery funding in a career. Once I was under contract with England Squash, it meant I got funded regardless of England team selections, rather than only being paid if selected.

Despite our successes, we still had to deal with politics along the way, even around some of the most important events of our careers.

At the 2010 World Team Championships in New Zealand, Australian Chris Robertson had been given the job of National Coach after the job was taken away from DP. I must admit I was shocked – we all were – as DP was the only senior coach I had ever known. Everybody trusted him and valued his expertise and experience.

The decision to appoint Robertson was a bit leftfield in my view. We were a bit shocked that David Campion (Camps) hadn't got the job. He had seemed a natural fit as England junior coach, under DP for several years, and had been involved and nurtured in the England squash system for most of his career. The news didn't go down that well while we were competing in New Zealand, especially with Camps' wife (Sarah Kippax) being in the team with us, while Jenny Duncalf, whose game was heavily influenced by Camps, was raw about DP's departure and also saw Camps as a natural progression.

It meant at the 2010 Commonwealth Games in Delhi the England coaching situation was up in the air without any real leadership. So, when Alison got injured in the semi-finals and couldn't play the bronze medal play-off, big decisions needed to be made. I was due to play doubles with Tania Bailey and Jenny was partnered with Alison. The temporary coaches made the decision to split myself and Tania up. They felt that Jenny was World No.2 at the time and having no partner would have made her redundant.

In some ways it was great as I was paired with Jenny, but I had done all my practice with Tania and I believed we were a genuine medal chance. I had a bust-up with coach Fiona Geaves, who didn't want me to play mixed doubles because I might get tired, when I was the second in line to play. At least with DP and Paul Carter, the two England Squash coaches who were almost father figures, you didn't mess with team selection, we did as we were told and it was easier in some ways to accept their decisions.

Even though I always liked the individualism of squash, I've actually always enjoyed playing team events. In the World Team Squash Championships, I won five silver medals with England while we landed gold in 2014 with a brilliant performance against Malaysia in the final.

As far as the Commonwealth Games went, Jenny and I had won silver in the 2010 Delhi women's doubles – where the court is around six feet wider than traditional singles – and I was paired with Jenny again for the 2014 Games in Glasgow. I found the doubles really hard work mentally. I had to take my blinkers off and check that she was okay wherever she was on the court during rallies. I wasn't just looking out for myself. Jenny was great at doubles and I learned a lot from her. I am confident, know what I want and am clear at telling people, but playing doubles really didn't come naturally to me. We worked at it as a team.

I remember feeling a bit stressed in the lead up to the 2014 Commonwealth Games in Glasgow. There was the usual politics around squads and selection, and it didn't help that Jenny and I kept losing in practice to Emma Beddoes and Alison Waters, England's other women's doubles pairing. I thought a lot about the doubles and couldn't quite work out why we were losing because I really enjoyed playing with Jenny and building our relationship. She was convinced that when we got to the Games our form would change and that the glass court would play a part in our favour. She had enough confidence for the both of us.

In Glasgow, I was out of my comfort zone and had to adjust to everything being a bit different. By that stage in my career I was used to having a settled team around me at big tournaments but at Commonwealth Games it's different. It's a team structure and it's not just about you; it's about all the players in the team. The journey to the courts from our accommodation was long, the security was strict and I felt stressed with the media attention building for what was a home Games, even though we were English and playing in Scotland. As squash players, we were not used to it. I was sharing accommodation with Jenny but our personalities are different, so I found myself spending a lot of time on my own in the room. We both prepared differently and I needed to find downtime. I wasn't enjoying the overall feel of the Games setup.

In my last 16 singles match against Nicolette Fernandes, from Guyana, I played terribly. All my worries came out and it looked like she was really enjoying the experience that the Commonwealth Games could bring. I sulked at the way I was playing and the crowd got behind her, which shocked me. Then again, I was playing like I didn't want to be there, so what did I expect? I managed to get through the match 3-1.

After the match, I felt devastated. I found Danny and managed to get him in behind the court, through all the barriers and security. It was probably all a bit dramatic in hindsight given that I'd just won a match, but at the time I was really upset and I think it was just a release of stress. I cried to Jade, our physio, as well as Danny and I got all the tension out.

Feeling my way into the event, I managed to set up a semi-final against Alison. It was a huge match, with the winner guaranteed a silver medal and predictably it was very edgy and tense on court, as it often was against Alison.

I had had a long British rivalry with Alison, which started when we played each other in the under-14 National Championships and went on for the next two decades. We played and won at European and World Teams together, and started on tour together but we also had some disagreements over the years, which you would expect being rivals and wanting the same things.

When the squash is finished, most players are genuinely different people with not a great deal in common. You will be lucky if you come away from a career with two or three very close friends you played against, that you can count on long after you have retired and you've hit your last squash ball. I know my rivalry with Alison probably made me a better player though, especially when we first left the juniors. Alison rocketed off at the start of our senior career and left me behind, really. It was a huge motivation to catch her and we had some huge battles over the years, all culminating in that semi-final in Glasgow.

The fourth game was heated, there were lots of lets and the match turned physical. Alison pushed me fairly hard into the side wall at one point and it showed how much we both wanted it and how much tension there was in front of a capacity crowd. Alison said I was blocking and I thought I took my space when the ball was loose. The clash got a bit of coverage, with even athletics great Kelly Holmes tweeting about the 'aggro'.

Nevertheless, I played well to get through to face Nicol for gold. I lost the final match 3-0 and I didn't really perform to my best. It was really hard in that pressure situation to not have Danny between games and I couldn't hide my disappointment after the match. I was crying when Nicol came into the training room where I was with Danny, but I didn't care. I wanted her to know how much it hurt me.

Once I settled down, I started to appreciate my silver medal. I got great media coverage – a group of the English players even ended up chatting on the sofa on *BBC One's* primetime Saturday afternoon coverage – and that's where the Commonwealth Games are so special. Normally, no one cares when you lose in a final. You're just the loser. But, at the Commonwealths, you're a silver medalist. So, fairly soon after coming off court, the cameras were in my face and people were saying: 'Congratulations, how does it feel to be a silver medalist?' I was genuinely thinking 'Congratulations? I just lost. Did you see the match?' But that's where it's so different to normal. Every medal for Team England counts.

The squash had been well attended – the largely Scottish crowd of two thousand had made for a fantastic atmosphere at Scotstoun – and the viewing figures for finals day reached a million on TV, so it was great to be part of that. In the men's final, Nick Matthew beat old rival James Willstrop to gold and every national newspaper was there to cover it. Nick had carried the England flag at the opening ceremony in Glasgow and five weeks previously had been lying on a hospital bed recovering from knee surgery. How he came through that lung-busting, five-game epic with James I will never know.

No time to rest after the singles, we were straight into the doubles the next day. We beat the Papua New Guinea, Wales, Trinidad and Tobago, and Australia teams before finding ourselves up to face Emma and Alison once more for a place in the finals; the gold-medal match. Jenny and I agreed that we both needed to get stuck into them, to make it tough and not let them have their way. The match was heated and messy, and I clashed with Alison during one point, which left her knocked to the floor on her back. But, for the first time all year, we beat them to set up the match for gold against India.

In the final the Indian pair didn't wait for an opportunity, attacked and were skilful throughout. Considering our form, we were pretty happy with silver and we had backed up our silver medal from Delhi four years previously.

———

After I had won my first world title, I thought I would be retiring before I had reached 30. I had won the British, the Worlds, now the singles silver at the Commonwealths and been World No.2 for a good few years. Deep down, I probably never truly felt as if I would get the World No.1 spot from Nicol.

As the 2014/15 season began, it felt that I was getting bogged down with my career. I was physically feeling fine but mentally tired from the tour, the travelling and the matches; while in the back of my mind there had been the relief of winning the two big titles and all I had achieved. After all, as DP had said several times to the media, if someone had £10 at the start of my senior career, they wouldn't have put it on me to become British or World Champion.

In February 2015, I played Sarah-Jane Perry and lost in the finals of the British National Championships. It was perhaps an unexpected result at the time. I was devastated. The loss was obviously part of it but I knew that SJ was talented, so it was more the manner of defeat. I had given effort, as always, but not in the right way. I was just running and hitting. That's just not good enough against top quality opponents.

I remember feeling exhausted on court. Why was I so tired? My legs felt rooted to the floor and I couldn't see a way through. I couldn't think straight or concentrate on my game plan. I couldn't remember where I was supposed to be hitting the ball and then because of all that, panic set in. Panic that I was going to lose playing this way. I couldn't change things or do what Danny was suggesting between games because I was too busy panicking.

Not surprisingly, I lost and I was left with the feeling I had spent most of my career trying to avoid. The feeling of letting people down, of failure and disappointment, for myself and those around me. These were just crappy emotions all round.

Danny was as disappointed as me. He was angry at the performance and the next few days were not much fun for either of us. When we had both calmed down I was describing how tired I felt. His analogy at the time was that, if I was a racehorse I would be put in the field to recuperate for a bit.

We had booked our flights to go to Chicago a few days later for the Windy City Open and Danny insisted we should cancel the trip and take a few days off to train at home. I hated pulling out of tournaments and how it would affect my ranking with the points deficit. From my point of view, I felt the loss in the Nationals final was down to a physical issue and if I could train harder I would be fitter. I was hell-bent on going to Chicago.

Danny was clear that I shouldn't go. He said that if I was going to fly to Chicago, I would be doing it on my own. He cancelled his flight and I decided to travel anyway. I had won the Windy City Open a few years previously and I knew I could draw on a few good memories. But it all felt very strange. I was sharing with Egyptian Salma Hany at the tournament hotel and after spending so many events with Danny, I missed him.

I was tense and frantic in my opening encounter against Malaysia's Delia Arnold and I knew I couldn't keep to my game plan, but I came through the match. I decided to have dinner on my own that night and sometimes there is no better therapy to spend time alone, gather your own thoughts and not have anyone else chipping in with what was going on in your head.

For the one and only time in my career, I decided to do what I had never done before. I ordered a gin and tonic during a tournament. G&T has always been my downtime treat but I had never, ever had one during competition. I was normally so controlled about everything I ate and drank and it wasn't how I thought a professional athlete should behave but I was pissed off and I knew it couldn't get any worse. I sat at the back of the restaurant and ordered pasta. I had my back to the door and I didn't want to make eye contact with anyone I might know who came in. I knew I shouldn't be drinking but I was also way past caring as well. No point in hiding it. I told DP about what I'd done and he said he was always an advocate of trying anything which may loosen me up.

I lost to compatriot Emma Beddoes the following day. In hindsight, it was the best thing that happened to me. It was messy and horrible against Emma, and I didn't enjoy it for a second. In my mind, my career was done. It wasn't the defeats, more the performances, and it probably didn't help that I had been ousted by two English girls for good measure in my last two defeats, which I must admit stung just a little bit more.

I changed my flight and went straight home. The decision to retire had almost been made after the Sarah-Jane match but the extra proof had been gleaned after losing to Emma.

Tears followed for the next three days. We drove up to Lytham St Annes beach and, as we pulled up, ready to feel the rush of the sea air and the walk over the dunes onto the huge expanse of beach we loved so much, I couldn't get out of the car. I was in a total mess.

I sat on the passenger side and it felt like I was back in Hong Kong airport, huddled against a wall, sobbing. I didn't really want my career to be over but there was a massive part of my mind telling me that I wasn't accepting what had happened in the last two tournaments. My mindset was telling me that I would never play again, that my career had been a success, more successful than I probably ever dared to hope. Maybe I should just be grateful for what I had and move on from squash. It was an internal fight between wanting more and being grateful for what I had already.

Danny and I had some deep conversations and eventually decided nothing could be done while we were at home. We needed a break and we booked a resort an hour outside of Dubai. The season was still in full swing, I put my rackets away for a month and we ate, drank and talked a lot. As far as I was concerned, I was retired. It was done and we were going to tell people once we got home.

Towards the end of the trip, I got really upset again. I was doing some writing and I downloaded my thoughts on paper. One day, as I wrote, it began to dawn that I had more in me, more in my career to give and it would be a huge waste to end it if I stopped now. We had another chat and Danny asked why I wanted to continue and play. 'I just want to win, Danny. I want to win. I know I've got more, I know it.'

We set about putting down some financial goals and achievement targets, something that would give me more power to chase and go after. Meanwhile, DP told me I should give it another week, so that it wasn't just a knee-jerk reaction. We spoke about trying a new coach after nearly four years and DP said I may need a fresh direction. Because it had come from him rather than from someone else for the first time in my career, it made it so much easier for me to deal with. It was typically selfless of DP to offer to step aside to allow someone else to get me back on track.

We jotted down some of the world's best coaches and I felt that there was no one else who could better DP. There was Peter Nicol, who I had always admired and respected; David Palmer, the Australian nicknamed 'The Marine' for his penchant for fitness; Frenchman Thierry Lincou, or Sarah Fitz-Gerald but working with anyone of them meant potentially relocating to the US or Australia for a few months to be trained by these greats. We were prepared to do it but it was so left field.

I went back to DP and told him that he was the only one who I could be coached by but I wanted us to come up with new ideas together. Over the years I had tried to make myself adaptable, with the aim of making it harder for my game to be broken down against opponents and to strengthen my weaknesses. DP had coached Peter Nicol and Cassie to be World No.1 and this was what was missing for me, and I realised that this was what I really wanted. DP rebuilt Cassie's game and made her movement world class. He had great experience in dealing with women and making them better. That experience showed in handling me and my personality, and bringing a calmness to my intensity.

It was actually Peter Nicol who became our inspiration. DP said that Peter was a class apart at making his weaknesses less exploitable. He once said that Peter's strengths were 10 out of 10, but his weaknesses were still eight out of ten. If you could get marks like that, then you would be very tough to beat.

For the first time in months I was happy and rejuvenated. And I had a very clear goal in my head – the World No.1 ranking.

(Above) With Danny when I thought I was retiring from squash back in 2015

See my full photo gallery at lauramassaro.co.uk/photos

12. A BIG SHAKE-UP

Getting to World No.1 was going to take everything I had. It meant taking everything I had learned up until this point and then getting even more committed. Diet, coaching, training and mentality.

The goal I set for myself was big and it was bold. It made me feel scared but alive as well. I had something to aim for and the numbness had gone. I was anticipating my future rather than waiting for it.

I only trusted those really close to me with my new goal. The shake-up meant new additions to my team but only with people who would complement those already around me.

Getting to that goal meant looking again at my fitness to see if I was getting everything that I could out of my body. My physiology had evolved over the years to simply be good at squash and its related movements but was I a good all-round athlete? Probably not. I realised this when my brother, Christopher, and I went for a gym session one day. He led the session and was coming up with some ridiculous repetitions which I found really hard to do. He was amazed and said that, as an elite athlete, I should be balanced enough to do a variety of different exercises. He was right.

When I was young and perhaps up until this point, I had never really gone to the 'next level' of physical development. It had always come as a natural progression as my squash improved.

It's not as if squash players aren't fit, but they're fit in a very specific way. Squash is a sport of lunges, short sprints and complex, twisting changes in body movement – it's incredibly dynamic compared to other racket sports. After more than 20 years in the sport, I can testify to this and also to the fact that the sport is only getting faster and more explosive.

In a bid to give the wider audience a greater insight into players' physique and the dynamism of the sport, the PSA tracked players' heart rate, distance and movement patterns in real-time. It tracked a men's match with Egypt's Tarek Momen and Frenchman Mathieu Castagnet over a 100-minute match and found that Momen had covered close to 5km during 100 contested points in that match, averaging nearly 50m per point over nearly 1,000 shots.

Effectively, Momen was doing more than 500 court sprints back-to-back, not to mention all the lunges and backward and forward movements. He was in-play for 60 per cent of his match, while the average heart rate was pushing at around 171 beats per minute. Bear in mind, in squash your recovery period is around four to 10 seconds, compared to 25 seconds in between points in tennis.

I wasn't getting any younger and, although I was still physically in good shape and into my seventh successive year inside the world's top ten, I needed to look at a change of fitness trainer to give myself an edge when matches went the distance.

At England Squash, I held a majority of the personal best scores for their squash-specific fitness testing, which means that you are awarded what they call a 'gold standard' for completing various drills. I held three gold standards on our squash-specific test including squash-specific agility, multiple sprint ability and multiple sprint ability fatigue index (percentage drop-off in speed from round 1 to round 10 of the test). However, in the 5m sprint test and the jump testing, I never came close. There were players who were faster and far more powerful than me. So, I certainly don't hold the gold standard for being England's most physically fit and strong female ever. I hold the gold standard for being the most efficient in movement – thanks to DP's work on my game and movement which unlocked me being able to do the test quicker.

I knew that there was room to improve myself physically and make myself a better all-around athlete, so I set about finding the right fitness coach to push me to my limits. I chose Mark Campbell, a New Zealander who had been so successful with Nick Matthew. He was based at the EIS (English Institute of Sport) in Sheffield. That meant a fair drive every week to see him but I was prepared to do it. However, when I rang Mark, he wasn't as keen because he was short of time and he felt that I was based too far away. In the end, my persistence paid off and several calls to England Squash later, they, Mark and I found a way to make it happen.

The biggest thing Mark had going for him was that he understood how hard the sport is. He used to get down to The Hallamshire Tennis & Squash Club in Sheffield to get on court at 7am before work. That in itself gave me huge respect and a deep trust in that what he was doing for me was going to be the correct path.

He was also all over the details and the data. He never had to ask how I got on when I went back for a session as he was always following the results, which was a complete first for any strength and conditioning trainer I knew. He had a genuine passion for the game, a real understanding on how the body coped on court throughout a match, what it needed to get stronger and the importance of efficiency in movement. We had done the standard testing and watt bike sessions, and our relationship began with him watching me train and play and knowing what my game was like. There was a link between who I was as a person and how I played the game. It was all so fresh and being at the EIS in Sheffield for the first time was also a new experience for me.

Previous strength and conditioning coaches had generally tried to get me to lunge the same way. But I earned my nickname – Longlegs – because I have a different leg length to everyone else. Mark understood that and he knew my style of play. He would top and tail my sessions to include a warmup, mobility and cool down; something that I had never really done before. At first I would turn up with a 20-minute warmup in mind but I wouldn't have enough time to do all the pre-session work that Mark had set me and, instead of a 45-minute session, sessions with Mark would be closer to two hours in all. It was a huge mental and physical adjustment.

Mark's training plan was to make me go out on court much harder and faster than I had ever done before. And then hang on. Again, this was a first as my fitness technique had always been based on me starting matches at moderate pace and then being able to hold that pace for a really long length of time. We began to think about how we would start with more intensity and get opponents off court in around half an hour, especially in the early rounds, because I'd set a pace that they wouldn't be able to match.

It was hard for me to understand this intensity at first. I couldn't get my head around it. But Mark kept insisting to me that 'you are winning in under 30 minutes and you are done'. In essence, the plan was for me to stamp my authority, not to put work in my legs and still make it tough going for my opponents. And, if I did have an opponent who could go with me – someone who was fit, fast and equally dynamic – it was about going the distance and being able to prevail over five games.

This was the biggest change Mark gave to my game and, boy, I had to work hard to get there.

The sessions were brutal. After I'd done some weights, I would do four rounds of a circuit and my last would be the fastest. He said that until that changed and the last circuit was the slowest, then I hadn't done my job. Knowing my mindset, I was never going to take my time on the fourth set. It wasn't about steadily getting quicker over the sets before seeing the finishing line. It was about taking those four circuits, or a similar sort of session, and the first one had to be quicker than I had ever done it before. The second one had to be at least equal to that, not to be quicker but to match it, which I generally did.

Then you can ask serious questions of yourself. I would be at the end of the second circuit and the tell-tale sign would be whether or not I would be saying to myself, 'God, I don't want to do a third one'. We would do circuits where it would be 'eyeballs out' for the first two sets and then I would be hanging on for the third and dying on the fourth. But, eventually, I would be less exhausted each time between the circuits.

And then there was the watt bike, which was actually a demon in disguise. I don't think I've ever hated a piece of equipment as much as I despised that instrument of torture. Everything on it is measurable, which is a complete nightmare because all the numbers you had to hit were written down and compared. And you always had to match your personal best.

I had to have a little chat with myself before going on and sometimes the excuses would start. Can I get out of this? Could I perhaps say to Mark whether I can do three sets, instead of four? It was all complete fear about the pain which I knew was going to come my way.

I might say: 'Mark, I feel a bit heavy-legged today.'

He was always very understated. 'No worries, just do your best and we'll see where we are.' There was never any pressure or expectation other than that you would always go flat out, as hard as you could, every time.

I would do circuits which were a combination of the prowler sled (a heavy metal frame on the ground with a flat underside that you push along), watt bike, kettlebell swings and skipping. I would finish with the watt bike, usually hanging over the handlebars with my lungs feeling like they were about to burst. Mark was stingy with his compliments but he was always warm, factual and never cold. When he said, 'Laura, that was a great set,' that was a proper little perk. I got so much confidence from that.

Once off the bike, I could feel the lactate in my legs pumping. One down, three to go. Back on the prowler and straight away the spiky chunk of metal felt heavier. Once through the second set, it was back on the bike and Mark would be there holding the shoe slip ready for me to pedal.

'Go, go, go!'

There would be serious heat in my legs, it felt as if they were actually bulging and getting wider. The timings would change sporadically, too. It could be 500m or 40 seconds but what didn't change was how knackered I was at the end.

In the short rest periods between sets, I quite often sat on the bike for most of my rest thinking I'll just recover here and not worry about walking. I would try to walk and a few times I remember thinking that my legs could buckle at any second due to the lactate and the blood in my quads. When I remember back to Chrissie Wellington's book and her not being able to feel her legs, these were the only sessions that came close. I was numb but in pain at the same time – it is such a bizarre feeling to describe.

People must have thought I was bonkers. When I used to complete these sessions at David Lloyd, I would have my headphones on and quite often couldn't hear myself breathing but I caught people looking at me, almost as if to see if I was okay.

With Mark, the sets weren't long, perhaps two to three minutes, with 60 or 90 seconds rest. But it was the intensity and power that I was constantly asking of my body all the time that was the killer. I would sit down on a bench and try to get some movement going: 'Thirty seconds, Laura.' 'Okay, now to get through the fourth set.' As Mark is counting me down, the final seconds seem crucial to get that final bit of recovery in my legs. 'Three, two, one … go!'

By the fourth set, it felt like I was pushing the prowler through mud. I'm trying to drive and go, however hard it is. I used to motivate myself by imagining what Nicol and the other girls might be doing, and how all this will get me over the line at 8-8 in the fifth game against them. I knew that there's no way that they'd be training this hard and it gave me a lift and helped me finish the sessions.

Session over.

There was something about getting through each one that gave me a huge sense of pride, so much so that I would be emotional afterwards. I would be so proud of my efforts. I would often have tears in the shower, a sense of pride of the depth I had been able to push to complete the session. I hated it but loved it. I knew that's exactly where I needed to be physically and mentally. How can you be mentally strong in matches when you haven't trained as hard as you possibly can?

If a session was exceptionally hard, Mark would quite often get an abusive message from me on how awful the session was and how awful he was. I put those emojis to good use and I always finished with a thanks or a wink at the end because I knew he had done me a huge favour. I genuinely felt like his sessions were my secret weapon.

When I spoke to Mark at Nick Matthew's retirement party in 2018, he told me that I would go down as the toughest female athlete he had ever worked with. And there were some seriously fit boxers and swimmers

Mark had trained, all of whom had a ridiculous work ethic. It wasn't that I had worked harder than them, Mark told me, it was that he had never seen anyone that tired after a circuit session and still be able and willing to go again.

I told him that was the biggest compliment he had ever given me and it was a relief to hear. Not bad considering where I had come from and how I used to hate doing any physical work back in the day.

———

Fitness and diet had to go hand in hand. I had always struggled with my weight in terms of putting it on quite easily. I don't have a fast metabolism and it was something I had to be wary of, which is why I got hold of a copy of *The Calorie Carb & Fat Bible*. I became obsessive in writing down what I was eating, how many calories it held and trying to figure out a daily amount. It was my first introduction in trying to get an understanding of what I was eating and how it was affecting me.

As part of our lottery funding, we had access to physiology. We got our skinfolds measured with calipers and it was my first foray into understanding 'skinny fat' people, those who look thin on the outside but have a high skinfold count and vice versa, with people who look bigger but it's actually muscle and they have a very small amount of fat layering. Measuring consists of eight sites on your body where fat is measured, for instance the quad point of measurement comes exactly halfway between the bone on the knee and the hip joint and is marked down on the skin, usually with eyeliner. With this process, the site is re-measurable weeks or months later because even if skin changes, due to weight loss or gain, the bones don't move.

I remember one player who was always in great shape and looked thin. She had significantly higher skinfolds than me and she used to live on fizzy drinks and a lot of sugar. When we had our skinfolds done, hers were higher than mine even though she looked much skinnier. It highlighted the different body shapes and how you store fat. It was surprising and I realised that you have to compare yourself to yourself and not other people. This is really important for female athletes in particular because women and girls in sport are often judged on whether or not they 'look' fit and are subject to society's idea of the perfect – ie. thin – body type. Women, whether they are athletes or not, come in all shapes and sizes and physiologies.

When I was young and at high school I didn't really think too much about my weight, body shape or my body image. I was aware that I wasn't overweight and that I had an athletic figure for a 15/16 year old but without social media and the so-called 'influencers' that really are influencing our young people, I only had the athletes I looked up to on the TV and my friends to compare to. I loved Sally Gunnell growing up and so my role models were the athletes I wanted to be like.

I was in good 'athletic' shape as I left high school for college, even winning 'best legs' in the end of year awards! However, that free and easy attitude started to change as I hit college at the age of 17/18. I put weight on as I came to the end of growing into a woman. I had to start thinking about what I was eating and I certainly became a lot more aware of my body. Maybe that coincided with actually being a bit bigger as well, I am not sure.

Part of the reason I gained weight at 17/18 was because it was around the time I started on the contraceptive pill. Don't worry, I am not about to make a turn here that takes this book super personal, but I think it's important to say that this is completely normal for female athletes. My periods had become extremely heavy. I was getting severe backache and stomach cramps and feeling very lethargic overall. It was an issue that came to a head while trying to play the first round of an event with all this going on.

I spoke to people I trusted and I listened to the older girls and women around me, and booked an appointment with my GP. We took the decision that starting on the pill was the right decision for my squash. Within the first couple of months, my periods had become significantly lighter meaning no worries of wearing white skorts anymore for my matches. I was getting significantly less cramps and fatigue and, also massively important, I knew exactly when my periods were due. Before starting on the pill I knew within a couple of days but what use is that when training or preparing to compete? You need to know something like this isn't going to pop up in the middle of a warmup or, even worse, a match. Obviously, there is also the bonus of being able to skip a period which could be so important if the start was due to land right on round one.

Let's be honest, winning at world level is hard enough without all the extras going on for women. However, with the pill did come some weight gain. Although I can't actually be sure it wasn't partly down to diet, as later on when I did lean down I was still taking the pill.

Your body is changing so much at this young age, so everything was evening out. Body image for women is spoken about all the time. Not only in a way of, 'Oh, if she was lighter she would be better'. Of course I believe this, otherwise I wouldn't have paid money and bought into a nutritionist. The lighter you are the easier it is to move, the less impact there is on joints and the better you recover. It's not about winning single matches, it's about staying injury free and being recovered round after round to keep on winning.

That is just on a performance level. What about the personal level? It's so tough as a woman, whether people are or not, you believe most people are commenting on how you look. Is her belly flat, is she toned, has she got good muscle definition or the worst of all, she's got cellulite. I have thought people are thinking every single one of those comments while playing. I have always had and, probably now retired, always will have, parts of my body I hate. I'm a bit too big here or a bit oddly shaped there. It honestly doesn't matter what people say to you, it's what you see and how you feel. It is totally normal as a woman.

I think it's just so delicate for men and women. It's always a difficult conversation to have with anyone, especially when it is between a coach and an athlete. I think it's important to be aware that just because you are shining a light on issues doesn't mean the person involved isn't already aware of those issues.

The difficult thing is, one person takes a comment as constructive feedback and the next person takes it as personal abuse. It's so hard to get a balance and I haven't had to deal with it as a coach yet but have experienced it in a couple of different ways as a player and, in my experience, care, softness and discussion rather than telling is always the best way.

Chances are whatever others are thinking it's at least equal to if not worse in terms of what the player is thinking. These things take time to even out and the player simply has to be ready to make the changes they are prepared to make. You calling them too big, or better yet 'can't you get fitter' – fitter meaning lose weight – is not going to help.

During warm ups I have worried my kit is too tight, my dress too short and have even done crazy changes during a match because I was worried about how I looked. You cannot concentrate on a game plan if that's in your mind! I have looked in the mirror countless times and thought, you can see cellulite at the top of my legs there and then sat with my dress pulled over my knees trying to give it a bit of extra length. Yes, I have got better. I got older and learned to accept my body. It's done amazing physical things for me and, at the end of the day, I firmly believe we could all eat and train in exactly the same way and we would all look completely different. That's just body shape and type. The question is, are you doing what you can to shape and mould your body into the best tool for you? Maybe that's adding on more weight for power or maybe it's losing it – it's totally individual.

Once I had set the big goal and felt comfortable with my coaching and fitness trainer, I set about seeking the right person to help me on the nutritional side. That person was Chris Rosimus, who had previously worked at the English Institute of Sport but later with England cricket and England football. I wanted to get a deeper understanding of nutrition and how it could help my match performances. Chris was the first to teach me that all calories aren't equal. If I took in a calorie as carbohydrate, it reacts differently in your body to if you took it as protein. Depending on how hard I was training, we tried to match up not only the amount of daily calories I was taking in but also where they were coming from. We worked out how many grams of protein and carbs I needed per day to fuel my training and calculated that, on a hard day, I needed 2,200 calories and within that I needed so many grams of carbs and protein. He helped me monitor my intake via an app where I logged my calorie intake.

At the time, Chris was working part-time at Manchester University, which was brilliant because they had a Bod Pod. The Bod Pod is like a massive egg in which you sit, wearing the smallest amount of underwear and a swimming cap, with the machine measuring your body mass by air displacement. The ears pop, the air gets sucked out and the machine sprouts out a load of numbers at you which tells us how much bone, muscle and fat weighed. It was a different level of information than I had ever had before and the first time we could see that my muscle mass and body fat were both moving in opposite directions. It was far more detailed.

Alongside the work I was doing with Chris, he would also ring Mark to link up with what he was setting me at the EIS. Chris would tell me he wouldn't mind what I was eating if I was training hard with a tough block. He didn't mind if I was putting on weight, as I needed to build up muscle mass. But when the training blocks would taper down with a month to go before the season it was time to shave down my layer of fat, leaving the muscle with very little fat on top. Chris and Mark would chat, then give me guidance. I always had to be honest about what was going into my mouth.

I would be at home making lunch and the difference would be having one slice of rye bread instead of two and it was the extras going on to your

plate which made all the difference. I couldn't allow it to happen. Even
a dollop of hummus with my salad. Who knew hummus was so high in
calories? Those were the extra few hundred calories that added up over the
days and weeks.

The discipline was something I could control and it harked back to my
childhood. I had a huge amount of guilt if ever I felt that I wasn't doing
things 'right'.

It's been a hard character trait to live with most of the time in my life
and career. There was a lot of feeling of being owed something, that I
had done everything the right way and thinking 'this better pay off now'
because I deserved it or had earned it. But sport doesn't work like that.

With the changes I was developing in fitness, nutrition and physiology, I
felt as if I was squeezing every little bit of potential out of myself. I was
now confident that no other female player was pushing themselves as hard.
I was driving towards my ultimate goal – the World No.1 spot.

Physical Assessment Feedback 07.09.15

Athlete Name: Laura Massaro

England Squash & Racketball

Power / Reactive Strength			
	21.07.15	07.09.15	Gold Standard
Power - Counter Movement Jump (cm)	34.4	35.6	38
Reactive Strength Index (30cm Drop)	2.72	2.81	3.8

Agility & Repeated Agility			
	21.07.15	07.09.15	Gold Standard
505 Linear Speed (secs)	2.95(L) / 2.81(R)	2.73(L) / 2.68(R)	2.2
Squash Specific Agility (secs)	9.02	8.39 New Gold standard	8.4
Multiple Sprint Ability (overall time secs)	203.5	186 New Gold Standard	190
Multiple Sprint Ability (fatigue index %)	5.8%	2.5% New Gold standard	6%

(Above) My fitness results: Gold standard

See my full photo gallery at lauramassaro.co.uk/photos

13. THE FITNESS TRAINER

By Mark Campbell

Iknew what it took physically to play elite level squash. In New Zealand, a young friend of mine was playing international senior-level squash aged 17. His squash-playing capabilities exceeded his own body's capabilities to handle that level of squash. He got exposed to a high level of squash too early without the physical underpinning in place to support it.

With squash, it was an added advantage that I had played the sport and, because of my love for the game, I would watch matches in the middle of the night if it was in Asia or America. In one respect it was a huge advantage but so is being one step removed.

I started with the English Institute of Sport in August 2007 and, since joining, I have worked across two dozen sports. We say to our strength and conditioning coaches when they start in a sport that you need to immerse yourself into it with the coaches and athletes, and understand what they are going through, with a particular focus on the physical demands.

I worked with Laura for just over three years. What really stood out was the clarity of her thinking and what she was coming to me for. The reason it sat well was that it was similar to my work with Nick Matthew, in that I was dealing with an intelligent, mature athlete who understood herself really well and wanted expert consultancy. She wanted input to enhance her level and this wasn't going to be a one-way relationship, which was a really good place to be.

She had an incredible drive. We talk about what is the difference between a female and male. Well, in respect to someone like Laura and her approach, it's not a gender thing, it's an elite athlete mentality. I believe that transcends someone's gender – obviously there are biological factors that go around training – but the drive and motivation is very similar. Laura and Nick both had those in abundance and I could draw incredible similarities between the two of them. You could put much of Laura's success down to that mentality.

The main aspect was to balance out her physical training with her squash. Previously, some strength and conditioning coaches had treated them as separate entities but I learnt the level of intensity that goes into squash practice, which then allowed me to balance out the physical training to complement this.

It was clear that Laura drew on the physical capacity to dovetail or support her mental approach. There were many sessions where at the end she got quite emotional about the session because of how hard it was, but she also knew that her opponents weren't doing what she was doing. It would have given her an added confidence, knowing the fact she had prepared that well and gone to the physical effort needed to achieve.

I started working with her when the tin height was lowered in the women's game and it placed an added demand on speed and attacking qualities. That wasn't Laura's forte previously but she adapted and worked on a way of manoeuvring opponents to limit their strengths to allow her to still be effective.

Squash differs from other sports in that the athlete has a large responsibility to piece together their training schedule to be effective. The individual nature of the sport doesn't always lend itself to strong interactions between a coach and a sports science team. So the key to getting performance improvements lies with the athlete themselves assimilating knowledge and communicating this clearly within their team. With Laura, she would tell me what she was working on technically with David Pearson, her coach, so I could understand it and then give her strategies from a physical aspect to work on to support this. It wasn't as if DP and myself weren't interacting but the athlete was the fundamental part of owning the programme. The really good athletes have a group of expert consultants and it's the athlete who owns the programme – it's down to them to consult with the people who they trust to really get the performance gains.

I would also contend that fundamentally it's whether the athlete has the capability. I believe in physical talent, not sporting talent, in as much as Nick Matthew had the ability to be an incredible squash player, but practice, discipline and the mental approach was the key driver of his success. I've worked with lots of players but only Nick and Laura got to that level and I think that reflects on their mental capacity to challenge themselves to look for improvement, to take on the information and put it into their programme across all aspects of what is required to excel.

Former England player Adrian Grant, for example, came to me and after two sessions I could see that I wouldn't be the difference. He was physically phenomenal, gifted beyond belief. It wasn't that which made the difference on court and actually his ranking went down when I worked with him. There were other things that he needed to address to make the most of his obvious physical talents.

With Laura, we had some interesting interactions where I was getting frustrated but I wasn't letting her know that. It was around the time when it was clear that it wasn't her physical capabilities which were holding her back, or she was focussing too much on that as the game changer. Her natural tendency was to work harder. It felt at times she was primarily concerned about the physical output of a squash technical session, whereas my feeling was that these sessions had to meet the technical requirements first, regardless of the physical load. She wanted to know how hard the squash session should be.

Early on, we had to prioritise physically what she was trying to get out of the squash court, what we could intelligently do to make that impact at the right time and to ensure we did it efficiently, so she could spend time on technical aspects to unlock her performances.

Continuously training hard all the time was just not possible. With Laura in particular the body wouldn't be able to handle it, as she was always willing to work as hard as possible. I certainly had to be careful of what I wrote down in her training programmes as she would do it to the last letter.

She is the type of person who had to get it done, no matter what.

———

It wasn't in my nature to scream and shout during sessions but Laura never asked me to. I never had any doubt that she would do the work, more often than not I was giving her guidance to ensure it wasn't too high.

The rumble circuits (continuous 40-60 minute mixed aerobic sessions) that I had created for Nick Matthew had gained some legendary status within the sport, but Laura's sessions consisted of more high intensity endurance work that I described as metabolic resistance training. Essentially, they were shorter, more intense mini rumbles, with anything from two to four-minute efforts with two or three minutes of rest where you would back it up with five or six sets. I chose exercises that the athlete was good at and asked them to go for it. You might have six exercises in a circuit, 30 seconds on each one so that you reached and maintained that level of high intensity for a long period of time.

Laura would dread those sessions and I would build her up to make
sure she was positive in doing them. They were probably worse than the
rumbles at times because the intensity is so much higher, because if you
do something continuously for 40 minutes you can't maintain the intensity
as high as you could in shorter blocks. If you try and repeat those shorter
blocks they come and get you and become a very potent physical stimulus.

One story sticks in my head when it came to the sessions I called
completion circuits – one which never happened with any other athlete I
trained.

You might have 12 to 15 exercises and a number of repetitions attached
to them, such as 100 body squats, 500m watt bike efforts, 50 burpees, 100
kettlebell swings etc. You could split the repetitions up any way you wanted
and the idea was to get through them as quickly as possible, ticking off
all the exercises. This particular completion circuit took Laura about 24
minutes to complete.

Most athletes would tell me afterwards, 'Ah, that was great, I feel really
good, that was challenging and really pushed me. Next time I will try and
do it faster.'

And Laura?

'I tell you what, if you give me four or five minutes rest I reckon I could
do that again.'

I was stunned but this epitomised Laura's 'more' factor. I had no doubt
that she could have gone again because she was always set on doing
everything she possibly could to get the most out of it. They say you
remember things that give you an emotional response. I don't know what
my emotional response was to this. I just laughed. I said, 'Are you crazy?'
What was I dealing with here?

It gave me a real insight into an elite athlete. It's not so much a talent than a discipline. It was a sheer mental determination to push herself physically. Nick Matthew would be up there as well, but Laura's resilience to keep going was her super strength.

And therein lies the interesting thing with her approach to squash.

Laura knew that if she could absorb the pressure of someone who plays a more attacking game in the first two games, and if she could sneak a game and stay in there, she would know that by games three, four and five they wouldn't be able to stay with her.

That was the level she needed to go to keep with the top girls. It was a tough realisation as it essentially meant you had to empty yourself every time you went on court. So, the physical training (and mental challenge) I put in place had to complement and support this approach as part of enhancing her overall sporting performance. Her willingness mentally to do the physical work required was the real quality that propelled her forwards and allowed her to reach the top.

And she also would look at more things than I could ever imagine in leaving no stone unturned: sleep, different nutritional strategies and psychological approaches. Everything was always about making herself better as an athlete.

14. SCALING NEW HEIGHTS

In 2015, the PSA World Tour sought to standardise and bring more parity to the sport by announcing a trial to change the height of the tin in women's squash. The tin is the area below the lowest red line on the front wall of the court. If the ball hits this line or below then it's down and you lose the point. It would be a bit like changing the height of the net in tennis.

The women's tin height had been set at 19 inches, with the men playing to a 17 inch tin after lowering the height several years earlier. When the two tours merged, it was deemed to be confusing – not to mention a bit patronising for the women – to have two different tin heights, especially as lowering the tin height had undoubtedly made men's squash more attacking and exciting to watch. At the start of the 2015/16 season, the PSA conducted a four-month trial, which was met with universal approval … almost. Nicol and her coach, Liz Irving, were fully against the idea, which is not surprising given that she'd had years of dominating the sport with the tin higher.

There was also the chance that lowering the tin would help the Egyptian players, many of whom thrived with attacking play and wristy, risky winners. It was obvious that it would affect some players more than others, so I immediately started to work on how to make it work in my favour. I wanted to protect my movement so that I could access the front of the court when balls were put short. This was going to be key. You now had to be able to pick your speed up off the mark, with explosive movements to get to the front.

There were a handful of players at the time whose movement was world-class. According to Liz, I was on the list of players who couldn't move with a lower tin. She also said that the initiative would ruin the women's game. I may have dipped to World No.5 by the time the tin trial experiment had been implemented in September 2015 – my lowest ranking for nearly four years – but this motivated and spurred me on so much. I was used to these comments during my career and it wasn't as if Liz hadn't said similar things before. I knew that she didn't rate me.

In some ways, it took some of the expectation away from me. In other ways, I could use it in my armoury. Sometimes even compliments sounded like quite faint praise. People would say that I was such a hard worker. That I was good technically and tactically. That I could change a game plan, always find a way. That I was mentally strong, really gritty and determined.

But, all you want to hear is that you are also a good squash player.

I couldn't start looking for recognition from the outside, I had to look for it from the inside. I knew that I would never be seen as the world's most talented player but I knew that from when I started out to the moment I closed my career, I had kept on improving. Sometimes talent lies in getting the hard work done daily, keeping to a programme, however gruelling it is. To use one of my favourite quotes: 'Commitment is sticking to what you said you would do, long after the moment you said it has gone.'

It was all self-motivation and, after our self-enforced mini break from the game in Dubai and my training and diet plan now in place, it was time to test the water on tour.

No sooner was I back than it was the final tournament of the season, the British Open in Hull. I had a brilliant run, which included coming back from two games down to beat Nicol in the semi-final, and even though it was the longest match of the tournament, I felt in good shape heading into the final against Camille Serme of France.

Camille was a player who had all the attributes to become a major winner and she shone in the final. Playing Camille throughout my career was really tough for me. She plays at a high pace and volleys across the middle of the court brilliantly. I always felt rushed playing her. Against most players I was too accurate for them to rush me but against Camille, she could make me panic despite my accuracy. I made silly choices against her more than anyone and, in that final, she beat me over four games. It was little consolation that I was the first Englishwoman to reach three finals in a row for nearly half a century. In retrospect, the five-game win over Nicol had taken its toll, but I knew that the work I would be doing with Mark Campbell over the summer months would soon pay dividends.

With a fresh block of training under a new regime with Mark and the lower tin now enforced, I started the 2015/16 season in fine form. It turned out to be the best run of my whole career.

———

I had been going to Manchester Northern Lawn Tennis and Squash club in Didsbury, Manchester since I was a junior. It was always one of my favourite junior events to play because there was a £100 prize pot for the winner. That was a lot of money to me and meant that I could buy the family the traditional Sunday night curry and still have plenty of money left over.

As my career developed, I made the short journey over to Disbury to play Andy Whipp (Whippy), a former PSA player who coached out of The Northern. Former coach Phil Whitlock had initially suggested the idea of going to play Whippy as a training aid but at the time I was dubious. I hadn't really spoken to him over the years and although I didn't know him very well, I guess I had made my mind up on what he was like as a person and certainly didn't think he would want to play me.

Phil told me in no uncertain terms to get my hand in my pocket and pay him to play me. I have always felt easier about paying people for their time. At least it's worth it for them then. I was reluctant but as the matches dried up at my club and players of a good level seemed harder to find, I bit the bullet and got Phil to ask Whippy if he would play me. From what I could hear, it was a quick answer: 'Yes, of course, anytime. It's £15 a session.' It turned out to be great value for money over the years and it was especially helpful in the latter part of my career. I can't put into words how grateful I am for the time Whippy gave me.

Initially the sessions were 45 minutes of beasting. Whippy said very little and we started and finished on the dot. If I asked he would provide feedback in a very black and white way but I liked that. I knew what I had done well and what I hadn't, and I knew I could trust his opinion because it was always honest.

He was unbelievably fit. Even on the rare occasion that I was his first or only session of the day, I turned up and warmed up thoroughly for Whippy to stroll through the door one minute before the start of our session and play flat out squash barely five minutes after stepping on court. It still staggers me. Moreover, in the four years I had sessions with him I only knew him to be injured twice. Once in the lower back and once in his calf, both of which he recovered from in less than a week. He put it down to drinking copious amounts of green tea.

Whippy was no nonsense, honest, stubborn but hugely reliable. If I was having a bad day I would normally get: 'Well that was sh*t'!' Equally, if I was having a good day, it might be: 'Well done, see you next week.' Compliments didn't come often but I learnt that was his way and no criticism normally meant you had a good session.

He was like a machine, where I could say I wanted him to feed me forehand drops for an hour and he wouldn't even blink. I had a tolerance for long routines – generally it would be the other player in practice who would say 'switch' as I would get so engrossed in it – but Whippy went above and beyond. Maybe I gravitated towards people who were firm with me, who punished me when I got it wrong. I'm quite a strong character but when someone led me, I responded quite well to that, so I struggled when people were soft around me. I just wanted people to toughen up and I couldn't stand it when people I was playing with pulled faces or were down.

What started as a session with a little feedback morphed into Whippy watching my PSA World Tour matches, giving me advice on where he thought I was beating my opponents, where I could improve. Soon, we increased time on court to hour-long sessions. His level, speed and accuracy of feeding balls to me was higher than anyone else I have ever been on court with; he could feed the ball in the same spot over and over again for a longer period of time than anyone I have ever known. Looking back now, I like to think that his extra level of input was down to the work he saw me put in and the professionalism I had everyday. But mainly because no matter if he had beaten me easily or killed me with routines, I was always quick to get my diary out and book the next session in.

Another time, I had turned up for my session with Whippy to find a *BBC Sport* crew at the Northern. I had expected them to come for an interview after our session but it turned out they wanted on court footage. During this session we did some channel games so that they could film us on one side of the court. After a loose drive by Whippy, which didn't happen very often, I swung my racket to volley the ball and caught him on the shoulder.

I had initially thought I had caught him in the face but as I stopped abruptly to apologise he said: 'I'm fine, it's just my shoulder.'

I remember thinking it felt like I'd caught him hard but he hardly seemed bothered at all. It was only that night that I got a text from him saying: 'What have you done to me? I'm in A&E with a suspected dislocated collar bone!' I couldn't believe he carried on for a session with a dislocated shoulder. He replied: 'Oh yeah, I forgot you hit me! Must have been that.' He had a seriously high pain threshold.

More than anything, it was a chance of playing a male player I wouldn't get otherwise.

———

It was also at The Northern during one of my Whippy sessions where I first met Lawrence Jones. Unbeknownst to either of us, Lawrence was soon to become somewhat of a mentor.

I had been on court with Whippy and Lawrence was lined up as his next lesson and had arrived to see the last 15 minutes of our hit. After we had finished, he had asked Whippy who I was and he told him that I was a top-ten player in the world rankings. This was before I had won my first British Open title and I soon got chatting to Lawrence. Within a few minutes, he asked me what struck me as a very strange question.

'If there was a way of teaching you to get to World No.1 without any extra effort would you be interested?'

I didn't know who he was at the time and I remember laughing and replying: 'Of course I would!'

He told me about his entrepreneurial background and how he had founded a series of companies including one of Britain's biggest hosting and cloud space companies. Lawrence gave me his details and told me to get in touch and, before he left, he asked if I had a website. He was interested in helping out and perhaps coming on board as a sponsor.

I got in touch and was invited to his office. We had a chat and he spoke to me about goal setting and about life-coach guru, Tony Robbins. It was nothing too detailed but it certainly got me thinking a little. He then left me with someone who would help with my website. I was over the moon that I had bumped into someone randomly, who was friendly, helpful and willing to build me a website.

The next time I saw Lawrence he came to watch me play at the British National Championships and asked why I didn't have his logo on my top like one of my other sponsors. I told him it costs extra, so we soon sorted a deal for a shirt sponsorship and in return he wanted more buy-in from me to try his ideas to get to World No.1. I had nothing to lose, so of course I agreed. We arranged another meet up and when I arrived he had every single audiobook or CD of Tony Robbins on a USB drive for me. My first job was to listen to them and ring him when I was done.

We had started working together before I became World Champion, but Lawrence says, after I won that title I disappeared from him, mentally. He thought that, in my mind, it was 'World Champion, job done' and I had hit my peak.

By 2015, I had dipped down the world rankings and had come very close to quitting the sport. It was during this period when I linked up with Lawrence a second time. We agreed he would come on board as part of my team and, if I was going after the goal to be World No.1, he was going to be around, hold me accountable for the goal I had set and the actions it would take to get me there.

We discussed what I wanted and how I needed to 'dream big' and then write it down. The goal we chatted about that day was to be the best squash player that has ever walked the planet. In my mind, I knew even if I caught Nicol I would struggle to surpass her achievements but what I could do was become a better player than she was. We talked about what that would take, the dedication, the effort and the commitment. Was I up for it? I had to actually think about it. When someone lists what that entails in terms of action, you're a little slower to agree. We discussed it and after everything I had been through – the trip to Dubai, the decision not to quit – I knew I had more in me. I still wanted to win. I said yes.

On that day, we wrote the goal down at the top of his whiteboard: To be the best player in the world and become World No.1.

He refused to let anyone wipe off that goal until I achieved it and it would regularly just be there during big meetings he had at his house. 'We'll wipe it off the board when Laura's done it.' I suppose his staff just learned to write around it!

Lawrence was relentless in telling me how good I was. He has incredible self-confidence and he was trying to instill that in me. But I was realistic. I worried a lot about losing and so it didn't come naturally to say how good I was. Saying that I am amazing, the best player to ever play the game? It felt fake. Yet, he always reassured me: 'You're not telling anyone else, you're just saying it to me and to yourself.' Whenever I did doubt, he would say: 'Ok, let's say you aim to be the best player that's ever played the game and you don't quite make it. Would you be happy with the second prize of being World No.1 and the best player you can be?'

'Of course,' I would say.

'Well then, let's aim for the stars and see where we land.'

It's amazing how much at ease I felt with that. I couldn't fail. I couldn't not do it right. All I had to do was attack it, commit, write my goals down and see where it led. He would make me say it to myself and constantly reminded me of it too. Dream big, write your goals down and close the book; your mind and body knows how to do the rest. I would even get the occasional text that would just say: 'You are the f****** greatest.'

And every time I received one, I believed it a little more.

There is an old story about J.P. Morgan, a banker and philanthropist, who was once shown an envelope containing a 'guaranteed formula for success'. He agreed that if he liked the advice written inside he would pay $25,000 for its contents. Morgan opened the envelope, nodded, and paid up. The advice? 1. Every morning write a list of things that need to be done that day. 2. Do them.

Lawrence also loved power-driven quotes, which I often added to my notebooks:

'Be the kind of woman that when your feet hit the ground each morning the devil says: "Oh crap, she's up."'

'I'm not telling you it's going to be easy. I'm telling you it's going to be worth it.'

'Not everyone deserves to know the real you. Let them criticise who they think you are"

'Two things will define you. Your determination when you have nothing. Your attitude when you have everything.'

As far as I was concerned, the new season couldn't come quick enough.

15. THE THERAPISTS

By Caroline Glain and Jade Leeder

By Caroline Glain

I've known Laura since she was just 14 years old and she's by far the person who I have treated the longest, which I think is the main reason we were a successful partnership. I am a French fasciatherapist. I work with fascia within the body. It is a manual therapy based on the discovery of how to work on the deepest part of the body, which is the source of all pathology.

When Laura was a junior, she struggled with a back injury. Whilst it wasn't serious, it was affecting her squash, so, of course, she and her family were worried. My experience has shown me all sorts of injuries, some of them very serious. Thankfully, Laura's injury wasn't one of the serious ones and I told the family so. Her injury was at a deep level within the body, where I carry out my treatments. Inevitably, all major injuries and problems come from the deepest part of the body. This is where I can feel what is going on and give treatment, which is exactly what I did with Laura for the back injury, and for everything I have treated her for since. In my mind, that particular back injury was like an onion. I needed to peel the layers back, one at a time over several treatments to clear the overcompensation and the protection the body had built up. Only then could I treat the cause of the problem. Once this happened, the injury was clear and it never returned.

Since that moment at 14 years old, I've been able to treat Laura over the years and keep her body clear and clean – to prevent compensations and therefore prevent her developing injuries. This is the reason we worked so well.

Since that first meeting, I have seen Laura grow both as a person and as a squash player. She is professional and determined, but she also needs a lot of reassurance with her body. That's just who she is. The way Laura's personality ticks is perfect for a therapist; she asks questions, listens and she follows advice brilliantly. On the odd occasion when I would tell her that this is serious, that she needed five days off or it will be worse, she would ask why, understand and ask what she could do while she was resting. Normally, I suggested swimming and non-weight-bearing work, either way, she would always do as I had asked.

Besides helping Laura over her career with injuries and their prevention, I also helped by talking to Danny. We spoke about Laura resting and trying to not let herself get stressed. Laura, as I said, is very professional and like most athletes she didn't always want to rest or take time off, but I could feel when she needed it. A prime example came every summer when I would always encourage her to take a month off at least. She would inevitably argue that two weeks was more than enough time but, certainly as she got older, she came around to listening to me.

When she took her mid-career break in Dubai 2015, it was brilliant for her. She was exhausted, her body drained, and she needed it. I would tell Danny: 'Get her to relax, stress makes the body more likely to injure, as does jetlag and the time of the month. Periods for a woman are also times of vulnerabilities, so be careful in these times and try to relax and be stress free.' Of course, this isn't always easy, especially as Danny and Laura took things so seriously, but I think saying this to both of them helped her to actually take the rest and accept it was ok to do so.

So, what exactly do I do? This is hard for me to explain. Laura calls me a 'witch' and I know what she means. The 'mystery' of fascia's success is difficult to understand if you haven't studied it. However, it is not a 'magic' treatment but rather a specialist technique for which I studied for five years at MBD school for Fasciatherapy in France.

When I go deep within the body, I feel things others can't. It's through energy and feel. It's an powerful holistic therapy which takes into account the whole body from the cranial to toe and, of course, the psychological dimensions. For me, when I feel an injury it's like feeling a stone inside a marshmallow. The body is soft when it is working at its best. Whether it's a muscle or a tendon, when things are not smooth within the body it has a problem. I treat the 'stone' until it's smooth. I can get bones gliding in the right place and I can feel the energy flowing up and down the body. Ligaments and tendons are notoriously hard to heal but I can improve them over treatments. Shin splints and tendonitis are both stubborn to shift but I have great success with both.

Most of the time, players will see me for an injury that a physio is struggling to solve and normally I can get improvements very quickly, so I have their trust immediately. Trust is vital between player and therapist; it's very helpful for me to get results.

An example that springs to mind was the 2013 British Open. I had treated Laura early in the tournament and we had got into a good routine. The day of the final she didn't really need to see me. She had no injuries and I had done the work the night before in aiding her recovery through the night but she asked to see me before she left for the glass court.

I walked to her room in The Village Hotel in Hull. We both knew it was partly superstition for her to do what had worked all week. I treated her on the bed in her room. She felt great, her body was flowing. I know her body well and, on this day, I could feel her energy and there were no blocks or energy restrictions. She had recovered well and I told her so. Putting a hand on either leg, I said: 'You're ready Laura. Your body is ready to go, it's full of energy.' I remember her looking back at me a little shocked. 'What do you mean, I am ready?' she said. I replied, 'Your body is ready to push, so take confidence in knowing that.'

I wasn't sure what she thought at the time but she has since told me that it gave her a huge amount of confidence. Mainly because she trusted what I said and knew I was straight talking. Laura said she thought of it while playing that final against Nicol. As a therapist it was fantastic to watch her all week, coming away with a major title at the end. I had known her body was ready but she still had to perform on court with the racket. That is down to her. On that day when it came off, how her body responded was not a surprise to me.

After Laura won the British, we carried on our treatments. It became more of an injury prevention tool rather than curing problems for the most part. I would see her and check her body and its flow. I can only describe Laura as having a 'clean' body. By clean I mean at the deepest level. There were few 'stones' and the energy flow was good up and down the length of the body. The positive side of this was when there was an issue with Laura's body, she felt them very early. This was brilliant for me because it meant I could treat many of her injuries before they became a bigger issue for her training or competition.

The downside, as Laura saw it, was that if she had pain it worried her a lot. So, while I knew an injury wasn't serious, Laura worried that it was going to stop her playing and training. It's not really a negative but if you feel pain then pain is pain! Laura was sensitive to these feelings, so to her it felt bad. I just used to say to her a lot, 'You feel this early, you have a long way to go before this is serious.' I think this helped her, as if she was away at an event and felt pain, she normally knew she could play through it while not causing a lot more damage. Unlike a lot of other players I saw.

In recent years, I have started treating more athletes, tennis players, Premier League football players and other squash players, including Greg Gaultier and other French players. The body doesn't change so I can help anyone in any sport. The key is that whoever the person, whatever the sport, they need to trust in me and think outside the box. That isn't always welcomed, particularly by very scientifically minded therapists but the best ones always embrace my uniqueness and want to work together.

One of the only injuries Laura had that wasn't preventable was rolling her ankle. Over the years, she has rolled her left ankle three times. The first was bad but not horrendous. The second was extremely bad, made worse that the timing was on matchball up for a big win, followed by contracting food poisoning at the hotel in Malaysia where the event was held.

She was in a bad way and had to postpone her flight home because of how sick she was. By the time she arrived home, she was a bit of a state. She came to see me after landing in Manchester and I had never seen bruising like it from rolling an ankle. It was deep purple on the inside and purple, fading into brown on the calf and shin. It had drained up to two thirds of her calf. The only explanation to the bruising was that it was constantly elevated in bed because of the food poisoning after doing the injury. The swelling was massive. It was about as bad as an ankle can get without a break. Luckily, we knew it wasn't broken as Laura had taken my advice while in Malaysia and had an x-ray.

I treated the ankle for almost an hour. There was a lot going on and I couldn't get to a deep level because of the swelling but by the end of the treatment I had reduced the swelling and enabled the body to start healing. I saw Laura's face as she sat up on the bed. She looked at me to the ankle and back several times, 'How on earth have you done that?' I had reduced the swelling by about 70 per cent and it looked once again like an ankle – or the shape of one at least! She didn't know what to say.

I reassured her I wasn't actually a witch and the swelling would return over the next few hours, but while the swelling was down the body could start to heal. It's times like these I honestly feel the old RICE acronym of rest, ice, compress and elevate is wrong. Well, it's wrong for my treatment. All I need is the rest, ice and elevate part but certainly not compression. I can relieve the swelling myself, the compression for me just locks the ankle up and freezes it in the position. Ideally, I want the ankle to move and keep a good blood supply. The injury was serious and unfortunate, but I genuinely believe it would have been far worse if I hadn't helped Laura with that and later, an ankle injury to happen mid-event at the US Open!

By Jade Leeder

I used to joke about Laura that if I told her to stand on her head for 30 minutes at 2am each morning in order to make her recover better, she would have done it. Not that she was naïve or just a 'yes machine', far from it, but Laura always gave my expertise a proper go. She would do things to the exact detail.

I met Laura when I first started working at the English Institute of Sport (EIS) in Manchester. We took a long time to get that trust working, for her to build up confidence in me. Once our relationship got going, and we realised we liked each other, she opened up more and more to my methods. From that point forward she was an absolute dream to work with. She valued the personal element of our relationship and the professional part. When an athlete does this, it helps me believe in what I am doing as well because so much is about a shared understanding. The trust and communication really are part of the physiotherapy.

Laura is a strong character but she still carried insecurities, like most people I work with. I always felt that having another female around her, particularly at tournaments with all the pressure and free time gave her the opportunity to let off steam in a way she might not have been able to around the men. I could give her certain reassurances too about all sorts of things, in fact we helped each other that way, which was nice. We would go for coffee, have some quiet time or I'd just let her download her emotions on the treatment bed. The high emotions and the low ones. The squash tour can get intense with all the other players and everyone seems to know everyone else's business so to have the trust of someone, a confidante is helpful. Laura was very intense and focussed on the squash, and I was able to calm that side of things down and make it more normal, away from the constant pressure of a tournament environment. Her tendency would be to overthink things and then worry. So, I had to snap her out of that sometimes by being very straight and to the point with her. Not all the time, just when she had gone too far.

The mind is connected to the body, so half the time when at tournaments it wasn't always the physical treatment that was most valuable, it was the chat and her ability to vent whatever it was which was stressing her out at the time and for me to give her a non-squash perspective.

She surrounded herself by positive yet intense characters and that can get overwhelming, I think. Naturally, coaches focus on the outcome and performance, but my aim was to highlight the enjoyment element of the sport and to reassure her that she was good enough to overcome it all. I made her realise that other players, all players in fact, are human. They all have faults and doubts too. They might pretend all is perfect and under control, but they are vulnerable like anyone is. In a way, this took a bit of pressure off Laura too because it was a clever way of reminding her it was okay to be softer sometimes. As she got better and better, she retained her steely side, her 'ice queen' stare and persona, but she allowed herself to relax a bit more and show that vulnerable part sometimes, especially to those she trusted. There were even a few smiles on court now and again!

With her injuries, we could understand them quickly and get on with the recovery. Laura understood her body well and that really helped me understand what's going on. Before the 2010 World Team Championships, Laura had a serious ankle injury and the ankle looked black and blue. Her attention to detail and dedication to that injury was incredible. We had six to eight weeks to sort it out and have her match sharp. When you're on those time frames, you need to have someone to do exactly what you're saying, religiously and she really did. No excuses. She would be straight in for the specialised equipment she needed to use, appointments all planned, always on the phone, replying to emails straight away. In that way she really kept me on my toes and that was quite a challenge at times, that level of demand. Yet that is what it's all about, it is a two-way process and you had to be at your most professional to be part of her team. It just becomes automatic with players like that. You knew she was doing the basics and the boring rehab work so you could concentrate on what needed to be done. It is a standard that has been set by the player and you don't go below it.

When at events there was always a little bit of support for Danny required too. It must have been difficult for him! He's so passionate, vocal and her husband. And so, for David Campion or DP and myself, it was always a balancing act. I would take Laura away, distract her and have a coffee and just be girls. And Camps or DP would be with Danny; letting him calm down, listen to all his ideas, offer some simple input and do it in a way where we didn't undermine him. They were good mates, so a few beers helped too, to let off steam. It all helped balance the team and took pressure away from Laura. Although, one time I do remember Danny overdoing the beers before a quarter-final in Philadelphia and Laura was far from happy about it when we talked in the morning. Let's just say I stuck up for Danny a lot and kept him from the doghouse that day! It helped save a lot of unnecessary stress. She won from 2-0 down to Nicol that night, so all was forgiven!

I am quite bubbly and loud, and I guess it was a distraction for Laura and if she was feeling a bit flat or an edge, I was also there to help get her up on days like that. It helped to see some positivity on our faces during matches, and if it looked like we were panicking you could tell she wouldn't be best pleased! Laura thrived off the positive vibes. I always felt it important to support and shout for Laura, along with Danny of course. 'Camps' even started joining in, although I never once heard DP! She needed to have people to believe in her. She knew she could do it – and when others did too and they expressed it with her, then it really geed her up.

A treatment that became a standard ritual before her matches was to release each of her big toes. Why? Well, one summer Laura came in to see me with a tight calf issue. I remember she had been doing beach sprints, which caused her big toe to stiffen up and it was manifesting in her calf. Beaches are uneven and can cause things like this, I recommended the track instead, but she was adamant she preferred the beach. When we told her about the toe, Laura looked at us as if we were crazy at first. How can my toe cause my upper calf to tighten? But then it would be one of the things we would continually work on with her. She would come in and want her big toe wiggling. Part of that was a mental thing, a comforter, but the important part was that she felt like her ankle and her toe was now loose and she would have that dynamic spring and push off.

Squash is high up there in intensity and players are working with ferocious forces going through the body, multidirectional repeated lunging with minimal recovery time.

So, for Laura, it was about making her legs feel fresh after matches, ready for the next one, often less than 24 hours away. Laura was starting to get to the late stages of most events and play for England at No.1 in the team events, so it was vital we got recovery bang on. With rallies always getting longer and more explosive as time went by and the tin lowered, we really had to keep developing our methods together. The emotional come-downs from matches were just as important as the physical elements, so not only the massage, icing, recovery garments, nutrition and manipulations were required but the release of adrenaline through laughter, chilling out or chit-chatting about life was much needed.

I've never known anyone to drag so much out of themselves and to be prepared to make some difficult decisions to change things. There was never a time, to my knowledge, where Laura felt afraid of those challenges. At times, some of us would doubt the changes but most of the time it proved to work.

At her 2013 World Championship title win in Malaysia, I was sitting watching her matches with Danny and Camps, dazzled by her ability to come through matches. It was at this tournament where we started to call her 'Find a way Laura.' She would find something from within to force herself over the line and win. It became a bit predictable. I'd be sitting there watching, whilst Danny would be panicking like crazy and I'd just be sat there expecting the comeback, like it was bound to happen. Obviously, she had that in her training application but, my word, she could pull it out on court when she needed to in those high-pressure moments. I really don't know how she did it half the time.

When I saw Laura before that world final, she was concerned because she had prepared mentally to play Nicol David and knew what to prepare for. I was able to tell her that Nour El Sherbini, her opponent, was not expecting to reach the final and it didn't matter who you were playing, they were all the same playing field. I'm no psychologist but I learned what kind of conversations helped Laura when she worried. It just became part of her overall treatment, our relationship.

It's amazing to look back on these successes now in English squash. My heart bleeds for Nick Matthew and Laura. What they accomplished, what they won (world titles, world number ones and titles galore) was so special. They were both completely committed to all aspects that could make them better and have retired knowing they couldn't have done a single thing more. They are so undervalued in British sport for what they did on the world stage. I worked closely with both and neither of them let it get them down. They were never resentful. They loved what they did and did it to the best of their ability.

I always wished Laura the recognition that her achievements deserved. She won everything in squash. We were all in a treatment room at the EIS with some well-known stars and Laura was way up there professionally as any of them. It was an honour to watch her grow, to become friends and to help her along. It was special to be involved in some of those moments as they happened. We felt like a squash family. That's unusual in some of the sports I've worked in and it meant a lot to me.

I think Laura is a special role model for the younger players, especially the girls. The way she did it and the path she left behind. There were lots of players who helped her on the way up and, very simply, Laura wanted to do the same.

16. 'YOU DO REALISE, IF YOU WIN YOU'RE NUMBER ONE?'

Until January 2015, I had spent 21 successive months at World No.2 behind Nicol. But Raneem El Welily's form had seen her close in and the Egyptian was now chasing Nicol thanks to her form on tour and the blistering start to 2015.

Generally, when I played Raneem, it was probably the biggest clash of styles you could get on a squash court and our games in the past were always intense and closely contested. Countless matches went 3-2. She is one of the most talented players I have ever been on court with. She had unbelievable touch and ball control, and always looked relaxed. It seemed like she went for her shots without a second thought. She had even admitted that trying to play winners all the time was like 'an addiction'. Raneem had so much talent, I can imagine it being hard to resist the attacking shot knowing you could play outrageous shots at will.

There were times against Raneem when I was made to feel like a dog chasing its own tail or being controlled like a puppet as she sent me all over the court. When Raneem was in this form she was horrible to play against;

I would be hanging in rallies and accepting that I would have to look like an idiot chasing balls, being sent the wrong way. The tough thing was that when she presented me with a chance, I had to make sure to take it.

On the other side you had my typically English style of play: attritional, precise and calculated. I played a basic, accurate and simple game very well and people didn't realise when they were watching off the court exactly what my shots were doing to my opponent. Based on subtlety, it could be a shock when you had to retrieve balls over and over when playing me. One time, I was playing a young Nour El Tayeb for the first time. I won 3-0 but knew she was a player to watch, even when just out of the juniors. She seemed to fancy her chances in the match but I was older and much more experienced at the time. She said to me afterwards: 'I knew you were good but I didn't know you were that good.' I took it as a compliment but realised how much the simple and basic tactics could be very tough to deal with. However, with Raneem that wasn't always enough.

There had been several matches over my career where I had managed to get the victory but it felt like Raneem lost it as opposed to me winning it. The squash felt all about her, waiting for her to hit an unretrievable nick or a tin.

That June, as I was setting about my second coming after nearly quitting the sport, we played each other in the semi-finals of the Alexandria International Open, hosted in Raneem's home town in Egypt. The day before, I beat Nour El Sherbini and there is a photo of me shouting over Sherbini, who was on the floor after one particularly fiery rally. It was quite a battle and that image really does paint a picture of the sport and how confrontational it can be sometimes.

Raneem came out with a determination that shocked me. She played so well that day and there was a steeliness about her that I hadn't felt before. We were having another five-game battle in some serious heat and the crowd were shouting their heads off, all with all their Egyptian flags waving. Danny was the only person who clapped or shouted for me, whereas the place erupted every time Raneem won a point.

At 5-5 in the decider, I suddenly hit upon a negative thought, which I am convinced lost me the match. I thought: 'How is she still playing this well at this point in the match when I feel so bad?' I questioned myself, my fitness and wondered why she was still looking so good. She normally would break before now and I knew the work I had put in. Yet, I was shocked she was still staying so solid. It only took one negative thought and a slight drop in belief, and the match was gone. I lost the next six points.

I sat in my chair in disbelief.

How did that get away from me so quickly? Did that one thought just lose me the match after an hour of brutal squash? How did she have so much left when I didn't? It is one of the only times where I felt like Raneem broke me a little mentally. Normally, that was my strength and I couldn't understand how she stayed so tough when I was wobbling. I got up and walked around behind the glass front wall. The further I ventured from the court and crowd, the more annoyed I got. Danny came to console me and I started shouting at him. 'I lost that match, she didn't win it. I questioned myself and I lost it!'

Typical athlete, thinking it's all about me.

The more I shouted it, the more angry I got. I was getting louder and then tears started emerging. I believe that ultimately I am responsible for my actions. I took personal pride in knowing that, as I was introduced or at the end of a match, I had done everything I could to be the best I could be. I wanted no regrets and, for me, that's all I could ask of myself. I had an honesty with myself that meant if I lost, it wasn't in vain. However, this was a shock. I had been mentally beaten that night and, boy, it was tough to take.

I didn't know it at the time but I later found out that if Raneem won that tournament, she knew that she would overtake Nicol to become No.1 three months later, providing no other events came on the calendar, which they didn't. I guess at the key moments of the match in Alexandria she pushed harder knowing what was potentially at stake – on the line was a major slice of women's squash history. I could break Raneem mentally but I couldn't that day. In the end, she broke me. It all made sense now.

Her win that night changed the landscape of women's squash.

One silver lining that came from that match, for me, was that I vowed to be much more positive in my shots going forwards. Raneem was only getting better and it became clear that I would have to commit to finishing the ball and ending the rallies on my terms. I accepted I was never going to be an out-and-out shot player but I had to be more clinical when given opportunities to win the rally. We came up with the phase 'live and die by my own sword'. A little intense but it basically meant go for it. It's one thing to work your opportunity but another to refuse your opportunities. A fine line but if you get it wrong against the top players you don't have a chance. More on the 'sword' later.

In September, Raneem was duly announced as the new World No.1, finally breaking Nicol's nine-year dominance at the top of the game, one of the longest reigns in any sport. Raneem had also become the first Arab woman to become a World No.1 in any sport.

Of the 104 tournaments since February 2005 and her emergence on tour, Nicol had won 77 and was nearing a 95 per cent winning ratio over a remarkable decade. Wow. No other sportswoman had maintained this much dominance. In tennis, German great Steffi Graf had held No.1 for 94 months. Nicol's feats far outweighed anything or anyone near her. The question now was whether she could regain top spot or was the game, with the lower tin, becoming too quick and too attacking?

———

I seemed to be adapting well to the lower tin trial and was ready to take on the young talent infiltrating the game as the new 2015/16 season kicked in. Thanks to all my hard work with Mark, I felt fitter than I had ever felt and my motivation was back. In September, I travelled to the Macau Open and won my first title for 18 months, the first since the Worlds.

The humidity and heat in Macau were the most intense I had experienced at a tournament. The heat hit you like a wall when we went outside and I remember walking out of the hotel and worriedly asking Danny, 'How am I going to play in this?' He just said: 'You'll be fine. It's the same for both of you.' I played Alison Waters in the semi-finals and had a big learning experience in that match because I realised that the moment I let my body language go, because the heat was sapping me, was the moment I lost all my energy, dynamic movement and forward attacking play. I needed to keep myself up emotionally even though all I wanted to do was sink into the floor on the open air court in Tap Seac Square.

Against Alison, I got very vocal and told myself to stay up, stay strong and keep hitting the ball with punch and pace. Don't go soft, don't push the ball around and make sure you volley. It was all a mask of how I was really feeling, which was like curling up in a ball and going to sleep. I was so physically depleted after the match that I had a funny turn heading back to the hotel and came out in a freezing cold sweat and shakes. Danny rummaged around in my bag looking for a gel pack and it helped immediately. I tried to breathe and stay calm while the sugar kicked in.

When the final came the following day, I was much more prepared for the heat. I had ice and gel packs at the ready. I took ibuprofen before my warmup, as I was so anxious about not feeling good, but the plus side is that the worry of not feeling well had put the nerves to the back of my mind. I had a plan, of course, but I was relaxed about it and that probably helped as I beat Egyptian teenager Nouran Gohar in the final, mixing up my shots with plenty of height and lobs. I was patient and calm in my play but intense in my mood which was what was needed in that heat.

My tactics on court were coming off; my hard work was paying off and my belief and hot streak continued in October and November, when I lifted my second US Open title and followed that up with victory at the Qatar Classic. I had never seen a crowd as busy as the one at the Khalifa Squash Complex. At times, the spectators were so loud I literally couldn't think straight. Most of the support was for El Sherbini but generally it seemed to be all chatter, babies crying and just a constant murmur of distraction. The whole match was tight. At 2-2 and 9-7 down, and El Sherbini two points away from victory, I put in a real effort and I found a very clear focus to win the next four points and the title.

I played the Hong Kong Open a month later, my tenth straight visit there, ahead of the World Championships in Kuala Lumpur. My form couldn't have been better but during the tournament we received an email from the PSA stating that the World Championships – the last under the WSA's agreement with Malaysia – was in jeopardy due to various promoter problems. Although the PSA must have been disappointed, it was a flaky deal at best and although they tried to rescue it, the deal had never been sound. My first emotion was one of disappointment and frustration. I had trained so hard for three weeks after winning the Qatar Classic to be in the best possible shape for the World Championships. After the initial shock of the email, which seemed to come out of nowhere, I decided to mentally behave as if nothing had changed.

The World Championships would be going ahead unless someone told me that it was cancelled. I couldn't afford to let it distract me from the job in hand that week at the Hong Kong Open and, just as importantly, I didn't want to be involved in idle gossip with the other girls, who were quite rightly worried about the situation and were looking for opportunities to vent. I even made the decision not to go to the informal players meeting because I didn't want to speculate on the situation. This was easier said than done. I was still playing in the Hong Kong Open and my flight to Kuala Lumpur wasn't booked for another five days so I had time on my side. Meanwhile, some of the other girls had already lost and were in limbo about whether to travel to Malaysia, a situation that must have been hard to deal with.

Over the next day or so, I started to realise that the chances of the Worlds going ahead were getting slimmer. On the day of my quarter-final match in Hong Kong, where I was due to play Egypt's Nouran Gohar, I had another email stating that the World Championships was officially cancelled. It meant that Hong Kong was the last event of 2015 and I was now even more determined to finish the year well.

I managed a tough 3-1 win against a feisty Nouran. I had played her three out of the past four events and each time the matches were getting harder. I was overjoyed to be in the semis of the Hong Kong Open for only the third time in my career. When I was doing media afterwards with the PSA's Nathan Clarke, he asked me various questions before finishing with: 'With the World Championships being officially cancelled today, it now means that if you beat Raneem tomorrow you will become the new World No.1 on the first of January.' I was absolutely blindsided. I hadn't considered that the Worlds might actually be off and what that would then mean for me if it was.

People had always asked me would you prefer to be world champion or World No.1? For me, it was such a difficult question. Becoming world champion proved that in a period of just under a week you can perform at your best, back it up day after day and handle the huge amount of pressure that builds as the rounds progress. However, the challenge of becoming No.1 was more a matter of longevity and producing an extremely high level of squash round after round, event after event. The pressures are very different and playing that single match to become world champion is pressure like I had never known.

I knew I had been playing well and now I knew that the goal I had written down on Lawrence's whiteboard only a few months earlier was closer than ever. It had proven that writing that goal down had worked – I was playing a better level of squash than any woman at that time. So with wins in Macau, the US Open, Qatar Classic and now a semi-final in Hong Kong, I guess deep down I must have known I wasn't that far off the top spot.

It was fair to say that Nathan's question left me with a mix of emotions. Firstly, there was excitement that I was so close to a lifetime goal and it was achievable within hours. I was a little bit annoyed that he had so casually told me and I was a bit frustrated because I didn't really want to know the significance of what the match against Raneem meant. I walked away after we finished and I thought, well, it's not rocket science. I knew the Worlds' points were coming off and I hadn't performed at my best last year in Cairo so that meant I didn't have many points coming off my ranking. Nicol and Raneem had played an epic final a year earlier, both earning themselves winner and runners-up points respectively.

I told Danny what Nathan had said. He looked at me initially with a bit of shock and then it registered what we both knew.

'What's he told you that for?!'

I agreed that perhaps given the choice maybe I would have preferred for that piece of information to have not been revealed, but it was too late now and I would just have to handle myself emotionally.

Don't think about the pink elephant, a psychologist once said to me. This particular pink elephant was years of expectation and pressure, but at least I had the experience to know how to trick my own mind or play games with it to put a different spin on the pressure. I spoke to Lawrence, who was always great in these situations, and he helped me realise that this was the moment I had worked so hard for. He reinforced my beliefs, confidence, strengths and determination. Suddenly, it felt like an opportunity rather than a burden.

Together, we had set about becoming World No.1 and he was equally excited to see that it could finally become reality. We both believed it was just a matter of time and how that time was here. He had always told me I was the best player in the world and the rankings just hadn't caught up yet. But no one gets the No.1 spot by just thinking they deserve it. I still had to perform on court.

The next morning, as we walked onto the glass court for practice, Danny said: 'Are we going to talk about the significance of today or do you want to pretend like it's just another match day?' I looked at him to see if there was a hint of sarcasm on his face but there wasn't. It was time to be straight about what was happening. I said: 'I see no point in brushing it under the carpet. I have made that mistake too many times before and at some point you have to deal with it.'

I felt relatively calm and the nerves weren't anywhere near as bad as before the World Championship final. I desperately wanted to win the match but I also believed that I was playing well enough for the No.1 ranking to happen over the next couple of months if it didn't happen that day.

Raneem, who hadn't been in the best of form since capturing top spot from Nicol, knew what I was capable of and that I would never quit. There was a mutual respect for each other. I looked at Raneem as we warmed up and she didn't look like herself. I'd played her enough to know when she was up for it and when she was nervous – this looked like the latter. I had seen her sit on her own before the match taking in some deep breaths. Settling her nerves or preparing for the battle? Only she knew that but, from my own experiences, sitting with her head down just before you're about to step on court wasn't exactly projecting positive body language.

I ran to the toilet just before being announced into court. I looked in the mirror as I washed my hands, sweat glistening on my face from my warmup. As I finished, I wiped water under my eyes and leaned towards the mirror. I said out loud: 'How much do you want this? How deep are you willing to dig when it gets hard?' I wiped more water over my eyelids, almost as a wake up signal, and thought for a few seconds about the reply to my question. I was willing to be dragged off this court before I lost. I gave myself a steely look in the mirror and my reflection looked scarier than I realised. 'I am ready,' I thought.

When the match started, I lost the first rally but knew I felt good. My shots were precise and I was moving well. After those first few points passed it was clear my instincts about Raneem were correct. She was making uncharacteristic errors, playing loose shots and not moving as well as I would have expected. I, on the other hand, felt like a steely determination was just pouring out of me. I won the first two games and kept telling myself that Raneem would surely get better and to expect some fight.

It did come in the third and I was becoming a touch cagey with my shots. The last few points were a battle, the toughest of the match, but I managed to hold it together and take the third game 11-8. I celebrated as if I'd won the tournament, fist pumping to Danny, who was on his feet too. It was a brilliant feeling but more than the win, it was knowing deep in my own mind that I'd held myself together mentally on one of the biggest occasions of my career.

I never imagined that I would have a chance to play for the World No.1 spot. The ranking usually came out on the first of every month and, throughout my career, I had usually been training at home when they were released. As my ranking got higher, I always assumed that if I ever got to World No.1 it would be on a random weekday morning as I set off to training. I'm so glad that in the end I got the chance to fight for it, to show how much I wanted it.

The news went around and messages came through thick and fast that night. I learned that I would be only the third Englishwoman in history to go to World No.1 after Lisa Opie and Cassie Jackman. I was also the only one to have won the Worlds, British Open and No.1 spot. Who would have thought that after all those starstruck moments trying to clumsily speak to Cassie nearly 15 years earlier?

The following morning I felt tired, understandably. I prepared as normal for the final, against Nicol, and spoke to Lawrence right before the off. He had hosted his staff Christmas party – the company logo was emblazoned across my playing kit – the night before back in the UK but was still up at 6.30am his time to talk to me.

Showing his support for me was rock solid and, with a tired and husky voice, he soon started to fill my head with positivity. He told me how proud he was and how proud everyone in the company was too. He told me that he had announced at the party that I would be World No.1 and the whole office had cheered and yelled like he had never heard. He told me that one day he would sit down with my children and tell them stories of how their mother had been the most amazing squash player, had fought her hardest and made everyone around her proud. I was welling up at his words but felt utterly inspired.

Nicol had been unbeaten in Hong Kong for a decade. However, I had won our last two meetings and the first game we played was up there as one of our best games ever. There were long rallies, quality retrievals and it was as competitive as ever.

Lawrence's words were also still ringing loud in my ears and I played like I had nothing to lose.

The first game was tight the whole way and I found myself game ball up. I was just thinking to stay positive and continue to go after it, but Nicol still got some unbelievable balls back. A backhand boast of mine was hit so clean and low that I took one step towards the door after hitting it. I had thought it was good enough to win the game but it came back courtesy of a forehand cross-court lob. This was still the Nicol of old, even though she was then World No.3 and at her lowest ranking for 10 years.

She took the game and the next one too. I was emotionally gone and maybe I wouldn't have got near taking the first game if it hadn't been for

Lawrence's powerful words. Who knows? But I do know it wasn't often that I felt the way I did in games two and three of that match. I was physically and mentally gone, too. The lack of sleep, the excitement and all of the messages had clearly taken their toll. However, Nicol had played brilliantly and it wasn't all about me. She was up for it and, together, we had produced a brilliant first game. That much was realised when people came up to me saying the first game had been some of the best women's squash they had ever seen. It was something to be proud of.

Maybe there was a silver lining to it all. Although not officially No.1 until January 1st, in my mind I achieved that ranking the day I beat Raneem in the semi-final. Lawrence had been telling me for months that I was the best player on the planet, which I had kind of achieved with World Player of the awards in 2011 and 2013. He was also quick to tell me I just lost my very first match ranked No.1 in the world. I had the ranking but I had just lost the event. It was enough of a reason to get back to training as soon as possible.

There was no time for celebrating and enjoying my time at the top as I had perhaps done after becoming World Champion. It had taken 18 months to win the title in Macau and I didn't want to wait that long again.

(Above) Being welcomed home as World No.1

(Next page) Winning the game to become
World No.1 - Danny is up!

CATHAY PACIFIC
國泰航空公司
新鴻基金融集團
SUN HUNG KAI FINANCIAL
SQUASH
CATHAY PACIFIC SUN HUNG KAI FINANCIAL
HONG KONG SQUASH
SquashSite

17. THE HUSBAND

By Danny Massaro

The support team in a sport such as squash can be incredibly important if you have good relationships. For Laura? She had a strong marriage; a brilliant coach in DP, who was also like her life coach too; a good relationship with Phil Whitlock, they were always in contact with each other and had lots of daily dialogue; Peter McNab, an excellent confidante and NLP coach; all her strength and conditioning coaches, especially Mark Campbell; and she had Lawrence Jones as a goal motivator and sponsor.

Because the relationships were strong, Laura felt a lot of security around her. There was a trust and she didn't feel pressured, rather inspired to go out and perform for them.

This had a tremendous impact and, speaking personally, it took a lot of pressure off me. Knowing people are in your corner and they really want you to succeed is an amazing feeling. And that spreads. It's a mixture of confidence, support and trust. Not to forget the 'raw' expertise of each person. These people were highly successful people in their own right, so their advice and support were usually cutting-edge and top class.

Personally, I was learning the whole time, all the way to the end, and the dynamics wouldn't have been the same if I had already coached a World Champion. What was great, as I was pushing my reading and knowledge, was that whenever I met other coaches or professionals, my feeling was that everyone was a guru. It was exciting that I could tap into all this knowledge around me. I realised people enjoy giving their opinions and ideas if you ask, just look at how podcasts have taken off now – people love sharing.

My mission at events early on was to seek information out of the former players and coaches, like I did with Sarah Fitz-Gerald once in Penang. I was like a research student. I used to get them a coffee, or a beer or two, and try and soak up all the knowledge I could. I was genuinely in a place where I didn't know what I was doing and that was hard because nobody likes being out of their depth, yet it was exciting too.

Not everyone was forthcoming however and why should they be? Liz Irving, Nicol David's coach, was frosty. I could sense that she was going to stonewall me and keep her distance. Perhaps she was wary of us and, being the dominant coach on the scene, wanted to keep us down. It was strangely comforting. I took it as a sign of respect and it really motivated me. We got on much better after Laura had established herself at Nicol's level.

I'll alway remember when Liz admitted to me that it was good for women's squash that Laura and Nicol had a genuine rivalry. This was just after their British Open Final in 2014, which Nicol had won and reclaimed her title off Laura. Granted, Liz must have had that post-win 'high' we all get and was having a cold beer celebrating, but it still felt genuine. That was nice actually. I don't think it came naturally to Liz to be like that with rivals. There is pressure when you are on top; you can fear losing your status. I never took it personally for that reason.

Of course, other coaches would share information. Camille Serme's French coaches were good like that, particularly Philippe Signoret – body language, movement ideas, psychology stuff. Yet again when the rivalry got closer and Camille got into the top 10 we stopped sharing as much. When you start winning a few things, you can fall into the trap of thinking you have 'cracked the code' of success. It can bring a dose of over confidence and perhaps a tinge of arrogance. It's an easy trap to fall into.

I watched Phillipe go through this stage, it was like he was the man with all the solutions, yet Camille would suddenly fall short in matches. I would find it amusing because I had done exactly that myself. When Laura won the World Championships, I became a bit of an idiot for a few weeks. My empathy went and I would cut people off in conversation, talk at them. I thought I knew it all, that I had cracked it. I ended up in a fight because of it, which was totally my fault. It can all get to you.

Sometimes I was a better person in defeat than in victory. I can genuinely say that when Camille beat Laura in the 2015 British Open Final, I was happy when I saw Phillipe and Camille embrace. He had coached her since day one, had found a way through and done it his own way as a bit of an outsider from the establishment. I felt that way about myself. I made sure to tell him and from that day on I felt we always had a healthy respect for one another.

———

I fell for Laura on the day I didn't turn up for a running session. She came to my door where I lived in Preston. I remember I had been out the night before with my mates and it felt like I had loosely arranged the run, as I never said that I would definitely be there. She really told me off and stormed off, leaving me standing at the door with a mild hangover and a dose of guilt.

It impressed me though. She was tough, straight and different; something which came from her early years with her father, who is a strong personality. She was stubborn, strong and would shout back. I knew the boundaries from the off. As Laura grew older and more successful, she held herself really well, was reliable and not overconfident. There was no ducking and diving, and there was lots of honesty. What you see is what you get with Laura and she never hid away from the truth. That is where we are most similar. Different personalities but get to the truth quickly. That way, I suppose, you never have to worry about lies you've told or games you might have to play.

In my opinion, so many people struggle with straight talking, they just cannot take on board the next level of responsibility that comes with making positive choices. To me that is what 'resilience' is. It is avoiding most of those tempting lies we tell ourselves, 'willful-blindness' psychologists call it. It is fronting up to those comfortable, tiny excuses that lurk around all those choices you must make to go forwards. The responsibility of knowing you can fix things can crush you. Even when you badly want your dreams, it is still overwhelming.

Laura could take the truth more than most and I think that's why we make a good team because I am a very pragmatic person, known for it in my teaching, although a little softer these days. I demand action, I put my foot down and you get total honesty about what needs to be done. It is bloody annoying to people. Many people I have coached can only go so far with that. They are the best 'talkers' going, they read all the books and set all the goals you're supposed to. Some even ask the universe to help. Yet, they can only go so far before they slide away.

I noticed it on tour. Many promising players can operate in surges here and there but not day in day out, year after year, as the responsibility weighs too heavily. I know I couldn't do it myself. I marvel at those that can and I marvelled at Laura every time she went to work with that responsibility on her shoulders, the pressure she was willing to put on herself.

Another way to put it is that when I noticed up-and-coming players who clearly did have this quality – players like Nouran Gohar and Hania El Hammamy, like Nicol David and Raneem El Welily before them – as a competitor your heart sinks because you know they are coming right at you and, before you know it, they will be past you.

——

Some coaches wouldn't be able to give the love or the cuddles. I could. A lot was made of the negative side of our relationship, the 'husband and wife at work' problem. I never saw it that way, it was mainly a positive. I could give support and encouragement in the room and I could pick her up when she was down. I could look at her when she was upset and she could look at me immediately. That could stop a lot of scarring. I've seen so many players get battle weary as they have had too much emotional scarring after tough losses, days hanging around on their own, feeling a bit useless.

Those moments after losses are vital, yet they are very hard for players who give a lot. Debriefing can go on in many forms and there is no perfect way, but I got a knack for doing it better. Just being there is the most helpful part but it is no picnic. Emotions can really help but obviously they have caused me to say things and think thoughts that aren't nice at all.

There were never any shaming or nasty comments, but I could still suggest hurtful things. In the early days it might have gone off, with tears and shouting, and I regret those moments. But it can't have been that bad as she carried on playing and we didn't get divorced! It was always the clear-the-air moment that we needed and we never stewed on it.

Back then, Laura may have deserved it to be quite honest. She may have made herself too nervous, didn't try, she wasn't fit enough or failed to stick to the agreed plan. I needed to get things off my chest and, 'for better or worse', Laura was going to be told.

It could be tricky when I did get it wrong, as Laura has explained during the tense dinner we had at the 2010 World Championships. As I was living it and it was unfolding at the time, I was coming into a scene and feeling threatened as I had no professional background in the sport. Am I doing it wrong? Am I stupid? Am I like a pushy parent? But if a relationship is strong enough, the bumps in the road are far easier to deal with. It can be healthy, the over-emotional spat. Making up can be a great leveller and we could get to work with that energy.

The other positive to being married was that it certainly got to some opponents, which was a clear advantage. I sensed they saw that we were strong, married and loved each other. 'How can they do that?' they may well have been thinking. 'I thought it could blow up in their faces by now and it hasn't!'

I used to shout for Laura a lot from my coach's seat. Sometimes it would be sat at the front by the back wall gallery or sometimes in the crowd itself. Squash fans would be accustomed to me shouting: 'Come on, Laura!' I had heard a bit of mockery of me in that sense, so I knew that it was affecting players. Gossip usually emanates from insecurities, people feel temporarily safer in gossip groups and, believe me, they spring up all over the place on tour. So, I made more of a habit of shouting. It would annoy people and agitate them, not into better action but into more gossip! That was fine by me. I grew a thick skin by sitting in those coaching seats.

Our closeness wasn't out of the ordinary.

There were other couples and also a few mothers who travelled to some events and were in their offspring's corner. I saw it as total love. What's the problem? Their son or daughter are on court and they are world class. There are sons and daughters out in the real world who have been neglected, even abused by parents. Some think of it as pathetic or too smothering, that the parent wants it more than their children on court. It is an easy generalisation to make but the evidence goes both ways.

———

For Laura to win the world title? It was the biggest high you could imagine. I was also sitting eight feet off the ground on a stand which had been built behind the glass court. I could barely watch as Laura had match balls, but I got this strange sense she was going to take the second of them.

'Match to Massaro!'

I jumped immediately up from my seat in delight and realised my arms were then flapping like a bird as I then landed down on the ground. Relieved not to have broken my legs, I proceeded like a fish out of water, leaping up and down the arena, much to many people's amusement. To best describe it, I went for a little touchline run like a football manager, before returning to pick up Laura courtside.

My celebration was pure relief coming out. Without knowing it at the time, I believe that being so involved with my wife's career and the fact we still had such a deep love and bond, I had felt a huge burden of responsibility. I had advised her on so many key decisions, coached her through many sessions, given her these harsh 'home truths' and witnessed her early struggles.

I dared to believe in the type and depth of support I offered, despite much self-doubt and external criticism coming my way. Most of all, however, it was Laura's consistent faith in me that was probably the most overwhelming of all . There is huge responsibility when somebody believes in you that much, when somebody needs you on a daily basis, even when they need you to do absolutely nothing. It complicates matters further when you love that person more than anyone; it takes on a deeper significance and this is the 'pressure of love'. What I learned through all the pain and joy gave me huge empathy for other people.

So, everything changed for me after Laura's world title win.

There was no way anything was going to be a failure after that point. She had the big two: the British and the Worlds. For me, it was more than the squash, it was for us and that could never be taken away. It is so affirming to achieve things together, especially when somebody trusts you all the way. When Laura became number one in the world it really was the icing on the cake and the way she handled herself to win that match, I'll never forget it. She was ferocious, her mind was made up, she would WIN. The person who left me standing on the step with my hangover and guilt turned up that day – her opponent Raneem had little chance of defending her position, much like me 12 years earlier.

(Opposite page) My favourite pink kit to match the amazing Dubai Z court

See my full photo gallery at lauramassaro.co.uk/photos

18. HUNTER BECOMES HUNTED

S ay it out loud,' wrote former world champion Sarah Fitz-Gerald. I had received Fitzy's text message at Heathrow Airport, on my way out to New York City for the Tournament of Champions and my first event as World No.1.

'World No.1, Laura Massaro.' Say it out loud.

At first I didn't fully understand what she meant, so she wrote back telling me that I was now going to be introduced on court as that and it would hit me hard all in one go, if I hadn't already heard it said.

The Tournament of Champions, the long-running event held every January at Grand Central Terminal, always kicks off the squash year. And now, I was a lot more prepared after what Fitzy had told me. I did indeed say it out loud to myself and got Danny to do the same.

On court, I reached the quarter-finals in New York and I played decent squash despite the extra pressure. But, in truth, I wasn't really handling being a World No.1 player very well. Ever the massive worrier, to me it meant that I now had to make every single final and win everything going. As I've said, I knew I wasn't super talented. I believed I had achieved more than I had a right to achieve and so, when it came to handling a situation like being on top of the world, it was a challenge. I wish I could have handled it better.

People talk about women and girls suffering 'imposter syndrome', where you don't quite believe that you deserve to be where you are professionally. I don't think female athletes are immune to it. I definitely wasn't.

I had gone after it with total determination and I struggled with the pressure and expectation when I got there. I had the No.1 spot for four months and, by this point, there were challengers aplenty. Each event was an uncertainty as to who would be the winner and, after a decade of Nicol dominance, it was refreshing. Nour El Sherbini had started to play incredibly well, Nicol was still there, France's Camille Serme was on top of her game and Raneem El Welily was feeling her way back after her brief stint as World No.1.

I now know that it takes someone really special to win so much, get the top ranking and be able to hold on to it for months on end. Many players say that by their second time at the top, they are much more at ease with it but, as it turned out, despite the fact that for that period 2015/16 I was playing the highest level of women's squash, I wasn't someone who could reclaim top spot several times. I guess, as DP says, I overachieved in my career. I never had the luxury of destroying players through sheer skill. I had to earn everything through hard work.

I had wanted it so badly, but I didn't want what came with it. At the time, you can't say that to other people but I was so much better being the underdog, the hunter and proving people wrong. That was a better place for me because no one really says how hard it is to deal with the kind of pressure that comes with being No.1.

I never believed I could reach top spot, given Nicol's dominance in the game since I was a teenager. Mix this with everything that was driven into me – us against the world, being told I wouldn't make it in the game, the lower tin changing the dynamics of the game and all the things which had motivated me – there was nothing left once I was No.1.

The whole team had worked hard to get me to the top but I don't think I was quick enough to map out the next goals.

If Lawrence and myself had sat down and worked out a goal to win so many events or to become better in another department, that may have prolonged my stay and put me on another plateau. Maybe it's a little regret that I didn't stay longer at the top but I certainly can't get away from the fact that I reached the pinnacle in the first place.

We learnt a huge lesson. We had done all the work to be World No.1 but we should have regrouped; the line in the sand had moved. Instead we tried to stay still and everybody else tried twice as hard to beat me.

———

Finding a way to win is not always in Plan A or Plan B. It might be something you have thought differently about, something technical, a belief process, something you read in a book. It might be the way someone looks at you before a match. You can always find a way to do something differently and change what's going on. For me, it started to become 'Laura always finds a way'. And then it became a self-fulfilling prophecy.

People said it way before I believed in myself. Coach DP would always say that about his own playing career. He said that he didn't work hard enough and he was always about the touch and control rather than getting down to the dirty stuff to complement all the skills he had. For me, it came from all the work I did away from the court. If you can do it off court, why couldn't you do it in the heat of a major competition or a big battle?

People who can't do that will never win those tight matches as it gets too stressful, too quickly. It's what football managers call 'bouncebackability'.

Maybe bouncing back comes from hating to lose. Maybe it's mental strength. Maybe it's a maturity gleaned from years of playing. Or maybe it's just plain stubbornness.

For me, it could be a combination of all four of these things. I certainly know from personal experience that the losses hurt differently to the way they used to. They actually hurt the same amount, but the pain faded more quickly once I'd given myself a break, if I knew that I had done everything I could in a match and in the lead up to tournaments, in my physical training and preparation. I accepted that there would be an emotional sting lasting up to three or four days and then I had to get back to business to be better for next time.

The funny thing is that quite often that feeling of hurt caused by losing is so much greater than the feeling of the joy you get when you win. I've heard and read a lot of other athletes say the same. It comes back to that quality that I think is so important – hating to lose. DP has it at the top of his list of qualities to make it to the top of the game. The good thing is that, while the pain of losing is sharper and harder to take, it has normally gone within a few days, whereas the joy, pride and satisfaction of winning can last much longer. Winning is a softer, happier memory that lasts weeks, months and years.

For me, the toughest losses happened when I felt that I could have given more mentally to the match. It didn't happen very often, as I can honestly say that I never gave up on a ball in a competitive match. However, sport isn't just about the physical side. You hear the saying all the time that 'sport is ninety-nine per cent mental'. I don't believe in that ratio. I chose squash, not chess, so I firmly believe that the fitter you are the more success you will have. But, if everyone is fit, strong, rhythmic and efficient in their movement, it's mental strength that makes the difference. Often the physical and the mental are intertwined; when you know that you are incredibly strong physically, it makes you stronger mentally.

I worked hard on my brand of squash over the years: Solid, error-free and mentally strong. Players knew where they had to go physically and mentally to beat me and I found that, in crucial times, I could win a match without seemingly doing a lot. It's a past memory of a match you've played with a certain player, the scars you leave on them each time you beat them. It's impossible to forget. Or it might be the amount of times they've seen you come back from behind.

One example of this was playing Nour El Sherbini in the 2016 World Championships final in Kuala Lumpur. Her daring shot-making had seen off Nicol in the quarter-finals, which felt like a bit of a changing of the guard in women's squash partly because Sherbini was so much younger, but also because it was after the tin height was lowered. Sherbini had beaten Nicol in Penang on the higher 19-inch tin and if there was a match which had enforced this momentum shift, this was it. Now, Sherbini seemed even more unstoppable for Nicol.

The lower tin had really made its mark and from the start of 2016 until her retirement, Nicol didn't win another major title. Meanwhile, I came into the final with another five-game tussle against Raneem under my belt. A match where the learnings from the battle verses Raneem in Alexandria came into play. I was in another huge battle and at this point all mental. Fighting it out, point for point, and at 10-10 in the 5th, I looked out at Danny only to see him stand up in his chair and shout: 'SWORD!' Camps, sitting next to him just looked up at him in bewilderment but I knew exactly what it meant. If you're going down, go down on your terms. I finished the match swinging and attacked at the right times. It won me a spot in the final and the opportunity to play for my second world title. Needless to say, Camps quite often just shouts the word 'sword' whenever Danny gets over excited or has a couple of beers too many!

Preparing the next day for that final was tough. I had also lost to Sherbini 3-0 the last time we had played. Having played a five-set match, going down to the wire in the semi-final wasn't going to help my cause either.

Sherbini was a unique player to get to grips with mentally. She had such a successful junior career that her self-belief carried into her senior career. She had a great support network and family, and it's fair to say it made you doubt yourself as an older player when you see a 20-year-old dismantle a player like Nicol in only 26 minutes.

Despite everything in the lead up, I went two games up in the final playing well. Sherbini looked a little edgy and I was solid. After being 2-0 up, she came back and we were in a tussle at 8-8 in the fifth. She closed out the match brilliantly and took it 11-8 to win her first World Championship title. Looking back, I am not sure I fully believed I could win that championship final. Something that stings a bit to even admit. Frustratingly, I also surrendered my World No.1 ranking to her in losing that match. She had also become the youngest ever World Champion.

It wasn't much consolation for me but one good sign of the progress women's squash had made in a short time was that Nour won a Citroen car and $27,000, nearly double the prize money I had received when I beat her for my world title two years previously.

After the final, I went to warm down on the watt bike by the back courts. In one of my interviews afterwards, draped over the handlebars as I turned the pedals, I said: 'I want to be better and not to experience this feeling of sitting on a bike having lost the final. That's what will make me go back and train hard. When that's gone is when you know you haven't got that drive to do it anymore.'

Losing that final really hurt because I had to admit to myself that my belief flagged in the match. That wasn't me. I didn't lose matches from being mentally weak. It kept bugging me until, later that day, Lawrence asked me about it outright.

'You didn't believe you could win that match, I saw it in your eyes.'

Instantly my eyes started to sting, but I needed to hear it.

'Why didn't you ring me after the third or fourth game?' he said.

I had no answer.

We went on to discuss that he thought he could have helped. Again that stung. Could I have done anything differently? Or did I just doubt too much in the lead up and then couldn't rescue that once I was in the match. So much belief was decided before the match started.

The chat was so important because it was honest. It hurt but I admitted it to myself and to Lawrence, and I took it on the chin. I would be better and stronger despite how painful the learning curve was. When I was on tour I heard and saw a lot of excuses being made by players – the floors were bad or the ref was terrible. I think many players could improve their level, or at least their learning of the game, if they were just more honest with themselves and learnt from it.

A couple of weeks later at the World Series Finals in Dubai I would play Sherbini again and prove to myself that I was better than that World Championships loss.

———

The World Series Finals are squash's season-ending finals. Only the top players from the season's World Series events qualify to play. It had first been played in 1993 but endured a low profile history in the past, with 19 men's events and just two recent women's stagings, both won by Nicol in 2011 and 2012. Ziad Al-Turki, the Professional Squash Association chairman, had been involved with the sport since 2005 and was responsible for making the event incredibly slick. He had made it his mission to build the World Series Finals whilst improving things for players across the sport.

With Ziad's backing, there was now increasing gender equality on the circuit. The PSA World Series events created a combined $2.3 million in prize money so they signed a three-year deal with Dubai to stage a 2016 World Series Finals, the first of which was to be played in front of the Burj Park with the top eight women who had accumulated enough points at World Series events to make the trip.

The women's season-ending finals had hit sponsorship troubles in 2014 and the event hadn't been played until Ziad ushered in a new era in Dubai. This was an exciting finale for us, where we would be competing for a combined $320,000 prize pot across the two events.

At the start of the century, the women's event had been held in Hurghada, Egypt, before hitting sponsorship trouble. When Ziad had rejuvenated the event by hosting the Finals at the Queen's Club in 2011, it was the first event I played where it felt as if we were on a plateau. Sky Sports soon covered the event and, five years on, Ziad and the PSA had elevated the tournament and moved it to Dubai. There, an air-conditioned structure hosted the eye-catching 'Z Court', with futuristic lighting and a new front wall which could show highlights and sponsors' messages.

Ziad had learnt how to showcase the sport when he bankrolled his own Saudi International events but it wasn't easy and he pretty much had to start from scratch. His events always felt very special to be part of.

Squash has always had the capacity to be played in some of the world's most stunning locations. Although I never played in front of the Giza Pyramids, the images of the glass court there, with the Pyramids lit up at night, has always been used to promote the sport. We play at Grand Central station in New York, where the court is placed in the chandelier-filled Vanderbilt Hall and commuters can stop and watch the action behind the front wall. The buzz is simply electric every time we play there. Then there's the China Open, with the court housed on top of the Peninsula Shanghai Hotel, overlooking the famous Bund and where the winner's package includes a stay in a suite in the hotel for two and a Rolls Royce pick up when you come back as defending champion.

Before the event in Dubai, I took part in a brilliant darts exhibition with Aussie squash player Cameron Pilley, along with professional darts players, Michael Van Gerwen and Gary Anderson, who were both out there ahead of a darts tournament. Then it was straight into the squash. I had to be on it straight away when I found myself playing Nicol in the group stages. Looking back to my diary at the time, I was full of confidence:

'I always find it hard v Nicol, so many scars and memories. Although I believe I'm better than her now and I am higher ranked, I want to prove it. During the match, I suddenly realised I was being passive and I remembered what DP had said to me. Be strong and stand up to her. I did exactly that, I stood tall and started hitting the ball with more pace and I got on the volley across the middle. Maybe she felt the change mentally from me. Maybe I just played better, I am not sure, but it turned the match. From being down in the third I came back and won.'

Having topped my pool group I was playing Sherbini in the semi-final, less than three weeks after she'd beaten me at the World Championships and taken the No.1 spot from me. This time I believed in myself and, being a best-of-three match, I had to be sharp. Sometimes the pain of a tough loss can turn into a steeliness and I had a bit of that as a result of what happened in Kuala Lumpur.

After that Worlds loss to Sherbini, Danny, Lawrence and I hatched a plan and agreed that our next goal should be the World Series finals. It focussed me and gave me purpose. Danny said to me: 'Do you want to win that money? Do you want to put together a run in Dubai and right the defeat in Malaysia? If you do it starts now, right after the loss. You can't turn up in Dubai and expect it to just happen.'

The semi-final against Sherbini was tough but the training had paid off. Who knows what Sherbini did after she won the Worlds but I knew I had prepared big time for this event. I made a great start and won 2-0 feeling really good and comfortable on the court.

I so wanted to finish the season on a high note in Dubai and I believed I had put in more training than any of my seven other rivals. I wasn't mucking around and was out to win $42,000; the largest winners' purse on the women's tour at the time. It was hard though; the hotel was like a giant party and the whole thing had an 'end-of-term' feel about it. The squash fraternity was all there, there was constant music and drinks round the pool and all the players were celebrating the end of the season along with the hotel guests on holiday. It was just Raneem El Welily and myself left having to really focus on the final.

Although back in 2016 there weren't any ranking points awarded for winning the World Series Finals (like there are now), I knew if I could win it would show that I was still playing the best level of women's squash. So, again, as an underdog, I set about directing all my focus on righting the disappointment I felt in myself from not winning the Worlds and losing the No.1 spot as I faced Raneem in the final.

Even though Raneem possessed enough talent to have won more than a single world title at least, I think that her talent sometimes weighed heavily on her and that showed in a lot of our closest matches when I sensed that we were both dealing with our own doubts and beliefs. We played a lot of close matches and I really had no right to beat her as much as I did. In the final in Dubai, she had dominated big parts of the match and was within two points of taking the title in the fourth. When things got close in that final, she hit tins like I knew she could but I also felt as if our previous matches were affecting her, consciously or unconsciously. Only she knew if that was the case but, as a competitor, I could sense it. You can't describe it, you just feel it. It gave me confidence and I flooded my head with positivity and I claimed the match after a sting of errors from Raneem to finish the season on a major high.

I was proud of the fact that I still believed I had the better of more players than they did of me. Beating Nicol was always a big moment, just because of all the history in our matches and how much I'd suffered playing against her. Some losses against her were close and a lot of people had always said I had the game to beat her, but a few of my defeats were embarrassing, humiliating batterings in front of big crowds, friends and family. At other times I'd just been completely physically spent at the end of a match, with nothing to show for it.

That tournament gave me the chance to put a few things right, against Nicol, against Sherbini and in winning another big title. I had won the event on the pink 'Z' court sporting my favourite pink Asics dress with the iconic football legend Diego Maradona, watching from the front row. Sporting stars don't come much bigger. It was brilliant and so special for Danny and I to get a picture with him after the match. I had given everything to take the biggest pot of prize money ever won by a woman on tour and that was an added bonus.

(Above) Needed an ice bath, so out
went the energy drinks!

19. CHICAGO COMEBACK

It was the hardest I had ever pushed myself. I was on my own in a Chicago gym, fuelled by anger and embarrassment. I got on the bike and set it to the highest level I could manage for that session. I went eyeballs out doing bike, core, bike, core repetitions and just went hell for leather on the pedals and on the mat.

The reason for this sweat-induced fury unfolded at the 2017 Windy City Open quarter-finals, which had been played the previous day. We may have been competing high up at the University Club of Chicago in the stunning Cathedral Hall, complete with tall and atmospheric stained glass windows, but I obviously had no divine right to be on court that day. A teenager called Nouran Gohar had blown me off course and court in 37 minutes.

I had first seen Nouran when she played a tournament that my brother Christopher and I ran at David Lloyd in Chorley in 2013. I had never seen a player of her calibre for someone so young. She had an absolute relentless desire to hit the ball hard and not care about the opponent. She was incredibly feisty on court, which is why she was later nicknamed 'The Terminator'. Off court, she would avoid eye contact with you, almost blanking you. To her, there was no pecking order between older, more established players and youngsters like her; she had no fear. I later realised that she was actually just very shy and timid off court, which is why she didn't interact much but knowing that made her swagger and aggression on court all the more surprising.

Seeing the confidence that Nouran had so early, and the focus she showed, made me look back on my own early career and wonder why it took me so long to find that in myself. Traditionally, Egyptian players do come through much quicker than Europeans, which is one of the reasons why Egypt has become the dominant nation in squash in the last few years.

I was on the bike and when I felt my legs going weak, I channeled my aggression and replayed the defeat to Nouran in my head.

Over and over again.

After one lung-busting round, I was having a rest when she actually walked past. It was mid-morning and she was on her way to practice on the court, where she had won in straight games. I was making puffing noises as I attempted to recover after a repetition and I could sense that she was doing a double take back at me. No, I wasn't nursing a hangover and wallowing in defeat. I hoped that she understood that this is what she had driven me to do and that the next match was going to be very different.

As I was going full tilt, I replayed the match so much in my head that there were tears of anger that I had got such a spanking from a teenager. By the end of the session, I don't think anyone would have known I had been crying as I was dripping so much with sweat.

Right then, I knew that these were the kind of fitness sessions that I needed to get in the bank if I was going to avoid being beaten by younger players. I was the underdog again and my fitness needed a push in the lead up to the British Open, which was just three weeks away.

I felt that pride after that session. I changed and went downstairs to tell Danny and Camps what I had done. It was then that Camps told me that he'd booked the glass court for us. I was exhausted but I agreed to an on-court session that afternoon. If I was going to win the British Open I was going to have to push myself harder than I had ever pushed.

That evening I went to the Chicago semi-finals to check on my rivals. It was always difficult to watch when you felt it should have been you competing, but the note-taking and seeing them play in real time was necessary.

It had been a habit throughout my career to go and watch my opponent the next day. It was important to pick myself up, dust myself down and walk in the venue with my chin up. I might have lost but I wasn't sulking, I was learning. Watching live, you can see the extra details up close. Nothing is missed and you send a message to the person you lost to that you're plotting revenge. I was here to learn how I had lost and to show everyone else I was moving on.

Once I got home, I really went for it, so much so that any fitness drills and sessions Mark Campbell gave me, I simply added on to my workload at the end of my sessions. There was no way I would have put myself through all this that if I hadn't lost to Nouran in Chicago. I wasn't just motivated; I was completely inspired.

———

March 2017

Thursday before the British Open. I played Ashley Davies at Harrogate Squash Club and DP said it was a miserable session. He said it looked like I was coming from a place of expectation and fatigue. He was probably right. I need to freshen up physically and mentally. Danny and I went for dinner. God knows how many 'chats' we've had over the years. There's no doubt that they've helped, but here was another one! You'd think I'd have figured things out now. Or at least figured out how to deal with myself emotionally and gain some sort of mental control. It honestly feels like someone erased my memory after each event and I have to figure it all out again. The feelings I have during training, my weight, my expectation and my worry that it will be worth it. Then during the events. The nerves, whether I think I can win, whether I worry I'll lose. Am I giving my opponent enough respect? Do they think they can beat me? Have I had enough sleep? Have I eaten enough? Do I feel good? There is more to life than squash. Or is there? I am an absolute nutter! And people think I am mentally strong. They have NO IDEA! Either that, or everyone else is a bigger nutter than me! If that's the case, God help them!

Anyway, back to the 'chat'. When did winning the event become the only way to be happy? Of course I want to win the event but out of 56 players, if only one can be happy at the end then that doesn't seem right. Enjoy the journey! I just knew how much work I had done, I wanted it to pay off. I deserve nothing but to start on court knowing I've given myself the best chance. We spoke a lot about being on my phone. The differences between being on my phone and how it was when I started on tour with no social media, no texts and how the interaction fries the frontal cortex and tires us. Chicago was a prime example, a long day bored and a conversation that got me caught up in frustration. I knew I should stop but didn't because I was sucked into the drama. I should have known better. I turned up and I don't think I could concentrate as well. I'm not saying it's all this but it can't help! I decided to buy a colouring book for something to do in those bored hours before a match to stop me reaching for my phone.

———

It was my 16th successive British Open and thanks to the pasting that Nouran had given me, and my reaction to it, it turned out to be one of my best. In the first round, I overcame a qualifier, Mayar Hany, in straight games and the Egyptian opponents didn't stop there. I was up against my old rival Raneem again in the quarter-finals, who was a higher seed than me that year.

I have so much respect for Raneem, on and off the court. On court, she always had a lot of integrity, coupled with an incredible amount of talent.

Luckily, I started brilliantly against her and that settled me. I then made a great start in the second but I was playing at a high pace and I started to hurt physically. She snuck it on a tiebreak and I was gutted. I told Danny at the break that I had needed that game. How could I have let it slip? He said directly: 'No, you need this one. Get back to the plan. Get in front and volley.' That was a perfect bit of coaching right there and I closed out the next two games to win the match. After the pain of Chicago, I was over the moon. I had beaten Raneem and felt in great shape. It was a big boost that all that training had come together and we'd managed the taper down well, so that I had started the tournament feeling fit but fresh. I had trusted a lot in Mark and it had worked.

It was time to face another familiar opponent, Nour El Sherbini, in the semi-final. Sherbini was the defending champion and had looked on fire all week. Before the match, I warmed up behind the stand, hidden away in a tucked-away spot that I'd taken to using over the years of coming to Hull. I felt comfortable, I knew that I'd have plenty of support from the home crowd, my support team and everyone at England Squash. I felt calm but a little nervous. I didn't want Raneem's win to be the end of the road. I ran up and down the side of the stand and at one end I kept running towards a lifesize banner of myself in my 'come on' pose. I looked at it, taken from last year's World Championships, and thought about how this is another big occasion, another big semi. How many more will you get to play? Aged 33, I knew things were coming to an end. Not immediately, but soon.

Sherbini looked up for it in the semi-final. You could just tell a player's habits and body language over the years; she looked bouncy and maybe slightly angry. I'm not sure what that meant but I knew it was different.

During the knock up, Sherbini hit a cross-court nick and it started to roll back to her on her side of the court. I was up the court so intercepted it and played it down my side. I felt her eyes bore into me. She was angry! Sh*t, I thought. I hadn't done much wrong but her look warned me of how up for it she was. It shouldn't have but it rocked me a bit and she had made a great start to go two games up. I remember saying to Danny that I was being lazy, not volleying and not hitting those extra straight balls before catching her with the change up.

Sherbini played close to her best in those first two games, in my opinion. When she is at her best, she is a heavy hitter of the ball and keeps you pinned in the back of the court with pace and accuracy. She has an unbelievably simple and classy technique and, having done so much technical work with DP over the years, I really appreciated how repeatable and simple her technique is. We all know simplicity is not easy. It makes her extremely difficult to read. She plays every shot from the same swing, making it very difficult for her opponents to move until she actually strikes the ball. She stops you in your tracks and when she chooses to play short, it feels so far away from you. Especially when starting from a still position. Her accuracy all over the court is ridiculously hard to deal with. The drops, so short and the length, so deep. All shots seemingly always drawing away from you with fade and shape. It's always subtle but it makes you do so much work to stay in a rally or match with her. The work you're doing slowly building up over the course of the match until the ball seems further and further away from you. Strangely and completely opposite to me, she always looks like she's having fun. The more fun she has, the worse it is for you as an opponent as her squash becomes free flowing and creative, which only means one thing – more running!

Unless I was disciplined and hardworking, I had no hope against Sherbini. In the third, I found my rhythm, I dug in and made it hard, she wasn't liking it. I could start to sense Sherbini fret and panic. I took the third and it was a good sign that the work I was putting in was now working. After winning the fourth, I didn't want to come off as I was so in the groove. My legs had started to wobble at the start of the fifth, but I knew they could survive this one, however much it hurt. I backed myself to push through because of all the work I'd done. Towards the end of the fifth, I saw her legs wobble on a shot. She even fell over at one point and that's when I knew I had her. It gave me a lift because I was feeling the pain too, just not as much as her. Stick to the plan and it's yours. She was still dangerous with her shots but I kept it tough and played well to the end.

I was through to my fourth final in five years and this time it would be an all-British affair (for the first time since 1953) after Sarah-Jane Perry reached what was then her first World Series final. We had played at the Nationals a few months earlier, where I'd ended up winning my fourth national title. I had loads more experience than SJ but I knew how good she was.

At the last minute, Lawrence had been able to make the Finals and came via helicopter. We had a chat once I got to the club and it was great to hear and see his passion. He told me that he had also felt like Anneka Rice – who once had a TV show called *Challenge Anneka* going across the country in a helicopter – as he didn't have permission to land anywhere so he told the pilot to get as close to the Hull venue as possible and he landed in a next-door field.

I started my warmup for the final and, unusually, I allowed myself to think that this could really happen, a second British Open title. I don't think I had allowed myself to think it until that point but minutes before the final, it felt more realistic. I tried to focus on the large banner of me screaming 'come on!', just as I had done before my semi-final against Sherbini.

It worked. I took the first two games 11-8, 11-8. When SJ took the third 6-11, Lawrence had tried to get down in between games during the final but he wasn't allowed to get past the ropes. We did catch each other's eyes and I visually told him everything was fine. I still felt in control and I wasn't panicking. I was starting to feel the match from the previous day but I just put all my effort into a good start in the fourth game. I managed to do exactly that and took the game 11-6, without any dramas.

At 33, I had won my second British Open. My first British Open had been an incredible high but this was a very different reaction, less ecstatic and more an overwhelming sense of satisfaction and pride. I had no pressure on me the first time, I won it because I was playing Nicol in the final and I hadn't won that many big titles at that stage of my career. This time there was more expectation on me but at no point did I let that bother me. Instead, I had channelled my frustration and disappointment at losing so badly to Nouran in Chicago and worked hard to put things right.

It was a really important tournament for English squash. Nick Matthew, at 36, became the oldest finalist since Pakistan's Hashim Khan back in the fifties. He couldn't get past Grégory Gaultier to win the title, but to have a player of Nick's age and calibre still riding high was testament to the work DP and Mark Campbell had put in with both of us. That was an amazing achievement.

The British success in Hull, at a tournament billed as 'the Wimbledon of Squash', didn't seem to make much impact with the outside world. There was more written about Britain's tennis number one Johanna Konta reaching the third round of the Miami Open than the fact that three homegrown squash players had reached the finals of the British Open, in one of the most physically demanding sports of all. To top it off, I remember *BBC Sheffield* phoning me up for a radio interview thinking that I was from Barnsley!

So it was left to James Willstrop, another thirty-something Englishman still at the top of his game, to write about our achievements in his blog for *The Guardian*. If anything, it showed that our increasingly under-represented sport had a story to tell:

They are the cream of English sport right now and very few people have heard of them,' he wrote. 'Laura, Sarah-Jane and Nick are not asking for fame for its own sake but these are stupendous achievements that deserve to be saluted more widely. What these athletes, coaches and staff have done is remarkable. Despite essential funding being threatened of late, Sport England and England Squash have helped the players achieve and these bodies also deserve a little more appreciation for the delicate job they have done.

'With a little help these athletes and their homespun success stories could inspire people, young and old, to take up sport. We have an English champion and we aren't making use of her. Perhaps it's worth mentioning that Nick recently donated his prize money from the Canary Wharf Classic to eleven-year-old Sumner Malik, who needs treatment for cancer, a gesture that reinforces that these are the sort of athletes we want to be reading about more often.'

——

The British Open win took a lot out of me and, by the end of the season, I was starting to feel a bit jaded. Camps, as England coach, had suggested to me that I could miss the European Team championships. With my ranking and winning the British Open he said I had helped England enough and so I decided to take him up on the offer.

After the British Open, I travelled to the World Championships in El Gouna and was knocked out in the quarter-finals in a tight match against Raneem. I finished the match and event feeling emotionally drained.

Once home from El Gouna, and now without the pressure of the European Teams to prepare for, it meant I could rest and train properly for the season-ending Dubai World Series Finals. Deciding to miss the European Teams didn't go down well with fellow England compatriot, Alison Waters. She felt it important to text me and state her disappointment in my decision. I didn't see what business it was of hers but sometimes text can come across as overly harsh. I decided to pick up the phone to try and talk it through. On this occasion, the message was meant how I had read it and Alison had definitely taken my decision to heart. Even on the phone, when I tried to explain that I had represented England and always gave it my best more times than I could remember, she wasn't happy. She explained her side and said representing England should always be at the top of my list of priorities. I would agree with her in part but, after 100 caps for my country, I also prioritised winning major events and adding these big titles to my trophy cabinet. I told her this and we agreed that we went about our careers differently. I feel as athletes we are entitled to do so. At the end of the day, Camps said I was contributing to the England funding with my performances and wins at major events, and I had earned the right to sit this one out. It was my choice, I was just given the option. Alison suggesting I wasn't patriotic seemed unfair considering how many times I had represented England. She hardly spoke to me at the Worlds and she seemed to take it very personally. For me, I just wanted to perform well in Dubai on the world stage and that would make it the right decision in my head.

Two months after that win in Hull, I swapped the Airco Arena for the Dubai Opera House – a new setting for the World Series Finals – and squash was once again put on a pedestal. We had our own dressing rooms with our names on each one and I will never forget playing up on that stage – even if some of the matches finished past 2am. The late start times at the event were to coincide with Ramadan, so that the action wouldn't start until people had broken their fast. There were several Muslim players in the tournament and fasting must have an extremely tough exercise, especially when you need to fuel your body to compete.

As with my win in Dubai the previous year, I wanted to go in feeling as fit as I possibly could because I knew that would also intimidate the other players. I had got through some really tough sessions in the weeks leading up to travelling to Dubai. I had trained hard but re-grouped emotionally as well. I remember one bike session where I pulled up a picture of Sherbini with the Worlds trophy from El Gouna to help me fight my way through it. This was a session that I could draw upon when I got tired or doubted myself in matches. They say that your training should always be harder than your matches and I definitely tried to live by that mantra, at least to the point where I had to recover and taper down right before the tournament.

When I found myself face to face with Nouran Gohar again in the semi-finals, I could have been overwhelmed by the scars of how she'd beaten me in Chicago. Instead, I realised what a big favour she'd done me because I fed off that disappointment and played inspired squash in the months afterwards. Needless to say, she was still a massive handful and I had to survive two match balls as time ticked towards 1am but I got myself out of it and got the win. As painful as it had been to sit watching her play the day after she'd beaten me in Chicago, those notes I took came in handy.

I was one of the oldest players left on tour but I didn't feel it at that point. The decision to miss the European Teams had meant I came into the event feeling fresh rather than jaded, like you often do going into a season-ending event. Ahead of the final, I felt fresh legged and raring to go the next day.

I was absolutely loving this event. It felt so special. The Opera House venue was incredibly opulent, the crowds were great and you were made to feel like you were playing on a really big, important stage. With due respect to Hull, this was a bit different.

Looking back, I played really well against Nour El Sherbini in the final. It helped that she seemed out of sorts but I won 11-8, 12-10, 11-5. It was the first time that I had defended a major title in my career and I had done it by hitting hardly any tins and playing an attacking brand of squash which stifled Sherbini. I remember saying afterwards to the local media: 'I'm the intimidating one, I'm old and feisty! If you don't have an edge to you in the game now, you don't have a chance.'

To win the World Series two years in a row and to beat Nouran and Sherbini in back-to-back matches must rank as one of my favourite weeks. I moved well and felt the most fluid I had ever felt on court. A couple of seasons later, Raneem said to Danny that, after that final, her coach had told her that if she wanted to win titles she needed to look at my movement and learn from it. What a compliment!

Dubai 2017 was another big pay in squash terms – more than $40,000 – and I was the top earner for the year. It was also the last major win of my career. Meanwhile, Nouran's improvement continued and, just three years later, in summer 2020, Nouran, that teenager who had so terrorised me on court in Chicago, would be announced as the World No.1, aged just 22.

20. THE COACH

By David Pearson (DP)

Sometimes, when I watched Laura play, it looked as if she wasn't enjoying herself on court. She could start a match and it would be like watching a rabbit caught in headlights; nervy, stuck and therefore her subtleties missing, especially her flow of movement. Then suddenly 'bang', something would click. I think it was the fact that she was usually nervous or worrying, then when she realised the loss was closing in she dug in and almost relaxed by having to get on with it. Laura absolutely detested losing; I think that was a big part of it all. It was the reason she came back so often from losing positions. If she did lose to someone, usually she would get them back next time. She stored that memory and it drove her on. Not all players are like this, they obviously don't like to lose but it seems to bounce off them quickly. The best players I have helped store the loss and reuse it down the line for revenge or fire to win next time out.

Laura would always push to better herself and that meant bringing in the best people she could find to advise her. She was never afraid of leaving a coach to find the right balance for her, to get the information required to be a better player. I think she got every ounce out of what talent she had and all her success came from this approach.

As her career developed, Laura became more and more meticulous in her professionalism. I would notice she had everything mapped out: Her warmups, her physical training drills, her technical work that I gave her. She was disciplined in everything she did, in a career where she didn't have the luxury of having talent alone. She became a powerful presence and had an 'I'm out there to win' attitude. There's no doubt some of her competitors found that intimidating. There were those who said she got in their way and blocked on court, all the usual stuff when they are repeatedly losing but Laura was taller than most girls and she used to take the space, just like the men would do. This was all part of the things we learned, to have presence and authority through the hitting, with grace and subtle skills. It just frustrated the heck out of people because they never understood the subtlety and skill. It used to be the same with Peter Nicol, subtle skills creating confusion and doubt in the opponent, dragging them to places they didn't want to go to get the ball back from. It's a demoralising form of squash to play against, so it was obvious to me the complaints would pop up, just out of sheer frustration.

From where she began as a junior player, even young senior player, it was quite amazing how she reached the top. Few would have believed it to be honest. I always said that if I had a £10 note, I wouldn't have put it on Nick Matthew or Laura to make it to the top when they were both out of their teens. It was full-on dedication to the process. It was never going to be a quick fix; they stuck at it for years and years, slowly chipping away, changing small things that end up being big things. It is quite rare that quality, you wouldn't think so, but it is. Perhaps more so these days.

Laura never got above herself. She was humble and I don't think she could quite believe she became as successful as she did. I wouldn't say that her self-belief came naturally, there were always insecurities to overcome.

There were also incredibly good performances especially as her self belief grew but with that also came the natural ups and downs. She wasn't a naturally confident player, for example, Laura would never think she could go on court and win 3-0. Danny and I would sit down for a match and think this will be fine today, she is way too strong for her opponent, she's been hitting great. Then the match would begin and she wouldn't put her foot down, there would be strange shots and odd decisions, no drop shots when that was so obviously the correct shot. It was a deep rooted fear of losing and something she never fully shook off. I never understood it for someone so good but then, occasionally, I would remember my own playing days, my own nerves when playing. It can be horrible. It's not as easy as you think.

Laura became like a lone wolf as far as English squash went in the back end of her career. She was having to operate against a production line of Egyptians at tournaments. I think this is where the people around her played a huge part. Together with England Squash, everyone rallied around her and she was never alone in those matches against the Egyptian players – that showed in the results and in how comfortable Laura was playing them. She had fantastic support from an array of people and, of course, Danny and I would be there most of the time. Sometimes it's just company you need, sometimes a hug, a laugh, some information. It settles players down and Laura, like Nick, built good relationships with people and it helped very much.

In Malaysia, for Laura's world title win, I had a prior agreement to do some coaching in Kuala Lumpur. I was on court at a local club and Ong Beng Hee, a former tour pro, was giving me rolling updates of the final. 'It's gone to matchball El Sherbini.' Then he told me that Laura had lost. A few seconds later the smile came from Beng Hee. Joking!!!! 'Laura has won,' he said. I rang Laura and I got quite emotional, I have to say. It was a phenomenal achievement for her, while I had also become the only squash coach to coach a male and female to the world title in the same cycle. It was a really proud moment for both of us to share. It overwhelmed me for a moment. It shows that if you want to push on, trust good people and keep at it, you can do something quite amazing in your life. You really can.

After she decided to carry on in the sport after retirement talk, we always tried different variations on court to mix it up and find something fresh. To be a good squash coach, you have to be a good psychologist as well. So sometimes I would say, 'Laura, you're doing that really well now' when really nothing had improved that much. She would think it had happened.

With Laura, she might say she wasn't hitting the ball well during a session. On court, I would see that she was powering the forehand really well. So I would say, 'Well, your follow through needs to recoil a little bit more.' In reality, her 'recoil' was fine, but she needed to know it when, in fact ,we hadn't changed anything. It was all to do with the mind, her confidence and making her feel she was good at keeping on top of things. It made her feel good about herself.

With Nick, all it was about was making sure he didn't go back to old habits, over bringing new ones in, when he found success in his thirties. If the player feels that the coach is behind them, then you have done your job, even if nothing has pushed on. When you are coaching different people, everyone has a different mind, so you need to know the player to say things at the right time to get the best out of them. I always felt Laura was very respectful. She listened and, because of this, there was never any tension or aggro between us. It was honest, clear and straight. We also had good fun, teased each other a lot and I think it's always a good sign when people can take a joke, it relaxes the whole thing.

Whether it be a successful time or on a bit of a downer, Laura knew she could rely on her husband and coach. Their relationship was so strong and that was part of the success on court. Danny was older than Laura, left home at 16, lived by himself, came from an educational background and perhaps understood things a bit differently from his wife. He was able to steer her in the right direction. He was getting more experience travelling the world and, gradually, opponents knew that she had a team to rally her. Danny and I became good friends and found a good balance between having a good time and talking squash. It all certainly had an effect on her rise and her ultimate job in the middle of her career was trying to beat Nicol David.

When all the girls seemed to have given up against Nicol and couldn't find a way to win, Laura was different, even when she was losing to Nicol herself. Come hell or high water, she wanted to get on court and really challenge her.

Even when she lost a match 3-0, she wouldn't back down on Nicol. She found that way to win and she wasn't going to lie down against her. There was a mission: 'I am going to be able to beat Nicol David, one of the most dominant female players ever.' She never gave up on the challenge and her main raison d'être was to overcome this in a major tournament. Soon enough, that rubbed off on us and we worked on that all the time to try and make it happen for her.

I think one of the ways I helped Laura, aside from other things, was in the subtleties of her game. Her forehand boast and drive became subtle and skillful. The watching public may not have understood or seen that, but these were the areas that we worked on the whole time. She was fully committed to whatever suggestions I made and when I sent her away with a new technical task she would return a week later with it improved. She was never late, never cancelled and she would drive from Chorley to Harrogate, a good 90 minutes away, week after week, year after year. It was total commitment and hard work.

That simple philosophy – analyse, do it, analyse, do it – got her to become a World Champion.

(Above) Taking the win in Monaco

See my full photo gallery at lauramassaro.co.uk/photos

21. STEPPING OFF THE ROLLERCOASTER

It's difficult to know exactly when the moment hits you that it might be the end of the road. It builds over time. Perhaps it's because people slowly start to plant the seed. Aren't you too old? Shouldn't you be having a family? You're married, doesn't that mean you have other priorities? There were questions all the time about my retirement. At first they take you by surprise, then the questions become more regular and, before you know it, you're asking yourself the same thing. A bad loss, an injury, a particularly tough training session or a long trip away can provoke all these thoughts.

I started to confide in a few close friends. They cared and said: 'No, you have loads of time left,' or that 'age is just a number'. Mostly they compared me to other athletes, ones that wished they had continued for longer than they did or sportspeople who were hugely successful at an older age. At any rate, the retirement thoughts were beginning to become more frequent than I would have liked.

I spoke to a couple of former players who I could trust with their opinion. I told Vicky Botwright, an ex-tour player, that I wasn't sure how long I had left. It's hard work and everyone is so good, I told her. She responded that having been through retirement, she could tell me how good life was on tour and to enjoy it while I could, that she wished she'd taken more breaks rather than just retired at the first thought.

Immediately after retiring and getting a job, she played the World Championships in Manchester and lost in the final to Nicol. What an achievement that was. She even worked at the same time as playing the tournament!

I also spoke to Danny and Tania Bailey, a close friend and another former player. They both cautioned me against retiring too early and regretting it and most people I spoke to seemed to go with 'when you know, you'll know'. I'd told my friends and family and decided in my head I was done at the end of the 2018/19 season. Honestly, though, I thought if I played well I might continue. I knew the time was close, but I just didn't know how close.

It was a surprise when a sudden thought jolted my mind when I was warming up for a match at a tournament in San Francisco. It just popped in my head. What are you doing? Why do you still need this? It was a shocker for me to be thinking this way and I immediately pushed it aside. At the next event, my mind became cluttered with the same thought. What are you still trying to achieve?

I had finished the previous season so well, as British and Dubai World Series champion. To achieve those successes, I had put in a huge amount of work and it was hard going to replicate them. Was I ready for that? Did I want it enough?

I was still winning squash matches in 2017, my 17th season on tour. I was holding my own at the top events. I was still training hard, chasing balls with Whippy. Going into the 2018 World Championships in Manchester, my image was on posters across the city. I faced Wales' Tesni Evans in the second round of my home event. Tesni was on the verge of the top 10 but I had high expectations for the tournament. In the match before ours, featuring Nick Matthew, the floorboard broke. Maybe it was an omen. From then on, it certainly turned into a mess of a day.

Over the years I seemed to know whether I would play well or not in the warmup – the vibe that day wasn't great. My brain was a little scattered and I was distracted. When the flooring broke, I was two thirds through my warmup and organisers didn't know how long it would take or when Tesni and I would get on court. We might have to wait for hours so I came out of squash preparation mode and I held back from thinking about the match to stop building up nervous energy. But, in the end, the flooring took less time. To make things worse, I had picked a kit I didn't feel comfortable in so I changed it after the first game, doing so with a towel around me so nobody could see. I was all over the place.

Tesni turned into a difficult opponent for me at the back end of my career. And, as my speed and edge wore off, her game matched up with her hold and variation in play really troubled me. I lost that day in the second round of a home World Championships, and again when I played her at the 2018 Commonwealth Games in the Gold Coast. Those two defeats were major disappointments and there is certainly still a regret at not being able to win a Commonwealth Gold.

———

That World Championship in Manchester was a disaster for me really. I was in pieces after the match. There had been a lot of people there to support me and I felt I had let them all down. Lawrence, my manager Faye, Mum and Dad, along with DP and Danny. I wanted to hide and I did for a while on the track behind the court. I spoke to a few of them but, honestly, I wanted to leave and not see anyone.

DP drove over to the house the next day – that's when you know things are serious and he was worried about me. He asked how I was and I will never forget his support that day. For all the support he'd given me over my career, that moment when I was at my lowest and coming to the house meant so much. He had a brilliant way of putting things into perspective. We ended up in a local restaurant that evening and plenty of drinks later, it was just a squash match and we had found a way to move on. I knew that my husband and my coach would both love and support me whatever happened.

After a second-round loss at the China Open to Nicol, in the opening tournament of the 2018/19 season, I decided I was done. Whenever I got beaten 3-0, I always told myself that if you are any decent player, you shouldn't be losing by that scoreline to anyone.

That 3-0 loss really got to me and I really didn't want to go to the next event, the World Team Championships for England, which was also held in China. I just wanted to go home. I decided, however, that I owed England more than that so I went and we actually competed well before losing to Egypt in the final.

My 23rd tour title came a few months later, in December 2018, at the Monte Carlo Classic. This ended up being the last title of my career and it actually meant more than a lot of them, especially as I beat my bogeywoman, Tesni Evans, in the final. I was glad I had managed a great run through the event and, unlike other titles I had won, I really enjoyed the one in Monaco. Normally, it was straight on to the next event but I knew that winning and appreciating victory was right at that moment. For once, I soaked it all up and took the warmth of pride home with me.

Having made the decision to retire, I knew that I had to make it real by making an announcement. Faye and Nathan from the PSA helped me put out a very straightforward statement. I would play two more events, both at home, at the Manchester Open and then, fittingly, the British Open.

In Hull, if I needed any reason to think it was the right tournament to retire, then this was it; when you look at how I played, it was an absolute disaster. On the day of my defeat, I was doing Instagram Stories with Telegraph Women's Sport, charting a typical day in the life of a tour pro. It certainly would have reminded people following that sport doesn't always deliver fairytales.

I lost 3-1 to unseeded Belgian player, Tinne Gillis, in the second round. Two years previously, I had become the first female English player in nearly 70 years to twice win the British Open. Now I was on court, giving a farewell speech and trying not to cry. It felt right to do it in Hull and in front of a crowd who had got me over the line so many times at the British Open, but it still stung.

'No one steps on court at seven years old and thinks they are going to achieve that,' I told them. 'It has been down to a lot of hard work. It's been a complete rollercoaster, it's been unbelievable highs and lows throughout my career and I'm extremely proud of my achievements.'

Of course, the last match will always sting a bit – to be honest going out like that still hurts a bit now as I write this, almost two years later – but it showed that I was making the right decision. I could have gone on for another season in the world's top 20, carried on the emotional rollercoaster, earning some decent money, but I was playing to win and to be in contention for major titles. I wasn't there to make up the numbers.

I knew it was time to go.

Danny's view

Squash is a tough, tough sport. When I'm watching a rally back, I can't believe the amount of work the top players are going through. The accuracy, the movements, rally after rally, is insane really. But, at the time, you don't notice it. If anything, it is about looking at whether the opponent is getting weak. At the elite level, it is about having the strategy; to wear the opponent out and make them crumble so that they mentally can't take it.

So, even though they might be a trapped rat – as squash great Jonah Barrington once termed it – and still getting balls back, you should be enjoying them getting those balls back. Your strategy has been to get them knackered and, in some cases, it can scar them if they kept getting the balls back. That's what Jahangir Khan did to a lot of opponents and what Nicol David did when at her best. They crushed hope in their opponent.

Laura had that for a few years but, once the movement and speed goes a little, you can never intimidate opponents in the same way. Then, the psychological barriers evaporate, opponents sense blood and gaps start appearing. It can be one shot they notice that you don't retrieve in the same way. This is enough. It's enough to give them hope. Then, they build on that hope, chip away and eventually break through. Not immortal after all!

All of this was summed up perfectly in Laura's last ever match at the British Open. She was so upset when she lost that match because, naturally, she was still giving it everything to prepare and win. I tried my best to energise her between games, to take her mind off the occasion, all the usual tricks but it was too overwhelming. The time had come. I gave her a cuddle and told her it was alright. It upset me too because she felt she had let me down. Ha! How utterly preposterous is that? But that's the human mind for you.

I never doubted that Laura would move on in life. I thought she might miss being professional and the exercise but as long as she had projects on, no matter how big or small – painting a room, coaching at David Lloyd, overseeing Lancashire junior squash, coaching professionals – it doesn't matter what it is, as long as she is feeling she can do a good job at it, then all will be fine.

The only worry I did have is the drug of attention, that drop off, not being in the limelight anymore, the massages, the coaches' attention, the fans at tournaments. Who wouldn't miss that? That part that is hard but Laura will crack it. It has been a natural winding down and together we will sort it out. Squash is not the highest of profile sports and the limelight is fleeting at best. Some still can't believe it with the way the game is played today, but I love that about squash. I love the grounded nature of it, the fact that the celebrity side is minimal but the sense of achievement within is just as meaningful as any other professional sport.

Overall, I have a deep sense of peace and satisfaction that we did what we set out to do – and more. We stayed safe, met friends, expressed ourselves and won some big tournaments. Laura really did it. It sounds obvious to say but I never hit one single shot for her. My trophy is that I didn't screw it up for Laura, didn't let her down and I wasn't the mad scientist that I often feared I might be inside. We made it through stronger than when we started, and long may that continue.

The end: Emotional after
my last ever match

22. I FOUND MY INNER WARRIOR

When I first started out in squash, things were a bit different. For one thing, there were no mobile phones, at least not ones that worked abroad without bankrupting yourself. I used to have to go to a tobacco shop in some far-flung place to buy a $10 phone card to call home, to get on Instant Messenger in Asia, or to send an email to my parents saying that I had arrived safely. There was no way to watch or find out the results on the tour until the next day's newspaper. If I was on my own at events, I remember getting homesick or having that plummeting feeling in my stomach when I saw some of the hotel rooms or clubs where I would be spending the next week.

I remember one particular trip to Montreal was a real ordeal for me and, looking back, it was probably a bit reckless for any young female travelling on her own to a foreign country. It began by boarding a flight from Manchester to Newark, New Jersey. I arrived in Newark at around noon, just as a huge snow storm hit. Storms in the US are a different animal to the UK and I couldn't believe the amount of snow that was getting dumped on the tarmac and runways as I peered through one of the airplane's tiny windows. While waiting for my connection, slowly more and more flights turned red on the monitors stating CANCELLED or DELAYED. I sat there on my own as my re-scheduled options kept on being changed.

I was supposed to be arriving in Montreal for the Atwater Cup, a tournament I had never played before, nor a place I had ever visited. It was all going to be new. I was set up to stay with a family I had never met before, the Martins, and, while I had their contact details, I was reluctant to ring them until I knew exactly what was going on. After about four hours, I called them to keep them updated and to let them know they wouldn't need to pick me up at my original arrival time. Hours passed and I called again to say no further news. I explored the whole of Newark airport that day and, still to this day, I know it too well. I was stranded at Newark for eight hours before I finally got back on a plane – only to sit there for another hour as the plane went through a de-icing procedure. By the time I landed at Montreal airport I was tired, annoyed, frustrated and grumpy, to say the least. As I walked through the airport, I was hit by huge queues at immigration. By this point it was almost midnight. I had no mobile phone, no way to let the person I didn't know who was picking me up that I was still a long way from getting out of the airport. I stood in that line for over 90 minutes and, when I finally reached the front, I was in an horrendous mood and admittedly just plain sarcastic with the immigration officer. I was rude and I was past caring. I was at the end of my tether.

Well, that lady at immigration taught me the best lesson she could have that day. My attitude gave her all the reasons she required to take me into a back room for further investigation. I was grilled by the officers in that room as to why I was travelling there, what I was doing and for how long I was staying. They were aggressive and did not seem to believe anything I said. The thought of the billet waiting for me out in arrivals went straight out of the window as I now panicked about being sent straight home, back to England on another plane!

Luckily, after a grilling and leaving me to stew, they decided to let me into Canada. I have never been rude to an immigration officer since ... well, that rude at least.

Things were now looking a little better. It was late but, after the worry of going home, I was feeling glad to be through it all and looked for my bag to the side of the carousel. They had by now been stacked at the side of the belt – the belt stationary and baggage hall looking worryingly quiet. I searched and searched again. Yes, you guessed it, no bag! I mean could this day actually get any worse?! The hall was like a ghost town. Several people hadn't got their bags and we were all searching for someone to speak to who might help us.

Another queue and sometime later, I walked out of the baggage hall into arrivals with a slip of paper, stating my bag was being looked for, and my hand luggage that I had travelled with all day.

At 2am, I was exhausted, downtrodden and a little upset. I put a brave face on as I hopefully looked around arrivals hoping my day would be saved and at least there would be someone waiting for me.

In the distance stood a guy with a squash racket. I mean, he must be waiting for me, I guessed. I walked over and after a brief introduction and a big apology for the day and the time, we walked out. I got in his car and we drove back to his house. The roads were eerily quiet as he told me his wife was away and would return the next day. I suddenly had an internal panic, maybe it was the tiredness or maybe not but it suddenly hit me that I had got in a stranger's car in Montreal and was currently being driven back to an empty house. What else could I do but go with it? I talked myself down and said he had a racket; he knew my name and was there so late but I won't lie, I was worried.

Having survived the trip and the night, everything seemed clearer looking through refreshed eyes the next morning. From here, everything got a little smoother. The home was great. The family were brilliant and, luckily, I had my squash shoes as I always travelled with them for this very reason. I was missing my bag until into the start of the event and had to go and spend money I couldn't really afford on new socks, shorts, sports bras, tops and energy bars and drinks – hoping my kit would arrive as soon as possible and that I would be able to claim the costs back once home.

The event itself went well; I was the number three seed and beat the number one seed, Natalie Grinham, in the semi-final. Then, I lost in the final to Natalie Grainger. Overall, a trip that started as the worst ever ended fairly well and, boy, was I was glad to get home.

Needless to say, I still keep in touch with the Martins and will forever remember them introducing me to bagels with jam and bacon! It's a winner if you've not tried it!

—

For today's players, the challenges are different.

There is usually someone there to rescue you, to mull over a defeat or share the glow of a win with in the evening after a match. You can always watch a video of the match back with someone and analyse every last second for you, to the point where we almost seem to be over-coaching. Squash is a sport of problem solving – you need to go through the challenges to figure out the struggles on your own terms. In many ways, it builds a strength of character to do it individually.

Becoming a coach has helped me see that more and more.

As a player, I never used to have a plan in the early days. I went on with determination, fight and grit. It was only later on in my career that I learned how important a game plan was. I see a lot of the Egyptian players now go on court with a serious plan that takes in lots of different scenarios and outcomes that their coaches have worked out for them. It means that even those most talented players are very reliant on their coaches.

Even when I am helping some players, the urge is to go down courtside and start feeding them information because I want to protect them from losses, but there is also a big part of me that wants to leave them on their own to work things out for themselves. As a coach, I need to find that balance.

For young female players now, there seems to be the added pressure on how to have a social media presence and be part of the right social clique and, most importantly, look the part. I was definitely conscious of how I looked as a player but it was always linked to performance – did I look fit and lean; could I intimidate opponents with how in shape I looked? When I first started working with a nutritionist and taking care of my training, I could see the changes in my body shape. It might not have been the shape that I would have chosen, to look good in a dress, but I didn't care – it won me squash matches.

That's what could be hard for young women in sport today. They may not want the muscular legs or arms because that doesn't look so good on Instagram. There is a lot of research that shows that this is one of the factors that puts young girls and women off sport and getting fit – they don't want to look sweaty or muscly. Yet, whether you are a professional athlete or not, being physically fit can give you so much inner confidence which spreads to lots of other areas of your life.

In Danny's book, *The Winning Parent: A parent's guide for the journey of competitive sport,* which he wrote a few years ago, he talked about how there was an extreme philosophy to develop sports stars. The theory goes that if you throw 50 eggs at a wall eventually there would be one that doesn't break. That's the one you want to work with to become, say, a gymnastics World Champion. That was the mantra in places like Romania, which produced incredible gymnasts like Nadia Comăneci. Danny believes that the sportsmen or women who make it can take body blows, they don't crack and they're not fragile.

Maybe I was that egg. I certainly had to take some knocks to my shell, dating back to losing disappointing matches in juniors. Sometimes those knocks came from the people that I cared about the most – like Dad, my husband and the coaches I was close to. Those lessons in pain and disappointment helped me build up my resilience as a player. Without that resilience I wouldn't have achieved what I did.

It's not pretty, glamorous or sexy but you have to go through those horrible moments to get better, get stronger and have the joy of winning. The horrible, 'sick in the pit of your stomach' feeling of letting others down and letting yourself down; the crying, the misery, the doubt if you are really good enough; and the dark periods, these are all part of being a professional athlete and I have seen many people who have broken down during the hardest moments. Often their careers have fallen away and they are never to be seen again on the tour. You can often feel it on court when you play an opponent with that inner steel and grittiness and it's horrible to play against. If you don't have it yourself it will eventually just wear you down when you face it week after week.

There was a lot of mental work done in the middle phase of my career, building mental strength, resilience, bounce-backability, asking questions and answering with honesty. I remember a phase when I started reading more cycling and ironman books. The ultimate sport in going to the depths of your mental and physical capacity.

To me, mental strength is:

Being brave.
Beating your best level (setting a new PB).
Believing that life is not a script already laid out for you.
Being honest and having honour.
Having a sense of winning.
No regrets.

Not playing for second place.

Having self-respect.

Being courageous.

Having inner strength.

Playing for yourself and having pride.

Being aware of what's going on with yourself and your opponent. Take the blinkers off.

They are all just words and sentences. They don't mean anything without the feelings behind them. Everyone can talk about being mentally strong, not many can do it. Honestly, there is nothing worse than listening to someone tell you how to be mentally strong when you know they couldn't possibly do it in a million years.

When I read about Tour De France rider Tyler Hamiliton being in so much physical pain that he ground down his back teeth, it made me wonder if I'd actually suffered proper training pain. It made me realise there was still a long way to go in my own mental and physical discomfort. I had some real barriers to smash through.

I remember working with Danny through the middle phase of my career on all of the things listed above. We talked a lot about a match being a full circle. The start and the end of the match is the full circle and, along the way, there are obstacles and problems to solve. You have to finish the circle and keep moving around the circle to finish the match. At any point if you stop or quit you haven't completed your circle.

Here's a typical diary entry of me having a real word with myself:

You are not here to behave like the rest. You are here to win. Are you brave enough to push physically and mentally? You have to beat yourself long before you can even start to beat your opponent. Play and be true to your own identity and values, and with no regrets. This bravery is what a real sense of winning is.

You have to watch and be aware of moments of weakness in yourself and your opponent. As soon as they doubt, then you've got to push on.

I know I am at my best when I am focussed but relaxed.

Don't be soft!!

Honour what you said you will play like from now on and do it for yourself and for those you love.

Complete the circle, complete the match all the way round.

———

One particular match that sticks out for me and my mental toughness was playing Premier Squash League (PSL) for Duffield. I was on the come back from my 'near retirement'. I was fit, strong, mentally fresh and ready to play well. I had put in a lot of work and had driven down to play in the final of the PSL. My match was against Yathreb Adel and, although I knew she was a talented player, I felt good – confident but a little nervous. It was my first competitive match after my break and, on top of that, I knew Duffield needed me to win and get us off to a good start to have a chance of taking the PSL crown. The image I have in my head of this match is one taken mid-match of me roaring. I look like a woman possessed. I was 1-0 down and down in the second, and getting so frustrated.

Mid-match my brain was going bonkers: 'I deserve more than this.' 'You're letting everyone down.' 'Dig in and make it hard.' I just wasn't match sharp and it was showing. At midway through the second game, I gave out the 'roar' and everything changed, clicked into position, and I literally never looked back. That's how mental it is. I refused to let this pattern of play continue. I dug in, made myself tough to break down and refused, simply refused, to lose that match. That's how you play yourself into match sharpness. I could have given up that day – not given up in the sense of stopping running or quitting but given up in the sense of not fighting to find a way, even if finding a way shocked half the crowd at the time with the noise I created. From there, I went on to win the match 3-1 and followed it up by making the final of the British Open the week after! And, just to add, I followed that PSL match with a bolt-on from Mark on a back court. Winning the match against Yathreb wasn't enough, I needed more in the tank physically for the British Open. So, anyone who saw me sprinting up and down the court having just come off from an hour's hard play will have got an insight into what I felt needed to be done to be the best in the world.

—

For years, people used to praise my willingness to hang in there and keep fighting when I was down, even if I didn't always get the result. I used to think what good that may have been if I wasn't winning but, as time went on, I came to realise that all those matches I lost, but fought hard in, built up other people's perceptions of me. It won me matches further down the line and I won countless times when I had absolutely no right to; matches where I refused to give up and rallied hard to the very end. More importantly, although I never realised it at the time, I was building up my own belief that I had an inner strength.

I am starting to realise these areas in my coaching, too. I thought when I started I could make anyone the best. I did it, so why not them? But I am also coming to realise that while I think I can help most players improve, the work and success has to come from within the player.

That was my talent. The talent to dedicate, change, listen, have honesty, fight, commit, never give up, seek out the right people and push myself to the limit with them, respect and listen to them but, most importantly, to do it for a ridiculously long and consistent period of time.

That, I believe, is something you can't teach.

—

I get asked a lot how I worked on this mental strength and the answer is not simple. I think my junior career and early upbringing certainly played a part in that but I like to think it's also a big part of my personality. Hating to lose, as most professional athletes will tell you, is a necessary and normal trait, yet I've discovered that there are levels of hating to lose.

I regularly see players smiling not long after a loss or chatting in the changing rooms afterwards. It always baffled me, especially in my early professional career, when I could go up to a week before I'd snap out of a bad mood following a defeat.

When I was playing I would do everything I could to avoid the pain of losing. As I got more experienced it was something I tried to improve at; don't take the losses too hard and, equally, try not to get too high after a good win. Hating to lose can always turn into a fear of failure and, at that point, it stops being a positive force and starts becoming a self-fulfilling prophecy as you panic when defeat looks possible.

As a coach, I'm a believer in even putting targets in for practice matches because if you can teach yourself to win when there's nothing on it, then you certainly can when those points come along in the big competitions. I've bought myself shoes, music, handbags and makeup over the years because I've won matches or done so many balls on the trot without hitting a tin or into a target. There has to be a consequence to your practice, especially on those days where motivation is a struggle. It is about realising your brand of squash and executing it in your training and your match play. It's all about how you want to play and how you want others to perceive you.

There just isn't as much discipline with today's kids. I think people are scared of being honest with players because they want to protect them and their mental health. Obviously, this is incredibly important that there are lines that coaches and parents don't cross and that, in the very worst cases, players are protected from mental or physical abuse of any kind but some of the stuff that makes you stronger as a person and an athlete in particular, is going to hurt.

I believe there is a softness in players and parents not wanting to hear certain conversations and often wanting to push back against what they perceive as criticism. Even now in coaching, you judge the kid a lot on how they behave but you can tell a lot more from the parents and how they react when you are honest about where their kid is at and what they need to improve.

I guess players I work with shouldn't be surprised that I am ready to be tough on them if I think it's warranted. That was the image I had as a player.

In squash, the up-close-and-personal nature of two players working on court means you sometimes have to be aggressive and in each other's faces, in full view of everyone, before coming off and pretending like it hasn't happened. It's almost a front. And, before you know it, you read in the press or other players saying that you are mentally strong or a particular kind of person.

I was given the nickname 'the Ice Queen' by Squash TV commentators, who gave nicknames to all the players. Joey Barrington, the lead commentator on Squash TV and the son of the great Jonah Barrington, once described Nick Matthew and I as 'quite hard-nosed' and I didn't mind that. It is what a lot of the older girls try and do. You want to keep the younger ones down as much as possible.

Perhaps that old pecking order has disappeared a bit these days, in the modern game. Jenny Duncalf grew up in Harrogate with DP, who had a stable full of top players training there. She always says if she tried to make a silly comment at dinner, she would be laughed at because your time would come when you were at the top. DP was very careful to put young players in their place and make sure they knew they hadn't made it yet. It built character but it's not done as much these days. Conversely, if you say a comment to a young player today it's like they just want to storm off home, rather than go away, take it on board and work harder.

I actually always wanted my Squash TV nickname to be 'Medusa'. If looks could kill and all that, which I thought was really fitting. Once the nicknames stuck on tour, it almost fed into how I started to behave on court. It wasn't like I was cheating or being horrible, but it was now becoming accepted that I would stand my ground. It made me proud to hear myself being described as feisty and the female version of Nick Matthew.

Danny also allowed me to be that player. I knew it was a way to win and to perceive myself as a force to be reckoned with and for players to be scared of me. They knew going on court that there was going to be no messing. Once I realised it was going to have an effect on people, I was going to do it even more.

At the end of my career, I am proud to have spent 99 months ranked inside the top 10, to have been World Champion, have two British Open titles, 23 tour titles, three Commonwealth Games silver medals, and been ranked No.1 in the world. I overcame my personal hurdles in finding a way to regularly beat Nicol, tackled the shift in tin height and score changes to point a rally, and I managed to take a step up to deal with the emergence of great Egyptian and European players in Raneem El Welily, Nour El Sherbini, Nouran Gohar and Camille Serme.

It was far more than I ever thought I was capable of. But I'm proud of the lows too, of the moments when I was bawling my eyes out after a loss, or freaking out before a match because I was so nervous I could hardly breathe or dripping with sweat, slumped over the watt bike like a rag doll.

When I announced my retirement in Manchester, I remember three of my tour peers came up to me and said, 'I can't believe how nice you are, I've never seen you smile as much!' These were people I had been playing with for years but they'd only ever seen the Ice Queen persona. But I was relaxed now I knew it was all coming to an end. The ice could finally melt.

THE END

The roar in PSL v Yathreb

EPILOGUE.

The bit after the story has ended

L et's be honest, the year 2020 and the start of 2021 wasn't what any of us expected, so it seems strange to try to predict what might be coming in the future for me. My career was more than I ever could have dreamed. Over many years I kept the faith, put the work in and set the 'dream big' goals. Deep down, for the longest time, I didn't know if I would finish my career satisfied or having achieved everything I hoped to. Now, stood looking back, I am lucky, grateful and proud of not only the journey but my longevity. As the seven-year-old girl I was, volleying my first ball, to finishing on the big stage at the British Open 29 years later.

I toyed with retirement for a good year before I finally settled on calling it a day. It was an exceptionally hard decision not knowing if I should stop. I was constantly questioning if I still had more to give. When I finally settled on the decision, I had to battle not only with transitioning out of a professional athlete's lifestyle and no longer travelling the world but also (like everyone) being thrown into a pandemic and locked down at home. It's been strange but, at times, comforting. A simple life was forced upon me; opportunities were not presented at the same rate and it forced me to slow down. Decisions have been taken out of my hands. It's provided me the time and opportunity to get to know myself again. I have begun to understand the person I am without the squash, and to know the person who doesn't have the big dream to conquer the world anymore.

When I think back to my last professional match, in some ways, it seems like a lifetime ago. In others, like yesterday. That last match will always be a bit of a disappointment. Having said that, maybe it was fitting and proved it was the right time. We all want the fairytale ending to a career and that's exactly what it is, a fairytale. It rarely ends like we wish. However, all great journeys come to an end and, at the end, I was supported by my husband, parents, friends, coaches and the brilliant British squash fans. Losing on the same day as two other amazing players in Nicol David and Jenny Duncalf made it a strangely fitting but emotional day all round.

After I played that last match and consequently retired, I was still trying to play fairly competitively into my retirement. That included playing Premier Squash League (PSL). Unfortunately, in October 2019 playing for Pontefract against Lisa Aitken, I suffered the worst squash-related injury of my career – a dislocated kneecap and torn MCL (medial collateral ligament). I felt a huge pop and a pain in my knee, which what I now know was the kneecap popping off and back on its runner very quickly. A pain I have never felt before and hope to never feel again. During the lockdown, I have been able to recover from the injury, which has forced me to sadly quit the competitive game totally. I have managed to rehab it fairly well, which was one of the positives of lockdown. The injury and rehab meant it was the longest I have spent away from the court since I was seven years old. I haven't played a match since and injuring myself that way taught me a big lesson. Like many lessons, they are painful and sometimes forced upon us. This was no different. I went into the match desperately not wanting to lose. I played like I still had something to prove and was actually nervous. How pathetic! Not surprisingly, life put me on my ass and said, 'Girl, you're retired. RETIRE!'

When I think about the physical and mental toll that professional sport takes, I think it's fair to say that you can reflect back on that looking back. As philosopher Søren Kierkegaard said: "Life can only be understood backwards, but it must be lived forwards." This now makes more sense to me than ever. I trained knowing I would do whatever it took to be the best for the days and weeks ahead. If the nutritionist advised me that that meant eating less than 70g carbs a day for a lean-down phase, then I did it. Was I always a nice person to be around? No! I was hungry and angry (hangry!). But, if it meant I carried a better power-to-weight ratio, then it got done. I now accept that is not true health. Yes, I was lean, yes, I was the lightest and fittest I had been but my skin and hair were poor and I had energy fluctuations daily. For many top females, it also includes irregular or no menstrual cycle at all and this certainly is not the true health of a woman. I knew ingesting so much protein wasn't good for me. Meals in the form of a shake or a bar are not food and I knew eating so little carbs was damaging to my energy but positive for my weight balance. So, I did it without question. Now, I know that is not a lifestyle I wish to continue for my own long-term health. It served a purpose to stay lean, strong and aid a quick recovery. I definitely do not regret that professional lifestyle choice. However, that is not my priority now, so I aim to eat well, stay in a weight zone that feels nice and eat more full meals. Now in retirement, I have accepted my body for what it is: Hugely resilient and reliable but at the same time fragile. I accept being a little bigger and a little softer round the edges.

I cannot remember the last time I drank a meal or a protein shake, and I have no intention to do so ever again. I have nothing to prove in my body shape now and health and happiness is the goal. My body, skin, gut, mood and hair are thanking me for it.

———

Since retiring, surprising opportunities have presented themselves. Working for HEAD was a brilliant opportunity. As one of the world's leading racket manufacturers, they supported me for eight years of my career and I won all my major titles with their racket. Now, I get to work for them and see the brilliant ingenuity and passion that goes into every racket design. If you ever get the opportunity to see how a racket is made from scratch by HEAD or by any company who are pushing forward the technology of our game, then you won't be disappointed; it is total craftmanship. I came home from my visit to their headquarters in Austria feeling the need to give my racket a hug.

The role in many ways hasn't been what I expected. However, it has meant I've learned more on the marketing and social media side, while trying to support our #teamhead players remotely.

Coaching is more fulfilling and more frustrating than I thought it would be, in equal measures. I have to stop all the time when the thought pops in, 'just do it like this', 'why can't you do that?', 'that worked for me, just listen to me'. It's not my journey anymore and I can't make players better through doing it for them. They have to find their own way and it's so hard to sit back and watch them try. As DP always said to me, players are strange. They want help but at the same time, they want to be really independent; that's a tricky balance.

With the coaching roles I have, I love the mix they provide at different levels within the game. It's fair to say as I start my coaching journey, I am going to be a heavily technical coach. For me, this underpins the mental and tactical side. In many ways it also helps the physical side too in efficiency and longevity. Being a very technical player and having the career I did, I don't see any argument as to why I would teach any players I work with differently. For me, it's how you hit the squash ball more than where you hit it. It's how it affects your overall rhythm, energy and tactics. In high performance coaching, it frustrates me to see coaches teach where to hit the ball. Squash, as I see it, is a movement sport where you hit balls, not a ball-hitting sport where you have to move. If you can't get the ball back in this ever-changing dynamic era you have no hope. Tying in technical movement and swing, for me, is where total brilliance and complete competence occurs. Less like teaching a static golf shot and more like teaching a ballet dancer where all the moves link together. Like the great Muhammad Ali said: 'Float like a butterfly, sting like a bee.'

I hope as my experience as a coach improves, I can find a way to really make players better through technical competency. In my years on tour when I was winning major titles (2013-2017), DP said to me, 'You and Nick are the last of the English technical warriors.' that says it all for me and my goal is to recreate some more of those English technical warriors. Another element that I noticed from some of the best coaches is that they have charisma, maybe even a bit of eccentricity. The widely experienced DP, Malcolm Willstrop, Neil Harvey and, back when he was still coaching, Jonah Barrington, have bundles of it. It comes across in their leadership, magical ideas and personality skills. Being able to read people and sum them up quickly. This is hard when you're a 'conformist' and this is something I don't want to become. The aforementioned are the coaches who have been able to take players from No.3 or 4 in the world to the absolute peak. There is a big difference in my opinion. In DP's case this was both male and female players. Non-conformists can teach their beliefs to the letter and those teachings, whether you agree or not, are pushed with a fundamental attitude of how the game should be played in their view. Fundamental in the best and worst sense of the word. They don't shy away from conversations; they push back and discuss it. They are older, set in their ways and know absolutely how they want and see their players playing. I know I would prefer a coach like this rather than one who is looking over their shoulder worrying about other factors. That style of coaching creates sterile sessions that become about facilitating rather than delving deep into technique that will create ultimate change. I have been a part of many group sessions where you turn up for two hours and get told what to do in conditions or routines, with stoppages being slight tactical corrections. I often come off thinking I could have put myself through that at home.

Away from coaching, I have also learned new skills in the world of online Zoom workouts, setting up a YouTube channel and, of course, being able to write this book, which has been a therapeutic process and also a learning one. A new skill gained as I move from the competitive squash world to the creative writing world. I have loved it.

Since then, I have simply enjoyed life. I've been to concerts, eaten, drunk, spent time with friends and family in ways I hadn't ever done and for anyone following me on social media I have made some pretty epic cakes during lockdowns.

I wish to wrap up the book, just as I started in my acknowledgments: Thanking you, the reader, for trusting me with your time. My goal in writing this book was to try to simplify my processes, to give you an insight into the world of women's professional sport and the women's squash tour. I hope every reader can take away at least one piece of information that will stay with you. Maybe finding yourself telling one of my stories or using what I did as an example to a player or junior. If this happens, then I have succeeded in writing this book with love, care and in letting the art of storytelling do the explaining.

Let the fun, learning and coaching processes continue.

Thank you,

Laura.

THE ACTUAL END.

(Opposite page above) On the BBC Breakfast
sofa talking about recieving my MBE

(Opposite page below) With my mum
celebrating her birthday

(Above) Girl Power!! At the Spice Girls concert in 2019 with my
friends (l to r) Dara, Jenna, Jacquie and me

(Opposite page) With my freinds from school / college (l to r)
Becky, Alex, me, Lynne and Gina at my retirement party

(Below right) With my friend Clare. We played squash together
when we were juniors and she's been a close friend ever since

MY NOTEBOOK

S&C with Mark Campbell

Here are two sessions I referred to in the book which add some depth to the story behind Laura's mentality around her drive and dedication.

This session was actually split across five weeks; so the first week at the end of a strength and conditioning session Laura would do Metabolic Resistance Training (MRT) ONE; the second week, MRT TWO, and the third week, MRT THREE, etc. Each one of these, although short (between 2-4 min), was very intense. It all culminated in week five, where she performed this session (again after a full strength session) where she did all five of the efforts at maximum intensity and minimal rest.

To help bring the sessions to life, the MRT BLITZ consisted of four workouts:

MRT ONE: 3:44 ON 0 MINUTES

KETTLEBELL (KB) SWINGS x 15

DB SQUAT AND PRESS x 10 (7.5kg)

PROWLER PUSH x 2 (10m per length)

LEG LOWERS x 10

3 x THROUGH CONTINUOUSLY

MRT TWO: 2:14.00 (ON 8 MINUTES)

KB SWINGS x 10

WATT BIKE 500m EFFORT

2 x THROUGH FOR TIME CONTINUOUSLY: 2:08.44

MRT THREE: 2:37.80 (ON 13 MINUTES)

DUMBBELL (DB) SQUAT AND PRESS x 10 (7.5kg)

BURPEE TO BOX JUMP x 5 (to 45cm box)

DB PRESS UP ROWS x 5 (5kg)

3 x THROUGH FOR TIME CONTINUOUSLY: 2:36.77

MRT FOUR: 3:04 (ON 19 MINUTES)

DB PRESS UP ROWS x 5 (5kg)

DB SQUAT AND PRESS x 5 (7.5)

BURPEE TO BOX JUMP x 5 (to 45cm)

PROWLER PUSH 2 MINS

KB SWINGS x 5 (16kg)

WATT BIKE 200m EFFORT

2 x THROUGH FOR TIME CONTINUOUSLY: 3:00.92

When running through the MRT circuit in full, so all four circuits back to back, it was done on a rolling clock. For example, MRT ONE would start on 0 minutes, MRT TWO would start on eight minutes, MRT THREE

would start on 13 minutes, and the final MRT circuit would start on
19 minutes. These times were determined to give Laura enough rest to
maintain the intensity from circuit to circuit.

The interesting thing here is the time in bold next to each of the session
titles. It was the time she did for the session as a one-off; the times at the
bottom of the session were when she performed all four in the one go
and, typical Laura, she beat every time even though she was under serious
fatigue. The interesting thing from these sorts of training blocks was
that I laid this out for Laura in advance so she knew what was coming
and, although she fully understood the effort that was needed and the
effects it would have, she pushed and challenged herself to perform at her
maximum and didn't hold back at any stage. It also showed why I didn't
need to motivate Laura by yelling and screaming, even in the middle of
such hard work. She was the one driving herself and I couldn't possibly
match this level of intrinsic motivation.

Here are two examples of the completion circuit that was the basis of
the story I describe in the book around Laura's unique response upon
completion of it. The numbers next to the exercise here are a total that
you can split up in any way and then complete in any order to get it done
as quickly as possible. No other athlete had ever considered doing these
sorts of sessions twice, but Laura did. We reflected on this story for the
book. The really important thing as an S&C coach was that it gave me a
really fantastic insight to the athlete I was working with and their mentality
and approach to hard work.

It meant that I had to give a lot of thought around many of the sessions
that I prescribed to Laura, as I knew that her natural tendency was to want
to work harder than most. This can be both a blessing and a curse when
it comes to getting an athlete prepared physically to perform. We also had
some challenging conversations around the tie-in between the physical
side and the technical aspect, and what needed to be the defining factor
for a court session. For example, Laura would always want to know how

hard a court technical session should be and my response would often be – as hard as it needs to be to meet the technical requirements your coach is trying to implement. It was a slight shift in thought process but one I considered key with an athlete of Laura's experience and physical strengths.

COMPLETION CIRCUIT ONE: 35:38

250m ROW EFFORT x 3

1min CYCLE EFFORT TO MAX INTENSITY x 3

SPLIT SQUAT JUMPS x 20 EACH LEG (EL)

SQUATS x 100

PRESS UPS x 40

BURPEES x 50

MOUNTAIN CLIMBERS x 100 EL

TRX ROWS x 40

LEG LOWERS x 100

KB SWINGS x 80 (12kg)

DB SQUAT AND PRESS x 50 (5kg IN EACH HAND)

LUNGES x 100 EL

YOUR WARM UP

HIT (LIGHT AND TECHNICAL)

20-30 minute foam roll and stretch

COMPLETION CIRCUIT TWO

TOUCHDOWN JUMP SQUATS x 50

SQUATS x 100 WITH BODYWEIGHT

PRESS UPS x 40

SIDE PLANK + LEG LIFTS x 50 (EACH SIDE)

DB MAN MAKERS x 50 (2 x 5kg) OR BURPEES WITH JUMP x 50

MOUNTAIN CLIMBERS x 200 EL

TRX ROWS x 50

SKIPPING x 100 DOUBLE UNDERS

LEG LOWERS x 100

KB/DB SWINGS x 60 (16kg)

DB SQUAT AND PRESS x 50 (5kg)

LUNGES x 100 EL

As I explained, you can split these up into any amount you want. So, for example, for 50 burpees, you might do 10 sets of five repetitions. For squats, you may split the 100 up into 10 sets of 10. You can then do these smaller elements of each exercise in any order you want with the goal of completing the total number of repetitions for each exercise is as short as possible an amount of time while maintaining high intensity and good form.

The exercises are done with as little rest as possible between them and mixed and matched to spread the work across the body. The goal is to complete all the repetitions as quickly as possible.

How Reading Shaped My Career

As I've mentioned, a number of books helped me in certain moments during my career. I kept a list over the years, and here they all are, in no particular order.

Sports books

A Boy in the Water, Tom Gregory (Penguin, 2019)

A Lifetime In A Race, Matthew Pinsent (Ebury Press, 2004)

A Life Without Limits, Chrissie Wellington (Constable, 2013)

Awaken the Giant Within, Tony Robbins (Simon & Schuster UK, 2001)

Black, White & Gold, Kelly Holmes (Virgin Books, 2008)

Boys in the Boat, Daniel James Brown (Pan, 2014)

Colin Jackson, The Autobiography (BBC Books, 2004)

Come to Win, Venus Williams (Amistad, 2012)

Every One A Winner, Jonathan Carswell (10Publishing, 2015)

Faster than Lightning, Usain Bolt (HarperSport, 2014)

Finding My Feet, Jason Robinson (Hodder & Stoughton, 2003)

Find a Way, Diana Nyad (Pan, 2017)

Iron War, Matt Fitzgerald (Quercus, 2013)

Knowing the Score, Judy Murray (Vintage, 2018)

Legacy, James Kerr (Constable, 2013)

My Story So Far, Paula Radcliffe (Simon & Schuster UK, 2005)

My Fight Your Fight, Ronda Rousey (Arrow, 2016)

My Life: Queen of the Court, Serena Williams (Simon & Schuster, 2010)

Mentor, Leon Taylor (Soap Box Books, 2011)

Murder in the Squash Court, Jonah Barrington (Hutchinson, 1982)

Open, Andre Agassi (HarperCollins, 2010)

Personal Best, Denise Lewis (Century, 2001)

Pressure is a Privilege, Billie Jean King (Lifetime Media, 2008)

Running, Ronnie O'Sullivan (Orion, 2014)

Racing through the Dark, David Millar (Orion, 2012)

Relentless, Tim Grover (Atria Books, 2014)

Serve to Win, Novak Djokovic (Corgi, 2014)

Shot and A Ghost, James Willstrop (Rod Gilmour, 2012)

Sweating Blood, Nick Matthew (internationalSPORTgroup, 2013)

Swim, Bike, Run, Alistair & Jonathan Brownlee (Penguin, 2014)

Twin Ambitions, Mo Farah (Hodder Paperback, 2016)

The Golden Rules, Bob Bowman (Piatkus, 2018)

The Outsider, Jimmy Connors (Corgi, 2014)

The Secret Race, Tyler Hamilton (Corgi, 2013)

The Winning Mind, Steve Backley (Aurum Press, 2000)

Unbelievable, Jessica Ennis (Hodder Paperbacks, 2013)

Unstoppable, Maria Sharapova (Penguin, 2018)

Winning Ugly, Brad Gilbert & Steve Jamison (Simon & Schuster UK, 2007)

Seventy-Seven: My Road to Wimbledon Glory, Andy Murray (Headline, 2014)

<u>Self-help, coaching books</u>

A New Earth, Eckhart Tolle (Penguin, 2009)

Braving The Wilderness, Brene Brown (Vermillion, 2017)

Body Mind Mastery, Dan Millman (New World Library, 1999)

Black Box Thinking, Matthew Syed (John Murray, 2016)

Clean: The Revolutionary Program to Restore the Body's Natural Ability to Heal Itself, Alejandro Junger (HarperOne; Expanded edition, 2012)

Daring Greatly, Brene Brown (Penguin Life, 2015)

Fast Food Nation, Eric Schlosser (Penguin, 2002)

Get The Edge, Tony Robbins (audio CD, 2000)

Giant Steps, Tony Robbins (Simon & Schuster UK, 2001)

Onward, Howard Schultz (John Wiley & Sons, 2011)

Hero, Rhonda Byrne (Simon & Schuster Ltd, 2013)

Here to Win, Chris McCormack with Tim Vandehey (Center Street, 2013)

Inner strength, Ralph Vernacchia (Warde Publishers, 2003)

Leading, Alex Ferguson (Hodder & Stoughton, 2016)

Leaders Eat Last, Simon Sinek (Penguin, 2017)

Lessons in Mastery, Tony Robbins (Simon & Schuster Audio/Nightingale-Conant, 2002)

Live with Passion, Tony Robbins (Simon & Schuster, 2002)

Living Healthy, Tony Robbins (audio CD, 2004)

Personal Power, Tony Robbins (audio CD, 2004)

Power Talk, Tony Robbins (audio CD, 2009)

Pig Wrestling, Pete Lindsay & Dr Mark Bawden (Vermillion, 2019)

Pressure Principle, Dave Alred (Penguin Life, 2017)

Rising Strong, Brene Brown (Vermillion, 2015)

Read Me: I Am Magical, Alinka Rutkowska (2010)

School of Greatness, Lewis Howes (Rodale Press Inc, 2017)

Shoe Dog, Phil Knight (Simon & Schuster UK, 2018)

Sleep, Nick Littlehales (Penguin Life, 2016)

Stillness Speaks, Eckhart Tolle (Yellow Kite, 2016)

Talk like TED, Carmine Gallo (Pan, 2017)

The Secret, Rhonda Byrne (Simon & Schuster UK, 2006)

The Body You Deserve, Tony Robbins (audio CD, 2004)

The Champion's Mind, Jim Afremow (Rodale, 2015)

The Success Equation, Michael J Mauboussin (Harvard Business Review Press, 2012)

The Outsiders, William N Thorndike (Harvard Business Review Press, 2012)

The Fighter's Mind, Sam Sheridan (Grove Press, 2010)

The Power to Shape Your Destiny, Tony Robbins (Nightingale Conant Corp; Unabridged edition, 2012)

The Inner Game of Tennis, W.Timothy Gallwey (Pan, 2015)

The Key to Living the Law of Attraction, Jack Canfield (Orion, 2014)

The Talent Code, Daniel Coyle (Random House Business, 2020)

The Edge, Tony Robbins (Robbins Research International, 2006)

The Courage To Be Disliked, Ichiro Kishimi (Allen & Unwin, 2013)

Winning the Mind Game, John Edgette & Tim Rowan (Crown Publishing, 2003)

The Inside Out Revolution, Michael Neill (Hay House, 2013)

The Chimp Paradox, Steve Peters (Vermillion, 2012)

The Space Within, Michael Neill (Hay House UK, 2016)

The Untethered Soul, Michael A Singer (New Harbinger Publications, 2007)

The Wisdom of the Enneagram, Don Richard Riso (Bantam, 1999)

Think Like a Winner, Yehuda Shinar (Vermillion, 2007)

The Surrender Experiment, Michael A Singer (Harmony, 2015)

The Power of Now, Eckhart Tolle (New World Library, 1997)

The Art of War, Sun Tzu (Shambala, 2005 /-500)

Tuesdays with Morrie, Mitch Albom (Warner, 2000)

Unshakeable, Tony Robbins (Simon & Schuster, 2017)

Unlimited Power, Tony Robbins (Free Press, 1986)

Way of the Peaceful Warrior, Dan Millman (HJ Kramer, 1980)

Winners, Alastair Campbell (Pegasus Books, 2015)

Win or Learn, John Kavanagh (Penguin Ireland, 2016)

Who Moved My Cheese, Dr Spencer Johnson (Vermillion, 1998)

What I Know for Sure, Oprah Winfrey (Flatiron Books, 2014)

Why We Sleep, Matthew Walker (Scribner, 2017)

You Go Girl, Kim Doren & Charlie Jones (Andrews McMeel Publishing, 2000)

Zen in the Art of Archery, Eugen Herrigel (Vintage, 1999)

12 Rules for Life, Jordan B. Peterson (Random House Canada, 2018)

My First Fishbone Diagram:

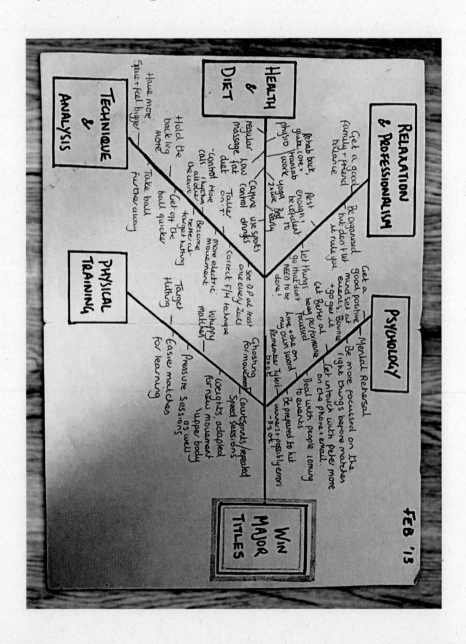

How the Organic Belief Change was set out, walking through the first pieces before turning around to work through the following three:

Rod Gilmour co-authored James Willstrop's Shot and a Ghost: a year in the brutal world of professional squash, which was nominated for the William Hill Sports Book of the Year in 2012. It was the first self-published book to be nominated for the award. He has covered Commonwealth and Olympic sports for the Daily Telegraph and national newspapers for over a decade.

Eleanor Preston spent 10 years travelling the world as a sports journalist for national newspapers, notably the Guardian. She co-authored Andy Murray: The Story So Far, the first Murray biography published, and continues to work as a broadcaster and media consultant to athletes, sporting organisations and events through her company The Emilia Group.